IT'S SPLITSVILLE

SURVIVING YOUR DIVORCE

James J. Gross

Apress

It's Splitsville: Surviving Your Divorce

Copyright © 2013 by James J. Gross

This work is subject to copyright. All rights are reserved by the Publisher, whether the whole or part of the material is concerned, specifically the rights of translation, reprinting, reuse of illustrations, recitation, broadcasting, reproduction on microfilms or in any other physical way, and transmission or information storage and retrieval, electronic adaptation, computer software, or by similar or dissimilar methodology now known or hereafter developed. Exempted from this legal reservation are brief excerpts in connection with reviews or scholarly analysis or material supplied specifically for the purpose of being entered and executed on a computer system, for exclusive use by the purchaser of the work. Duplication of this publication or parts thereof is permitted only under the provisions of the Copyright Law of the Publisher's location, in its current version, and permission for use must always be obtained from Springer. Permissions for use may be obtained through RightsLink at the Copyright Clearance Center. Violations are liable to prosecution under the respective Copyright Law.

ISBN-13 (pbk): 978-1-4302-5716-5

ISBN-13 (electronic): 978-1-4302-5718-9

Trademarked names, logos, and images may appear in this book. Rather than use a trademark symbol with every occurrence of a trademarked name, logo, or image we use the names, logos, and images only in an editorial fashion and to the benefit of the trademark owner, with no intention of infringement of the trademark.

The use in this publication of trade names, trademarks, service marks, and similar terms, even if they are not identified as such, is not to be taken as an expression of opinion as to whether or not they are subject to proprietary rights.

Author photo © 2013 by Carly Glazier

While the advice and information in this book are believed to be true and accurate at the date of publication, neither the authors nor the editors nor the publisher can accept any legal responsibility for any errors or omissions that may be made. The publisher makes no warranty, express or implied, with respect to the material contained herein.

President and Publisher: Paul Manning
Acquisitions Editor: Jeff Olson
Editorial Board: Steve Anglin, Mark Beckner, Ewan Buckingham, Gary Cornell, Louise Corrigan, Jonathan Gennick, Jonathan Hassell, Robert Hutchinson, Michelle Lowman, James Markham, Matthew Moodie, Jeff Olson, Jeffrey Pepper, Douglas Pundick, Ben Renow-Clarke, Dominic Shakeshaft, Gwenan Spearing, Matt Wade, Tom Welsh
Coordinating Editor: Rita Fernando
Copy Editor: Jana Weinstein
Compositor: SPi Global
Indexer: SPi Global
Cover Designer: Anna Ishchenko

Distributed to the book trade worldwide by Springer Science+Business Media New York, 233 Spring Street, 6th Floor, New York, NY 10013. Phone 1-800-SPRINGER, fax (201) 348-4505, e-mail orders-ny@springer-sbm.com, or visit www.springeronline.com. Apress Media, LLC is a California LLC and the sole member (owner) is Springer Science + Business Media Finance Inc (SSBM Finance Inc). SSBM Finance Inc is a Delaware corporation.

For information on translations, please e-mail rights@apress.com, or visit www.apress.com.

Apress and friends of ED books may be purchased in bulk for academic, corporate, or promotional use. eBook versions and licenses are also available for most titles. For more information, reference our Special Bulk Sales–eBook Licensing web page at www.apress.com/bulk-sales.

Any source code or other supplementary materials referenced by the author in this text is available to readers at www.apress.com. For detailed information about how to locate your book's source code, go to www.apress.com/source-code/.

Apress Business: The Unbiased Source of Business Information

Apress business books provide essential information and practical advice, each written for practitioners by recognized experts. Busy managers and professionals in all areas of the business world—and at all levels of technical sophistication—look to our books for the actionable ideas and tools they need to solve problems, update and enhance their professional skills, make their work lives easier, and capitalize on opportunity.

Whatever the topic on the business spectrum—entrepreneurship, finance, sales, marketing, management, regulation, information technology, among others—Apress has been praised for providing the objective information and unbiased advice you need to excel in your daily work life. Our authors have no axes to grind; they understand they have one job only—to deliver up-to-date, accurate information simply, concisely, and with deep insight that addresses the real needs of our readers.

It is increasingly hard to find information—whether in the news media, on the Internet, and now all too often in books—that is even-handed and has your best interests at heart. We therefore hope that you enjoy this book, which has been carefully crafted to meet our standards of quality and unbiased coverage.

We are always interested in your feedback or ideas for new titles. Perhaps you'd even like to write a book yourself. Whatever the case, reach out to us at editorial@apress.com and an editor will respond swiftly. Incidentally, at the back of this book, you will find a list of useful related titles. Please visit us at www.apress.com to sign up for newsletters and discounts on future purchases.

The Apress Business Team

*To my wife, Holly, and my sons, Jake and Nicholas,
in the hope that readers of this book will be as
blessed in their next marriage as
I have been in mine.*

Contents

About the Author... ix
Acknowledgments xi
Introduction xiii

Part I: **Facing the Prospects of Divorce**.............. 1
Chapter 1:   Timing.. 3
Chapter 2:   Things to Do Now 15
Chapter 3:   Research and Documents........................... 27
Chapter 4:   Can You Do It Yourself?........................... 35
Chapter 5:   Finding a Lawyer 45
Chapter 6:   First Meeting with Lawyer and Beyond............. 57
Chapter 7:   Custody in General 67

Part II: **Children** 73
Chapter 8:   Physical Custody 75
Chapter 9:   Timesharing 83
Chapter 10: Child Support...................................... 91

Part III: **Finances** 101
Chapter 11: Alimony... 103
Chapter 12: Property and Debt................................ 113
Chapter 13: The House: A Play in Three Acts 123
Chapter 14: Pensions, Retirement Plans, Deferred Pay,
             and Social Security 131
Chapter 15: Business Investments.............................. 143
Chapter 16: Bank Accounts, Stock, and Other Assets........... 153
Chapter 17: Taxes 163
Chapter 18: Prenuptial Agreements 175

Contents

Part IV: Settlement 185

Chapter 19: Separation Agreements............................. 187

Chapter 20: Different Ways to Get a Separation Agreement 197

Chapter 21: Tactics and Strategies for Negotiating Your Own Separation Agreement......................... 205

Chapter 22: Pleadings... 215

Part V: Trial 223

Chapter 23: Evidence: Proving Your Case......................... 225

Chapter 24: Trial Procedure 237

Chapter 25: Same-Sex Marriage and Divorce 245

Chapter 26: Postdivorce... 253

Part VI: Appendix 263

Appendix: Sample Forms 265

Glossary: Glossary 281

Index 289

About the Author

James J. Gross is a divorce lawyer in Chevy Chase, Maryland, who has been helping people solve their most difficult legal problems since 1976. He has authored or coauthored *File for Divorce in MD, VA and DC; Father's Rights;* and *Money and Divorce.* He writes for two blogs, *Father's Rights and Maryland Divorce Legal Crier.* He holds a BS in chemical engineering, a Juris Doctor, and a master of laws in taxation. He has been named one of the best lawyers in Maryland and Washington, DC, by Martindale Hubell, Avvo.com, SuperLawyers.com, and the *Washingtonian* magazine.

Acknowledgments

I'd like to acknowledge my law partners, John Thyden, Michael Callahan, Lois Finkelstein, and Nelson Garcia, with whom I work at Thyden Gross & Callahan. It is a joy to work with a team of such skillful and knowledgeable lawyers.

Thanks to our bookkeeper, Ruth Zetlin, who gets the bills out on time and makes our law firm possible and profitable.

And no matter how crazy the practice of divorce law gets during the week, I can always look forward to Saturday morning racquetball with my long-time friends David DeConcini and Jay Baraff.

Thanks to John Husband, the first person to encourage me to write.

And thank you to my excellent editors at Apress, Rita Fernando and Jeff Olson.

Introduction

There are better things ahead than any we leave behind.

—C. S. Lewis

As a divorce lawyer, I've heard a thousand stories from people like you, in the process of separation or divorce or thinking about it, sitting in the client chairs in my law office across from my desk. They are looking for answers to one of the most difficult personal growth experiences in life. I've made up the characters in the stories in this book, but they provide fair representations of what people are going through.

Tom and Emily

"Tom, we have to talk," said Emily at the breakfast table of their sunny suburban home. She was 39-years-old, tall, and trim. She was a registered nurse working part time.

Tom put down his newspaper with a sigh. He was 44, an engineer, and in shape from jogging every morning. "OK, let's talk."

"Are you happy with our marriage?" said Emily.

"Well, I guess I'm not unhappy."

"I am," said Emily. "You're never home. All you do is work. You go to work before I get up and you come home after I'm asleep."

"That's ridiculous, Emily. I work hard so I can provide for you and the kids. Where do you think the money comes from to pay for this house, the food, and your car?"

"I work hard, too, Tom," said Emily. "What's the point," she thinks. "He never listens to me anyway. But I've got to try."

"I have a job," she says. "I take care of the house. I take care of the children. Who helps them with their homework, bandages their knees, and gives them their baths? Who picks up after them and feeds them and does their laundry?"

Tom replies, his voice rising in anger, "I work full time. I take care of the cars and the lawn. I take the children to baseball practice and swimming practice."

Emily sighs. "You're not emotionally available."

"What are you talking about?" said Tom. "I don't even know what that means."

"Tom, I haven't smiled for years. Haven't you noticed? I'm so unhappy," said Emily.

"Emily, you just like to complain."

Emily is in tears now. "There's no intimacy. It's like we're roommates. We're living in parallel universes that don't connect."

"So what are you trying to say, Emily? Do you want to get divorced?"

"I don't know, Tom. What should we do? What about the kids? What about the house? I've never been in this situation. I don't know where to turn for help. What do you think we ought to do?"

There is a long silence as Tom tries to think of the right thing to say. "I don't know, Emily. I don't know what to do. I don't want to tear this family apart. I want the kids to have their dad. I'm as confused as you are. I'm late for work."

He gets up and leaves without saying goodbye.

About This Book

I wrote this book for people like Tom and Emily, and anyone else who is in the process of separation or divorce, or even thinking about it. No one gets married expecting to get divorced. In fact, if you had drawn a timeline for yourself from birth to death, you might have put down getting married, having children, buying a house, buying a vacation home, starting a business, making a million dollars, and retirement. But, unless you had been divorced before, I bet you wouldn't have put divorce on that timeline.

Yet the odds are pretty high that you will be one of the people who gets divorced. You probably already know many people that have been divorced.

Sometimes, divorce is necessary. It may be forced upon you, unwillingly, because it has been initiated by your spouse, and you have no control over the decision. Or you may find you need to correct a mistake and move on with your life.

The decision to separate or divorce is not one that should be taken lightly. There are many things for you to consider first, and it may take a long time to become clear about whether you should stay or go.

If you do decide to go, divorce can be devastating, both financially and emotionally. This is true whether you are the one who is leaving or the one who is being left. It can also seem overwhelmingly complex.

You may be feeling lots of different emotions. Anger, sadness, depression, rage, revenge, grief, and jealousy are normal emotions for someone going through a divorce. In fact, I would be more worried if you weren't feeling anything. But emotion can lead to paralysis. You need to be an active participant in your divorce. You can help yourself and your divorce lawyer if you are making decisions based on operating out of positive emotions like courage, clarity, tranquility, serenity, and peace. There is much to do and many decisions that need to be made with a clear head. This book will help you get control of your emotions and start taking action about your divorce.

Tip This book will help you gain control of your emotions and start taking positive actions steps regarding your divorce.

In these pages, we will break all the issues down into separate components that are easier to understand. The main issues that need to be resolved can be counted on one hand:

1. Children (custody and timesharing)
2. Alimony and child support
3. Property distribution
4. Legal fees
5. Taxes

We will drill down into each of these topics together and keep breaking them into smaller and smaller pieces so that you can understand them. We will also discuss the process of divorce that takes place during both the settlement and the trial.

Structure of the Book

There are five parts to the book.

Part I deals with preliminary matters. It discusses the factors that go into deciding whether you should stay or whether you should go. We'll take a look at timing factors and certain personality types. There will be some pointers on how to talk about divorce with your spouse. We'll discuss what you need to do now and things you have to research. We'll talk about how to find a lawyer and tell you what you can expect from your first meeting.

We'll also help you to determine whether you have the type of divorce that you can handle yourself or whether you need a lawyer.

Part II is about the children. You can skip it if you do not have children. But if you do, you know that children represent the highest stakes for the parents in a divorce. First, we'll talk about custody and break that down into the separate discussions of legal custody and residential custody. We'll also talk about dividing time with the children and various parenting schedules. Then, we'll discuss child support.

Part III deals with financial matters. These include alimony, property division, and taxes. Will talk about how different assets, such as the house, a business, or a pension, can be divided.

Part IV is about marital settlements. We'll discuss the advantages of settlement agreements and why it's almost always better to settle out of court. We'll take a look at prenuptial and postnuptial agreements and the different ways that are available to help you reach an agreement. We'll also give you some tips and tricks for negotiating an agreement with your spouse.

Part V is about the contested divorce trial. If you cannot settle with your spouse, you will have to have your case tried. We'll go over the rules of evidence, pleadings, courtroom procedures, same-sex divorces, appeals, and modifications after trial.

Divorce can make you feel helpless and hopeless, like it's the end of the world. Why is this happening to me? you may ask. When the future is uncertain, it feels like you are walking off a cliff into an abyss. But many people have sat in the client chairs across from my desk, and I have guided them all safely through their divorces. They all survived. Many found happiness and success. It does get better. Just not right away.

Why Do People Get a Divorce?

"I don't know why Tom and I fight all the time," Emily told her psychiatrist, Dr. Dory.

"In any group of people, there will be different agendas," said Dr. Dory. "And a group consists of two or more people."

So you and your spouse have different agendas. It's no wonder there are so many divorces. It's a wonder that so many people can stay together in a marriage.

Men and women are different. People are different. Can you respect and even admire the differences between you and your spouse? Or do you want your spouse to be exactly like you?

That would be boring. Differences make life interesting. It's only natural for people to have different agendas, interests, and ideas. Once you realize that, then it is a matter of reconciling your differences.

Some people find it easy to reconcile huge differences. Some people find it difficult to resolve even the smallest of differences. If you have no mechanism for resolving conflicts, then the same disputes keep coming up over and over again. The situation makes people unhappy and frustrated, and they begin to think about leaving the conflict and the relationship behind.

Specific Reasons for Divorce

Let's look at some of the specific reasons people get divorced:

Relationship Breakdown. Do you trust your spouse? Is your spouse reliable and honest in your relationship? Is your relationship one of mutual trust and respect? Or are you indifferent or even contemptuous of your spouse's interests and ideas?

A relationship is damaged over time by small discourtesies and unkindnesses. Conversely, it takes time and effort to restore a damaged relationship.

Imagine a big clock. Imagine that at one o'clock, there are the words "business relationship." Every relationship begins by establishing a business relationship at one o'clock. In a business relationship, you have no assumptions and no expectations about the other person.

Eventually, if you see this person often enough, you might suggest a lunch or a coffee. After a while, a business relationship can evolve into a friendship. "Friendship" is at four o'clock on our imaginary timepiece.

You have expectations of a friend. You assume they will be available for lunch or dinner. You may ask them to jump-start your car, give you a lift, or help you move.

A friendship can become more intimate. "Intimacy" is at eight o'clock on our imaginary timepiece. Now, you can expect more from an intimate partner than you would from a friend or a business acquaintance. An intimate partner will visit you in the hospital or give you money when you're broke.

When there is a breakdown in an intimate relationship, like a breach of trust, you would like to go back from intimacy to friendship, counterclockwise from eight o'clock to four o'clock.

But this clock only goes one way—clockwise. You cannot move counterclockwise back to friendship. The only way to regain the trust needed for a friendship is to go clockwise to one o'clock and start over by establishing a business relationship with no assumptions and no expectations.

Begin by making clear agreements and keep them, like, "I'll meet you at Starbucks at a certain time." or "I'll take the kids to church Sunday." Making and keeping agreements is the path to restoring trust and repairing a broken relationship.

Communication Problems. Sometimes couples just stop communicating with one another. One or both give up trying to communicate because they think, What's the use? We believe that if we just talk enough, sooner or later the other party will smack themselves on the head with their hand and say, Of course, you're right, I see it now! But it doesn't work that way. Maybe you want to avoid conflict. So you don't ask for what you want or try to negotiate a compromise.

Parallel Lives. Usually, you will have a different career than your spouse. You will have different interests and different hobbies. But that doesn't mean you can't be interested in your spouse's life. But some couples are just not that engaged in their marriage. So, it is an annoyance if a spouse calls them at work in the middle of a big deal to tell them their son lost a tooth. You might be married but living parallel lives that don't intersect or connect at home. You may enjoy staying at home on the weekends, but your spouse likes to take bicycle trips.

Adultery. Affairs are one of the major factors contributing to divorce. Sometimes affairs are more the symptom of a troubled marriage than the cause of a divorce. Marriages can survive infidelity. But if you are involved with a man or a woman other than your spouse, then you are not in a committed relationship.

Desertion. You can leave the house. That's called abandonment or desertion. You can even have desertion while still living in the same house if one spouse deserts the marriage and the couple no longer acts as husband and wife. If you are forced to leave by your spouse, that is called constructive desertion by the spouse who stays in the house.

Finances. Arguments about finances can torpedo a marriage. People fight about finances in goods times and bad times. When times are good, they argue about how their money should be spent. When times are bad, they fight about not having enough money to pay their bills. Donald Trump talks about financial infidelity. That's when one spouse intentionally hides information about purchases from the other spouse. This happens in more marriages than you might think.

Parenting Styles. Conflict may arise from different parenting styles. You may think your spouse is too strict with the children. Your spouse may think you are too soft on them. An inability to compromise and work together leads to strife in the marriage.

Abuse. No one should have to put up with abuse by another person. But domestic violence is a fact of life. And in many cases it can be difficult to break free from an abusive spouse. Abuse can be physical or verbal. Words can hurt as much as physical abuse and sometimes even more.

Avoiding Divorce

You certainly should try to avoid divorce if you can. Here are a few tips from a divorce lawyer on how to avoid divorce and stay married:

Tip Can you avoid divorce? Yes, but it's not easy to do once one or the other party makes up their mind to get a divorce. Talking is a good start.

Talking. One weekend I was doing some yard work. My wife drove by in my car. She rolled down the window and said, "I'm taking your car to the store because mine is out of gas. If you have time, can you take my car to the gas station and fill it up?"

I was busy and did not have time. Do you think that was a good excuse? No, I was in the doghouse. I had forgotten to check my "Man/Woman Translation Dictionary."

If I had, I would have seen that she meant, "Fill my tank or you will be in big trouble, honey."

What I took as a request, she intended as a demand. We were able to talk about our different ways of looking at things and communicating with one another. She agreed to try to express herself more directly and I agreed to try to be more sensitive to her indirect messages. We laughed about it and the problem was solved. The next weekend, I filled her tank without her even asking.

The solution to marriage problems can be as simple as just talking to your spouse about them. We go around with all these thoughts in our heads that we never express because we're afraid, or embarrassed, or we just expect people to read our minds. You've got to get those thoughts out of your head and into your mouth. Say what you think.

It is hard to talk about some issues in a marriage, like sex or money, especially if you have stopped talking to one another completely. You may need a third party, such as a therapist, marriage counselor, or mediator, to help you talk out some of the problems in your marriage. Men and women, and people in general, do have different ways of looking at things, different perceptions and thought processes, and different ways of expressing themselves. You may need a third person to act as a translator so you can each hear what the other is saying and so you can express yourself and be heard.

I recommend you set aside a certain time, day of the week, and place where you make it a point to talk to one another; for example, over a glass of wine at dinner on Friday night. You don't need an agenda. It can be a freewheeling conversation about anything and lots of things. The point is that you are talking.

There are all kinds of ways to talk nowadays. In addition to face-to-face communication, you can talk to your spouse by e-mail or text; on social-networking sites like Twitter or Facebook; or on your computer, tablet, or cell phone.

Conflict Resolution System. It always amazes me that some couples are able to resolve very big issues, like infidelity for example, while others cannot resolve the most trivial of issues. They keep having the same argument over and over again with no hope of resolution or solution. The difference is having a conflict resolution system. This may be made by a coin flip or a mediator, or just being willing to give in on issues that are more important to your spouse than to you.

Commitment. Both parties have to be committed to the marriage. A good marriage should not be taken for granted. It requires compromise. It requires effort. If you are not committed to keeping your marriage together, then you are going to have problems.

Courtesy and Respect. It is the small things that build a relationship. If you can compliment your spouse, greet him with enthusiasm, and acknowledge his presence each day, you will anchor your marriage. On the other hand, if you belittle, insult, criticize, embarrass, or ignore your spouse, then don't expect your marriage to be a bed of roses.

Summary

There are many reasons people get a divorce, including adultery, desertion, money problems, and lack of communication. You should try to avoid it if you can by talking to your spouse, developing a conflict resolution system, and showing commitment and respect to her. But, sometimes, divorce is inevitable. In that case, keep reading. This book will help you survive your divorce. Next, we will look at some timing factors.

PART I

Facing the Prospects of Divorce

You may not want a divorce. It may have been thrust upon you by your spouse. You may have loved well but not wisely. Or you may have made a mistake and married the wrong person. In any case, there are certain things to think about and certain things to do in making a decision to divorce.

CHAPTER 1

Timing

Breakups can be just as hard on the person who leaves as for the person who is left. But sometimes the emotional timing is different for each. The person who leaves may have been thinking about leaving for a long time, perhaps six months, a year, or longer. He has been trying out the separation in his head for a long time while still participating in the marriage for all outward appearances. He may already have one foot out the door. The other person may not know anything is wrong, and so the announcement comes as a complete surprise. This person then has some catching up to do emotionally. This chapter covers the issue of timing, focusing on financial, practical, and emotional issues, especially for those about to make a decision to separate or divorce.

Practical Timing Considerations

Whether to stay or go is a hard decision to make. It can take a long time to decide—sometimes years. It is not a frivolous or impulsive decision, and you want to get it right. Sometimes people come to a lawyer's office and even pay a retainer before they have really decided to get a divorce. I call this the inquiry stage. It is OK to stay in the inquiry stage for a while.

But I also have people who come to my office after being together with their partners for 5 years, 15 years, or 25 years. They say they knew they wanted out years before.

"Why didn't you leave?" I ask.

"Because I thought things would change."

People sometimes do change, but frequently they do not. Here are some things to think about if you're trying to decide whether you should stay or you should go:

- **Investment**: You've got a lot invested in your marriage in terms of time, effort, and cost. Is it time to cut your losses and move on? Or do you stay in the marriage and try to find a way to make it work?

- **Children**: What will be the impact of a divorce on the children? Children are always better off in an intact marriage with two loving parents. But if there is constant bickering and fighting in the home, would they be better off if you and your spouse separated? A split may mean the children have to move to a new residence, a new neighborhood, and a new school. Many parents time the divorce so that the kids don't have to change schools in the middle of a school year. Sometimes spouses wait to get the divorce until the children are out of high school.

- **Companionship**: It's lonely out there. Even though you may be unhappy living with your spouse, you may dislike being alone even more. Doing things alone, like eating, watching television, or sleeping, can make you feel very lonely. But you can also be lonely in a dysfunctional marriage.

- **Familiarity**: Have you heard the saying "The devil you know is better than the devil you don't know"? Some people keep repeating familiar habits after getting a divorce and pick the same kind of partner they just got rid of.

- **Dating**: Do you really want to enter the dating pool again? If you have been out of circulation for a while, the dating scene can be awkward and uncomfortable. You are older now. You may have children to deal with. You probably have more responsibilities and that can make dating more difficult.

- **Finances**: Two can live as cheaply as one, but not when they are supporting two separate households. The money available for one household is typically not enough to support two. Something's got to give, and usually it's the lifestyle of both spouses. Before you decide to divorce, make a budget and see if there is enough money for both partners to survive.

States Matter: Where to Divorce If You Have a Choice

Only the state courts can grant divorces. The state where you should go to court to get divorced is the one where you live at the time of divorce, not the one where you got married.

In the event that you and your spouse are separated and live in different states at the time of divorce, you may be able to file in either the state where you live or the state where your spouse lives.

Every state has different laws, passed by their legislatures, that govern marriage and divorce. When you look around for the best place to bring a legal action, it is called *forum shopping*. Although the term may have a negative connotation in some contexts, it is perfectly legal in divorce. If you have a choice, it may pay to do a little forum shopping in your case.

For example, in Maryland, you must be separated for a year before you can file for a divorce, but in Virginia and DC, the time of separation required is only six months. So, if you live in Maryland and are in a hurry to get divorced, you can move to DC and file for a divorce there.

However, if you have children, child support is required until age 18 (and in some cases 19) in Maryland and Virginia, but it is until age 21 in DC. That could mean your ex can sue you for your children's college expenses if you get divorced in DC.

And if you have acquired property or the worth of your property has appreciated after your separation, you will want to get divorced in Virginia. The court determines the value of your property according to what it was at the time of your separation in Virginia but calculates according to the trial date in Maryland and DC.

Tip Consider your options when filing for divorce. Filing in one state vs. another can sometimes be to your advantage.

Employment: Why It's Best If Your Spouse Is Employed

Without a prenuptial agreement, when you get married you are entering into a contract that you haven't read and don't understand. It's a contract that has provisions contained in the code of law of your state, and the interpretation of that law is done by the appellate judges, whose opinions are written in books known as reporters.

Part of that contract says that you have to support your spouse and children during the marriage. Furthermore, if you get divorced, you will have to continue to support your children. You may also have to support a spouse who is not yet self-supporting.

If you will be in need of child support and alimony, then you want your spouse to be employed so as to have the ability to pay these expenses. Despite this, many spouses are so angry at their partners that they are eager to make complaints to their spouse's employer, the IRS, or the police. Before you do that, remember that a spouse that's fired or in jail cannot pay support.

If you are the breadwinner of the family, the amount of child support and alimony you are responsible for may be affected by the amount of money your spouse earns or is capable of earning. Obviously, it's better for you if your spouse earns a good income. This will improve the chances that you won't get hit with excessive alimony payments.

In cases where one of the spouses quit working to be a stay-at-home parent and raise the children, the court can make up a fictitious income for that parent if the judge decides she is purposely not working to increase support. But even in that case, it will take the stay-at-home parent some time to return to the job market. Additional job training may be required. That means the working spouse will have to pay some support during this transition back into the workforce.

Should you quit working or cut back on hours during a divorce to show the court a lower income? No, because the court can base its decision on what you are capable of making, not just what you are actually making. And finances are tough during a divorce, so you will need all the income you can earn.

Finances: What Is the Best Time to Split with Your Spouse?

The timing of your divorce may have a significant impact on how financial issues will be determined. As mentioned, it is important for you to determine the date of valuation for property in your state. Some jurisdictions determine and value marital assets based on the date of separation. Some use the date of divorce.

So, if you are in a state that uses the trial date, anything you save or purchase after the separation may still be considered marital property. If you are the breadwinner, you will want to speed up the timing of your divorce. If you are a dependent spouse, you will be better off the longer the divorce takes.

If you know that your business is about to be sold for a big profit, or you are taking a new job with higher pay and stock options, then you will want to time your divorce so that it happens before those events.

If your 401(k) stock crashes, and you think it might recover, you will have an incentive to buy your spouse out of that asset while it is down. A similar strategy would apply to your business or real estate. In fact, many settlements are reached where one spouse trades their share of the house for the other spouse's share in a business or pension. I remember one case where the husband traded his interest in the stock of the wife's company for her interest in the couple's real estate. He thought real estate was the better investment and would do better than stocks in the future. She thought the stock was better.

If your income is down, and you are thinking about getting a divorce, this might be the right time to do it. On the other hand, if your spouse is a high-income earner, and you are thinking about getting a divorce, you may want to proceed now rather than take the risk of waiting and having your spouse lose his job in uncertain economic times.

The housing market has fallen on hard times, and many married couples now own houses that are worth less than the mortgage. This makes it more difficult, if not impossible, to sell the house in a divorce. There are no doubt couples who want a divorce but are living together in misery right now because they can't sell their house.

There are also cases where a business owner is about to sell a company or it is about to go public, and she wants to step on the gas and get a marital settlement agreement which places a lower value on her business before the sale or public offering.

The best timing was probably by Kevin Halstead, a 50-year-old British bus driver who had a divorce that dragged on for two years. When it was finally settled, he went out and got drunk with a group of his friends. The next day, he decided he would use his last quid (about $1.50) to buy a lottery ticket. On Sunday, when he got up, he checked the morning paper and—you guessed it—he won. His prize was £1.15 million (that's $1,773,990).

His wife Helen took the news well. "We've been separated a long time. We are the best of friends. In fact, we get on better now than when we were married," she said. "It couldn't have happened to a nicer bloke. I wish him all the luck in the world—he deserves it."

Timing Issues When Your Spouse Wants You to Leave

Bill is sitting calmly in his living room one evening, with no idea that anything is amiss, when there is a knock on the door. He gets up, opens the door, and is surprised to see two uniformed county sheriff's deputies.

"Can I help you?" he says.

Chapter 1 | Timing

"William P. Fritz?" asks one of the deputies.

"Yes."

"The court has issued an order for you to stay away from the premises for the next ten days. You have ten minutes to get your personal effects."

"What? Let me see that order."

The deputy hands the order to Bill, and Bill puts on his glasses to read it.

"My wife filed for this! She says I threatened her? It's not true! I was watching the football game, and I shouted, 'I'm going to knock your block off' to the TV, not to her!"

"You'll have a chance to tell the judge at the hearing in ten days, Sir. Please get your things. You have to leave now."

From there, things went from bad to worse. Bill was so depressed that he was paralyzed into inaction. He failed to show up at the hearing where he could have presented his defense. Instead, his wife accused him of threatening her with imminent bodily harm, causing her to fear for her safety. When the judged asked her what Bill's income was, she said she thought it was somewhere around $100,000 a year. In truth, it was much lower.

The judge ruled that Bill had committed domestic violence, ordered him to stay away from his house for a year, and ordered him to pay alimony and child support of $4,000 a month. Bill lost his security clearance because of the finding of domestic violence. As a result of that, he lost his job. His wife's lawyer placed a lien on his bank account. Finally, Bill just left town and went underground, still owing alimony and child support.

The lesson you can learn from Bill's case is that you must confront and deal with legal issues early in a divorce. Bill should have seen a lawyer as soon as he was asked to leave his house. Waiting only compounded his legal problems.

It may surprise you to learn that you can be removed from your house based on your spouse's suggestion that there has been physical abuse or that it has been threatened. This could, and sometimes does, lead to false claims.

In cases other than those involving allegations of abuse, you do not have to leave the marital home, even if your spouse asks or tells you to go. This is true if you are jointly on the deed or lease. Even if only your spouse is on the lease, some judges will still not let your spouse evict you until all matters are resolved in the divorce.

However, things may be so difficult for you in the marital residence that you want to leave. And leaving may start the clock on the period of separation running in states where timing is a consideration. You do not give up any property rights in the house by leaving. In other words, you are not abandoning your claims to equity in the house or its contents by leaving.

However, there is still a danger: Your spouse may allege desertion. This could potentially hurt you when the judge considers awarding alimony and distributing all the marital property.

You can avoid this by making a written agreement that says the move is agreed upon and neither party will use it to claim desertion. The agreement, which is sometimes called a *move-out agreement*, can also cover such issues as how the bills will be paid and dividing the time you spend with the children if you and your spouse can agree on those matters. The move-out agreement usually stays in effect until you reach a complete settlement or the final order of the divorce court.

Tip   If you plan to leave your residence, be sure to have your spouse sign a move-out agreement so that you are not accused of desertion.

Timing Issues When Your Spouse Leaves You

In many cases, spouses are taken completely by surprise when their partner leaves. That's usually because the leaving spouse has been thinking about leaving for a long time, perhaps six months or a year. They mentally have had one foot in and one foot out of the door of the marriage. But since they didn't know if they were staying or going, they acted as if nothing was wrong. If their spouses had asked them if they were thinking about leaving, they would have said, No.

The left-behind spouse, if they even at all suspected that their partners might leave, had been in denial all this time. Their alarms were turned off. If they noticed something was amiss in the relationship, they would still tell themselves that everything is fine.

So, when leaving spouses makes up their mind to go, they get an emotional head start on the spouses they will leave behind. They are ready to split up the assets and get on with their life. The left-behind spouse is still in the relationship and has another year to six months of catching up to do before they can even think about such things.

Lawyers can help you divide the assets and end the marriage with a divorce. But there is also an emotional divorce. Sometimes the legal divorce and the emotional divorce are on different schedules. It can take a long time to get over your emotional divorce.

Divorce is a stressful, traumatic event on par with death of a loved one. Your trusted partner suddenly becomes your worst enemy, with hostile intent and knowledge of all your weaknesses and secrets. In addition to legal and financial issues, emotions can run wild. Here are some of the emotions you may encounter and how to deal with them:

- **Depression:** Sadness is a normal human response to divorce. A divorce means the end of your marriage and the dreams you had for a future together with your spouse. It is perfectly natural and common to grieve for your loss. Depression, however, can lead to inaction, and inaction can lead to disastrous results. You can't protect yourself in a divorce if you spend all day crying or sleeping. If this describes your situation, you need to make an appointment with a therapist now.

- **Anxiety:** There is plenty to worry about in a divorce. You will naturally be anxious about the outcome, the money, the bills, the house, and your children. I could tell you not to worry, but you would probably worry anyway. One simple way to deal with anxiety is to write your problems down and think about what you can do to solve them.

- **Anger:** Rage and anger at your spouse are typical emotions in a divorce. But if you let them get out of control, you can harm your case. We have already seen that physical or verbal abuse can cause you to be put out of the home. The spouse who cuts off support for the other spouse and children out of spite will not win the judge's favor and will probably get a big judgment for retroactive alimony and child support payments.

- **Revenge:** It is not at all uncommon to feel like you want to take revenge against a spouse who has hurt you. But remember that living well is the best revenge.

- **Uncertainty:** The future is always uncertain. But getting divorced can feel like you are standing on the edge of a black hole and stepping forward. You are used to certain routines, and all that is being disrupted. Take it one day at a time. You'll make it.

We like to think we are rational, logical people and make decisions on that basis. But psychologists say that our logic is just the tip of the iceberg. Below the surface lies our hidden, subconscious emotions, which really make up 90 percent of our decisions. We just don't know it.

The legal system, however, is based on reason, not emotions. If you are making emotional and not rational decisions, you may encounter problems in your divorce.

Your friends and extended family can offer great emotional support during a divorce. There are also support groups for separated and divorced people. Or you can hire a professional therapist.

Don't let the things your spouse says upset you. They will probably regret those words or not even remember them later.

If you are feeling depressed or angry or crazy right now, don't worry. That means you are normal.

Remember There is legal divorce and emotional divorce. They operate on different timelines.

Family Finances: Can Cause Trouble When Handled by One Spouse

Some people are good at financial matters. Others couldn't care less. In many marriages, one spouse handles all of the finances and investments for both. This can be an efficient division of labor while you are married, but it can cause problems in a divorce.

One of the first documents your lawyer or mediator will ask you to complete when preparing for your divorce will be a financial statement. There are many different formats for a financial statement, but essentially they all include:

- your assets, which are things you own
- your liabilities, which are debts you owe
- your income
- your expenses

It's fine if you don't know enough about your finances to complete these forms, but that means your lawyer will have to obtain the information through the legal process, which takes more time and expense.

Knowledge is power, and the more you know about the family finances, the more you can control how financial matters will be determined in your divorce. You can prepare a budget based on what you expect your expenses to be after divorce. This will help you know what to seek in the way of support from your spouse if you need it, or what you can afford to pay in support if you are the one with more income.

You need to determine and identify what assets exist, whether those assets are marital or separate property or mixed, in whose name they are owned, and when they were acquired. Don't overlook retirement funds, which account for about half of the assets divided in divorces.

Likewise, you need to determine all debts; balances due; what the money is owed for whose name the debts are in; and which debts are associated with which assets, like mortgages and car loans, for example.

I use a spreadsheet in a three-ring binder with tabs to organize this information. The spreadsheet consists of a table of contents, which lists each asset and liability and has corresponding columns entitled "wife," "husband," and "total" with corresponding values for each. Then, in the tabs I place supporting documents like bank account statements, pension statements, mortgage statements, appraisals, and so forth. This is helpful for gathering information and keeping it organized and accessible. I find that it also adds an element of control and focus to settlement meetings and mediations. It allows you to keep bringing everyone's attention back to the notebook when they get off track and to patiently plod down the spreadsheet one item at a time. No one can argue with you because the paper statement is right there at the tab. You can even use the notebook to present your evidence at trial.

When Can I Start Dating?

You can start dating at the earliest judgment for your divorce or when your spouse signs the settlement agreement. You are married until you are divorced. So, if you have an affair while you are married, even though you are separated, it is still adultery.

If you date before you have a settlement agreement, your spouse may claim the divorce is your fault. In most states, even so-called "no-fault states," the judge can consider you at fault in determining alimony and property division.

That is the reason why some people's spouses hire private investigators to follow them and take pictures. Adultery may be proved by circumstantial evidence. This allows the investigator to testify that you showed inclination to commit adultery and had an opportunity to do so. For example, a private investigator might testify that he saw you holding hands at dinner and checking into a hotel that evening with an unrelated adult of the opposite sex.

If you have signed an agreement, though, adultery will not cause legal harm to your case. That is because you have already worked out alimony and property division, and the court will honor your agreement. In fact, in states where adultery is grounds for divorce, it may shorten the waiting period for it to take place.

Timing Once You Have an Agreement

If you and your spouse cannot agree to terms for settlement, you will have to try your case before a judge in divorce court. That may take days or weeks and require you to present your testimony, witnesses, and documents.

The judge will then decide your case and give you an order of divorce that determines custody, visitation, support, and property division. The judge will make an agreement for you in the form of an order.

If you are fortunate enough to reach an agreement, however, then when it is time for trial, your formal pleadings will send this message: "Judge: We have already agreed to everything. There is nothing left for you to decide. Please grant us our divorce."

In the latter case, the divorce trial lasts about ten minutes, or in some jurisdictions it may even be done by affidavit or deposition. It is almost clerical or ceremonial.

The agreement is 98 percent of your divorce. It gives you almost everything a divorce can give you except the right to remarry. You can begin living as though you were a single person. You can date. Your property is yours to keep. So, the irony is, unless you have someone else beating down your door to remarry, once you have an agreement, you can wait as long as you want to get divorced.

If Rome Is Burning, Stop Fiddling Around

While you don't need to be in a hurry to get divorced once you have a signed agreement, you may get burned if you tarry too long in coming up with an agreement.

In one case, a man in his 30s had $3 million in stock options in the dot.com company where he worked. At the beginning of the case, he offered to split the options with his wife. Her lawyer declined the offer and began seeking detailed and extensive financial information under the rules of court and requesting hundreds of documents from the spouse.

He produced these over the course of a year. That was the year the tech bubble burst. At the end of this process, no new assets had been found, the options were worthless, and the couple owed $100,000 in taxes related to the options.

A LAWYER'S SENSE OF TIME

You would think lawyers, who sell their time in minutes, would have a better grasp of time.

But when a lawyer tells the judge she will just need another minute, she means fifteen minutes.

And when a lawyer tells you he will call you back in five minutes, he means a lawyer's five minutes, which is actually closer to an hour.

An emergency to a lawyer is around two or three weeks, and an expedited hearing is about three months from the request.

Lawyer time is not real-people time.

It also pays to remember that lawyers are trained in law and not in business. They have an overly developed attention to detail bordering on obsessive-compulsive. A good lawyer can be very helpful, but don't let your lawyer become an obstacle to making the right deal with your spouse.

Divorce Is a Process, Not an Event

Let's say you file for a divorce on January 1 of next year. You set up the initial conference the following week, and you hire a lawyer. The lawyer sends a letter to your spouse on January 15 seeking settlement discussions and gives your spouse ten days to respond.

Your spouse hires a lawyer who calls your lawyer on January 25 and suggests the two of you exchange financial information. It takes about a month for this to happen. The lawyers start trading proposals and counterproposals over the next three months.

In June, the parties have reached an impasse, and negotiations are broken off. One of the lawyers drafts a complaint for divorce and files it on June 15. It is served on the defendant on June 30. The defendant answers and files a counterclaim on July 20.

The parties go to a scheduling conference where the judge gives them six months to complete discovery and sets a mediation on December 15 and a pretrial hearing on December 30. After discovery is completed, the mediation does not produce an agreement, and the parties go to the pre-trial hearing. At that hearing the trial is set for March 1 of the following year.

It's now a year and two months from where we started, and we haven't even talked about appeals yet.

Summary

In this chapter, we have explored various timing issues in divorce and separation, including the financial, practical, and emotional issues. Next, we will tell you what things you need to do first to protect yourself.

CHAPTER 2

Things to Do Now

"What should I look out for?" John says as he twists nervously in one of the big winged-back visitor chairs in his divorce lawyer's office.

Ways to Take Charge of Finances

"That's a question I get from a lot of my clients," says Henry, putting a thumb under his suspenders. "I tell them there are certain things I have seen over the years that they may experience in their case. Some of them have to do with protecting assets and others with protecting yourself and your privacy."

Bank Accounts

"Do you have joint bank accounts?" Henry asks.

"Yes, we have a joint savings account and a joint checking account that we use to pay the household bills," John says.

"I've had cases where the spouse cleaned out the bank accounts."

"She wouldn't do that," John says.

"You know her better than I do, but I wish I had a nickel for every client who sat in that very chair and said that. She may not be that way, but her attorney may convince her to take all the money. Some of those clients called me to follow up to say, 'You'll never guess what happened.'"

"So what do you recommend?"

"Take half the money out of the accounts and open a new account in your name with it. Then, tell your wife what you've done on my advice, but only after you've done it."

"Won't the judge be angry with me?"

"Maybe, but it's easier to give the money back—if the judge orders you to—than it is to get it back if your wife takes it first."

"Then how do we pay the bills?"

"That's what we have to negotiate. You don't want your children and their mother left out in the cold. So you'll have to give your wife some money to get by on. The judge will make you do that anyway."

> **Tip** Take half the money in joint bank accounts now before your spouse takes it all.

Stocks, Money Market Funds, Certificates of Deposit, and Brokerage Accounts

Henry begins polishing his wire frame reading glasses. He asks John, "Do you own any stock outside of your pension plan or IRA?"

"Yes, we have an account at Schwab," says John.

"I assume it is in joint names?"

"It is," says John, glumly.

"Call your broker. Tell him you want to divide the account equally and put half of it in a new account in your name alone. Different stocks have different tax burdens associated with them. So you want your broker to divide each stock holding equally or make sure the tax basis is equal."

Credit Cards

"Are the credit cards in joint names?" asks Henry as he leans back in his leather swivel chair and puts his fingertips together making a steeple with hands.

"The Visa, MasterCard, American Express, and some gas cards are," says John.

"Just like with the joint bank accounts and stock accounts, what if your wife goes on a giant shopping spree tomorrow with the credit cards and spends thousands of dollars?"

"That would be a rude awakening."

"Yes, and you may be responsible for paying all or part of the debt."

"So, what do I do?"

"Call each credit card company and tell them you want to close the account because you are getting a divorce. Don't worry. This won't be the first time they've heard that and they will know what to do. You can ask them to reopen an account in your name alone if you wish. To be on the safe side, send a letter, return receipt requested, confirming your instructions. Keep a copy of the letter. You will still have to make payments on the old account, but there will be no new charges from your spouse. Let your spouse know what you have done so there will be no surprises when the joint card no longer works."

"Wow, I never thought there were so many things to worry about," John says.

"Oh, there's more," says Henry. "Much more."

"You might as well give me the whole list. Do you have a piece of paper? I want to take notes."

Henry tears off a couple of yellow-lined sheets from his legal pad and hands them to John. John takes notes as Henry gives him the following list of various additional steps that he might need to take in order to prepare for his divorce.

Tip Call the credit card companies and tell them you are going through a divorce and want to close joint accounts and open new separate ones.

Loans and Lines of Credit

You'll want to contact the banks and any other lenders that have given you and your spouse any ability to borrow on joint loans, a home equity line of credit, or other lines of credit that you and your spouse can borrow on with one signature alone.

Explain your situation to the lender, and ask her to close the line so there can be no further borrowing. Follow up with a letter and keep a copy.

Another way to stop your spouse from any further borrowing on these lines of credit is to withdraw the money yourself up to the loan limits.

Health Insurance

You might be tempted to drop your spouse from your health insurance policy to save money—or to do so out of spite. This is a bad idea. First, most policies have individual coverage and family coverage, so if you drop the family coverage, you are not only dropping your spouse but your children as well.

If a member of your family experiences a serious illness or other catastrophe, you may be responsible for the bills. Medical expenses for children may be assessed against a noncustodial parent as child support. Medical expenses for a spouse may be assessed as additional alimony.

If you have group health insurance through your employer, your spouse is no longer your spouse at the date of divorce, and so they are not included in family coverage. However, an ex-spouse can keep the group health insurance for up to 36 months after the divorce for an additional premium. Children continue to be covered under the family plan until age 26.

Life Insurance

You may want to consider changing the beneficiary on your life insurance policy, especially if there are no children involved. Just contact your agent or the insurance company for the right form.

However, if you do have children and you change the beneficiary from your wife to your children, your wife will still get the money as the children's guardian in the event of your death.

Life insurance is usually used to secure payment of alimony and child support in divorce settlements, so you may want to keep any life insurance you have and not cancel it right now.

Bills

It's time to take a hard look at the family expenses. If you are separated, that means the income that previously paid for one household must now cover two. Usually, as the old army saying goes, "There is not enough blanket to cover the cot."

You are going to have to cut costs and cancel anything that is not a critical requirement like extra cell phones, Netflix subscriptions, gym memberships, or premium cable channels. Hold a garage sale for things you don't need and raise some cash.

Don't, however, cut off the utilities at the home of your spouse and children without plenty of notice. A judge won't like the spouse who cuts off heat and light in the winter for the other spouse and children.

Retirement Accounts

If you are making contributions to a retirement account like a 401(k) plan or an individual retirement account for yourself, you should be aware that these contributions are marital assets that can be divided by a divorce court. That means your spouse may share in contributions made before the separation or divorce.

To avoid this, you should stop making contributions until after the divorce. You will probably need the extra money to go to your paycheck soon anyway. Your employer will have a form for you to fill out to stop your 401(k) contributions. And you can stop making contributions to your IRA.

Snooping: How to Find Information Legally

It's OK to gather divorce information and evidence by looking in files, drawers, automobiles, checkbooks, and briefcases that are in your home. You can make copies and replace the original documents.

You can also check home computers and laptops in your home if you know the passwords because there is no expectation of privacy for these items. You can open mail addressed to both spouses jointly, but don't open your spouse's individual mail unless you have permission to do so.

You can access telephone bills, bank account statements, and pension plan statements online if they are jointly owned or if your spouse has given you his username and password and has no expectation of privacy.

Some states require both parties to consent to recording a telephone conversation on a topic. Some require only one party to consent. Even in those states that require consent from only one of the two, you can still be sued for invasion of privacy for recording a conversation. Information left on answering machines can be used as evidence in court because the speaker knows they are being recorded.

Inventory and Safeguard Your Stuff

In one of my cases, a husband told his wife to leave their home, and she did. Then, he started noticing that more and more things were missing from the house each day. First, the towels; then, the silverware and china; then, his coin collection.

He called me, and I told him there was nothing he could do. As long as the wife is on the deed, she can come and go as she pleases. She can also move the items that belong to her and even those that belong to both parties. Although it will all get sorted out in the divorce, that may be a year from now.

This is why you need to inventory every item in the house: furniture, appliances, draperies, jewelry, clothes, and everything else. Make a video or take pictures of these items. Record the date of your inventory.

This will give you a record and evidence of your belongings in case something turns up missing.

Collections and Other Valuables

If you have collections, expensive jewelry, original pieces of art, items of sentimental value, money, or any other valuables, you want to move these to some place safe, like a friend's house, a safe deposit box, or a storage locker. The objective is not to hide these items but to protect them from your spouse.

Documents

One client had made a list of everything he owned on one sheet of paper. He had made several investments in private businesses over the years. They were all speculative and unsuccessful.

Yet, he had put monetary values on the list that were wildly optimistic. His wife went through his desk, his briefcase, his car, his cell phone records, and his laptop for evidence to use against him in a divorce. This list became the centerpiece of her settlement negotiations and no doubt would have been admitted into evidence at trial if the case had not been settled.

He would have been wise to move his records somewhere else, like his office or a friend's house.

Safe Deposit Boxes and Storage Units

Open an account for a safe-deposit box to store your valuable documents and property. You may also need to rent a storage unit for larger valuables like artwork collections.

If your spouse has access to your safe-deposit box or storage unit, make a list of the items in them and photograph or video everything for evidence in case something turns up missing later.

Social Security

There is a special "ten-year rule" that applies to Social Security: if you and your spouse have been married for at least ten years, you can use either party's work record, whichever is greater, to determine your Social Security benefits.

Those benefits will be available to you as a divorced spouse if your ex-spouse retires or reaches age 62, whichever comes first, or becomes disabled, and you

- have been married at least ten years
- are unmarried (if you remarried, you will still be eligible if the new marriage ends in death, divorce, or annulment before you apply for benefits from the previous marriage)
- are age 62 or older and have been divorced for at least two years

If you ex-spouse dies, in order to receive benefits as the surviving divorced spouse, you must

- have been married for at least ten years
- be at least age 60 (or 50 and disabled) at the date of her death
- be unmarried (or remarried under certain conditions)

If you have been married for almost ten years and your spouse has earned more over their career than you, you should file for a divorce after your tenth anniversary so you don't miss out on these important benefits.

Tip If your spouse has earned more than you over his career, and you have been married nearly ten years, wait until your tenth anniversary before filing for your divorce.

Your Will and Powers of Attorney

In the event of your death before your divorce, your joint property will go to your spouse, and your other property will go to your spouse and children if you don't have a will.

Even if you make a will that leaves out your spouse, a spouse can take a portion of your property against the terms of the will before the divorce or settlement agreement. You still may want to make a will to govern the part of your estate that your spouse cannot take.

If you already have a will, take a second to review it. If you have left everything to your spouse, then you probably will want to have a new will prepared or make a codicil, which is an amendment to the original document. If you have given any powers of attorney to your spouse, revoke those immediately. The same goes for any advance medical directives.

Domestic Violence

If your spouse physically harms you or your children, or threatens to harm either party, you can file criminal charges and also obtain a protective order or injunction that will put her out of the house.

File a petition for a protective order with the court as soon as you can after the abuse happens. Most courts have forms for this at the courthouse, and the clerks will help you fill them out. Shortly after you have completed the forms, you will speak with a judge that same day. Tell him about what happened and any previous incidents of domestic violence.

The judge, if you ask, may grant an order that requires your spouse to leave the home temporarily; require the abuser to stay away from you and the children at home, school, and work; provide for support payments; and give you temporary custody of the children. The judge will also schedule a hearing where you and your spouse can both testify about what happened together with any witnesses. The judge may then continue or dismiss the protective order.

Once you have filed for divorce, you can also ask the court to prohibit your spouse from taking money out of the bank, disposing of marital assets, or running off with the children.

Some states have automatic injunctions that apply when the case is filed. In other states, you have to ask for that relief, and, usually, there will be a hearing.

The penalty for disobeying an injunction can be harsh. You can be required to pay your spouse's attorney's fees. The court may not allow you to defend or prosecute your case. You can go to jail. Even if none of this happens, the judge may not trust you if you disobey a court order.

Any allegation of domestic violence will be taken seriously by the court. Out-of-control rage can lead to serious injury or death. But abuse is sometimes hard to prove. It occurs behind closed doors, and it is the word of one spouse against that of the other. If you are the victim of abuse, you should call the police, get medical attention, and have pictures taken of any injuries to use as evidence.

In a few cases, people are tempted to exaggerate or even make up allegations of abuse to get an advantage in the divorce or get a spouse out of the house. You should avoid any form of conflict, control yourself, and walk away from any provocation. But if you find yourself in a situation where you are defending yourself against false allegations of abuse, you need to explore whether your spouse provoked the incident, could have walked away from the conflict, called the police, or sought medical help.

Find a Lawyer (and Make Your Lawyer's Job Easier)

It may come as no surprise that there are good divorce lawyers and bad divorce lawyers. Ask around to find a good one. Good attorneys are usually found by word of mouth. There are also Internet sites that rate attorneys and publish profiles like www.lawyers.com, www.avvo.com, and www.superlawyers.com.

A lot of people make the mistake of thinking they want a "shark" for a divorce attorney, thinking the shark's teeth will benefit them. That is not the way to handle a divorce. A shark will run up your bills and accomplish little else. Find someone who has some common sense and can be practical about your case.

Schedule an appointment for an initial consultation with the lawyer as soon as possible. It will usually cost you between $200 and $500 dollars for an hour of the lawyer's time, but you will most likely receive valuable information and advice about your case.

If you determine that this is the attorney for you, discuss fees with her. Attorneys charge by the hour and require a retainer, or advance payment, for divorces. The attorney will give you a written fee agreement.

Tip Don't sign anything your spouse wants you to sign until your attorney reviews it first.

War Chest

A divorce takes lot of money. You need will need money to hire a lawyer, pay the costs of filing fees, transcripts, and expert witness fees. If possible, start saving for these expenses. We know one client who saved the cash she found in the pockets of her husband's pants every night. If you have to borrow money from a relative or a friend, sign a promissory note to show that it is a loan. You want to show that it is a debt that needs to be repaid when the court considers property division, and you want to show that it is a loan and not a gift so the court won't consider it as income when deciding support.

Divorce Calendar

You will have many dates to keep track of in your divorce, like court deadlines and lawyer meetings. You may also track visits with the children to have a record if your spouse is denying you access to them. You can use extracurricular events and meetings with your children's doctors, teachers, coaches, and tutors to show that you are an involved parent.

> **Tip** Keep a detailed log of your activities related to the divorce and your children. The "divorce calendar" could become an important record that shows you to be a dedicated, involved parent.

Divorce To Do List

The period of your divorce can be a confusing time. You need to stay focused. It is also important to keep moving forward and not get bogged down or dispirited by everything you have to do. Organize and prioritize your next steps with a to do list. List everything you have to accomplish. Then mark off each item as you execute your list.

Divorce Notebook or File

There will be lot of papers coming to you in a divorce. One of my favorite ways to organize these is with a three-ring binder, tabs, and a hole punch. Keep all papers in order of time received, and create an index.

Alternative types of file folders also make a good organization system, especially those that have metal prongs to hold your papers neatly in order.

If you want, you can set up different files or different notebooks for different papers. You may make one for correspondence, one for agreements, and one for pleadings.

History of the Marriage

Preparing a brief written history of your marriage will help your lawyer get up to speed quickly on your case. It will also save you money because the lawyer won't need to dedicate time to finding out the basics of your situation. Include the following information:

- how you and your spouse met
- details about the courtship
- the date and place of marriage
- whether or not there was a prenuptial agreement
- whether or not it was the first marriage for both parties
- the names and birth dates of children
- details about both spouses' employment

- a description of problems in the marriage
- the date of separation
- both spouses' ages and state of health

Financial Statement

Clients tend to think that 90 percent of their divorce is about determining who was at fault, and so they spend 90 percent of their time on that. Lawyers and judges know that 90 percent of a divorce is about support and dividing property.

Some courts require that the parties submit a financial statement consisting of assets, liabilities, income, and expenses. Whether your jurisdiction requires it or not, prepare one early in your case.

A mediator will ask you to fill out financial forms at the first mediation session and bring them back for the second session. A lawyer will ask you about your finances at the initial conference. Completing a statement of them early on will allow you to focus your attention on the important aspects of your case, show you which items will need more investigation, and help you and your lawyer to be on the same page of the hymn book.

Tip 90 percent of a divorce is about finances, not fault. Spend your time and effort accordingly.

Summary

Taking some steps early on to protect yourself will save you problems down the road in your divorce. Next, we'll discuss how to organize your research and the documents you will need for your divorce.

CHAPTER 3

Research and Documents

Once you have decided to get a divorce and you have taken some initial actions to protect yourself, you will want to begin the process of gathering facts and documents. You could hire a private investigator to find information for you or you could wait until you have filed for divorce to ask for information under the court's rules for discovery. Informal and early discovery will save time and money in the long run.

Do the Research *Before* You Leave

Some records will be easier to find while you and your spouse are still living together. So start looking for the records you will need for your case now. Documents might be found in desk drawers, safe deposit boxes, file cabinets, briefcases, automobiles, and other places. You can have a meeting with your accountant, financial planner, and banker to go over the family finances. The following is a checklist of the type of information you should do research on before you go to court.

Assets (Before and After Marriage)

Assets are things you own, like bank accounts and furniture, for example. Here is a list of the records and documents you should try to obtain to identify and value your assets:

- **Bank accounts**: Collect copies of recent bank statements. If you are using these to determine income or expenses, or if you have questions about deposits or withdrawals, you will need more than just the recent ones. Keep updating these as well as other monthly statements available for assets during the course of your divorce.

- **Real estate**: Try to find a copy of your deed(s) if you own real estate. This will show how the property is owned. Also, look for the settlement papers (especially the HUD 1 form you signed at closing, which details the down payment, closing costs, and loan information). Find copies of any appraisals and real estate tax bills. Locate copies of the mortgages and home equity line of credit and recent statements for these. If you own rental properties, obtain copies of the leases and transaction record for the income and expenses of the leased property.

- **Retirement funds**: Locate statements from IRAs; 401(k)s; Civil Service Retirement System, or Federal Employees Retirement System; and Thrift Savings Plan statements for federal government workers, annuities, or other retirement funds. If you have a copy of the plan documents or the summary plan description, so much the better.

- **Insurance policies**: Find copies of the policies for life insurance, medical insurance, health insurance, and home owners' insurance. Life insurance has both a face value (the amount of the death benefit) and cash value (how much you can surrender it for now). Find out both values.

- **Safes and safe deposit boxes**: If you have access to a safe or safe deposit box, inventory the contents. Take pictures or make a video.

- **Stocks and bonds**: Look for copies of current statements for stocks, bonds, and certificates of deposit from stockbrokers, banks, or other financial institutions.

- **Business interests**: Look for evidence of any business interests, such as sole proprietorships, partnerships, corporations, limited liability companies, or professional corporations. This includes partnership agreements, corporate records, business bank accounts, ledgers, and checkbooks.
- **Inheritance or trust interests**: Look for bank records, trust agreements, copies of wills, and codicils.
- **Automobiles and other vehicles**: Find titles and loan documents for all automobiles, motorcycles, trailers, motor homes, and boats. Make a copy of any appraisals you may have for vintage automobiles.
- **Jewelry**: Collect any appraisals and receipts or credit card statements showing the purchase of jewelry.
- **Collections**: Try to find appraisals for coin, stamp, art, or other collections.
- **Furnishings**: Gather any receipts you can find for carpets, draperies, and other furnishings in your home.
- **Furniture**: Obtain receipts for furniture in your home.
- **Country club memberships, credit card reward points, frequent flyer miles**: Find any information available on country club memberships or credit card reward points for frequent flyer miles.
- **Time-shares**: Find agreements and any related correspondence on any time-shares you may own.
- **Tax benefits**: Obtain copies of your tax returns. You can order these from the IRS if you don't have copies. Your attorney or accountant may also be able to tell you if there are any other assets you don't know about by looking at your tax returns. There are certain tax items that can have value and be carried over from year to year. For example, losses that cannot be deducted in the current year may be used to offset income in future years

Note that assets can be considered marital property that the divorce court can distribute between spouses. Or they can be considered separate nonmarital property, which the divorce court cannot divide. Property you brought into the marriage, for example, is your separate property as long as you haven't made it into, or mixed it up with, marital property. Property acquired during the marriage, with a few exceptions, is marital property. Some property can be part marital and part nonmarital. For example, a pension plan started before the marriage and contributed to during the marriage will be considered part marital and part nonmarital property. In such cases, you will have to find historical statements showing the dates and amounts of your contributions if you want to be able to keep the nonmarital portion of the property.

Liabilities (Before and After Marriage)

Liabilities refer to things you owe payments on, like student loans or credit cards. You can order your credit report for free from one of the three reporting agencies, and that will give you a starting point from which to go over your debts. Here are other documents you want to find to identify and value your liabilities:

- **Promissory notes secured for real estate**: Look for copies of mortgages, mortgage statements, home equity lines of credit, and business loans secured for obtaining real estate.

- **Bank loans**: Find promissory notes and statements for bank loans if you can.

- **Student loans**: Gather all documents related to student loans, including promissory notes and statements.

- **Loans from friends and relatives**: If you have borrowed or intend to borrow money from friends or relatives for living expenses or legal fees during your divorce, be sure to document the loan in writing with a promissory note signed by you. Blank forms are available cheaply at most office supply stores.

- **Automobile loans and leases**: Obtain copies of automobile or other vehicle loans or leases and statements showing payments and the amount still owed.

- **Credit cards**: Acquire copies of monthly statements that show charges and payments for all credit cards.

- **Taxes**: Gather tax returns, which will show past amounts due. Collect copies of any correspondence from or to the IRS, state tax, and local tax authorities.

Income

Your income includes everything for which you receive payment—your paycheck, interest, stock dividends, lottery winnings, and so on. Pay special attention to:

- **Pay statements**: Find copies of your last two pay statements.

- **Employment contracts or letters**: Make a copy of any documents related to employment.

- **Bank and brokerage statements**: Gather any evidence of interest and dividends you have received, such as savings account statements, certificate of deposit statements, and brokerage account statements.

- **Trusts**: If you have any trust accounts, you will need the trust agreement and records of disbursements.

Expenses

Expenses are payments you make for goods and services. Make copies of canceled checks, bank statements, budgets, computer records, and other financial documents that relate to your expenses. Here's a suggested list of expense categories to help you get started. If the expense varies from month to month, you will need about a year's worth of records.

- Mortgage or rent
- Utilities
- Food
- Automobile
- Expenses for children
- Clothing
- Medical
- Dues
- Miscellaneous
- Charge account debt
- Taxes
- Other debt

Additional Records

You may also find useful information in calendars, diaries, e-mail, automobile mileage records, photographs, videos, letters, package tracking bills, cell phones, and social-networking sites on the Internet. Don't forget to Google your spouse's name and conduct a search on Facebook. If you or your spouse has applied for a loan recently, copy any financial statements that were submitted with the application.

Tip   People often keep information in their phones, day planners, computers, and so forth.

Organizing Your Research

You can put copies of all the documents you collect in individual file folders or tabbed, three-ring notebooks, as described in the preceding chapter. You will need to make an index that will also serve as a comprehensive list of all assets, liabilities, income, and expenses. This format is easy to update when new statements are issued, and you will find it very useful later during settlement discussions, mediation, discovery, and trial.

A Word About Fault and Private Investigators

Fault determines who was to blame for the breakup of the marriage. Traditionally, fault was the only way to get a divorce. Fault includes adultery, desertion, and cruelty. Now, many states have added or substituted no-fault grounds such as separation or irreconcilable differences. (I'll have more to say on this subject in Chapter 4.)

Even in "no fault" states, however, fault may affect the outcome of your divorce. The judge may consider who was at fault when she is establishing alimony or dividing property.

Adultery is the only fault ground that is usually proven by circumstantial evidence. Private investigators are hired to provide that evidence. The investigator can follow your spouse and perhaps testify something like, "I saw them having dinner together and holding hands. They left the restaurant and went to a motel. I put a chalk mark on the tire of the car and when I returned the next morning the car had not been moved."

The best way to find a private investigator is to ask your divorce attorney for a recommendation. Divorce attorneys are used to working with private investigators and will know the best ones to use. Investigators can also do asset searches for you if you believe your spouse is hiding assets and will not reveal them in the court's discovery process. Investigators charge by the hour plus expenses, so be prepared to spend several-hundred to thousands of dollars for their services.

Researching the Law

Researching the law is not done to gain the expertise of a lawyer. Rather, it will help you to know where the law is found and to read summaries of it written for laypeople so you can understand what is going on in your case. The law can be found in the following places.

Constitution. The Constitution of the United States, as well as of each state, is the document that sets up the framework for the executive, legislative, and judicial branches. It gives you the rights that you enjoy, such as due process and pursuit of happiness.

Code. King Hammurabi of Babylon, born in 1792 BC, is known as the lawgiver. He produced the earliest written collection of laws, known as a code. The code was written in stone on tablets over eight feet tall. In our democracy, the people elect a legislature, which considers, deliberates, discusses, and passes laws each year. These are published in book form, and you can also find them on the Internet. There is a code for the United States, and each state has its own code of laws. The courts interpret the laws and can decide if they are constitutional or not.

Cases. If you go to trial and don't like the result, you can appeal your case to a court of appeals. The appeals court consists of a panel of judges (who are different from the one who tried the case). The appeal judges do not try the case over again; they review the briefs submitted by counsel. These briefs are written arguments that one or more errors were committed by the trial judge. They may also review the transcript of the trial. They may affirm, vacate, modify, or reverse the decision of the trial court. Many of the orders of the appellate court are published in books called reporters. Lawyers may cite these cases as legal precedent in later trials and appeals.

Rules. Each state has rules for its courts. These are published in a book of court rules. The rules contain deadlines, descriptions of pleadings, how evidence is to be presented, and so forth. Some judges also publish rules for their particular courtroom. And there are unwritten rules, which are the customs and practices of various judges.

Where to Find the Law

The first place to look for information about the law is the Internet. If you don't have access to the Web, you can try the public library, but you will have better luck doing legal research if there is a law library at the courthouse or a law school that you can get access to.

Tip   A couple of good Web sites on which to find out about divorce law are www.divorceinfo.com run by Lee Borden and the "Divorce Support" page on www.about.com run by Cathy Meyer.

Visit the Courtroom

Nothing compares to actually watching a trial in progress. Courthouses and divorce cases are open to the public. You can gain a lot of knowledge and become more comfortable with the courtroom if you watch a few trials.

Summary

You've given your divorce some thought. You've done some research on the divorce laws in your state. You've begun to gather and organize the information and documents you will need. You're probably asking yourself if you can get a divorce without a lawyer. We'll discuss that topic in the next chapter.

CHAPTER 4

Can You Do It Yourself?

You are not required to have a lawyer for a divorce. Actually, most divorces are handled without a lawyer or with a lawyer for only one side. *Pro se* is Latin for "by yourself." A *pro se* divorce is a do-it-yourself divorce. Can you do it yourself or do you need to hire a lawyer? That depends on a number of factors, like how complicated your divorce is and the resources you have available for legal fees. You first need to weigh the costs and benefits of using a lawyer.

Benefits of Using a Lawyer

By all means, hire a lawyer if you can afford one. There are many benefits to having a good lawyer on your side to guide and protect you:

- You will know that things are done correctly in your case.
- You can stop worrying about your case and let your lawyer start worrying about it.
- Your lawyer will have the education, experience, and skill to handle the job.
- Your lawyer will know the law, the cases, and the rules of court.
- Your lawyer has dealt with the court before and will be comfortable in the courtroom.

- Your lawyer can negotiate for you.
- A lawyer can protect you and help you reach a fair settlement in your case.
- Your lawyer can prepare a settlement agreement for you.
- Your lawyer can keep track of court deadlines and guide you through the divorce process.
- Judges are lawyers and speak the same language as your lawyer.
- You may get more respect from the judge and your spouse's attorney if you have a lawyer.
- A lawyer will know what to do if complications arise in your case.

Costs of Using a Lawyer

There are also downsides to using a lawyer, and there are costs you'll have as well. And I'm not just talking about money, as you'll see.

Conflict

Some lawyers can increase the conflict in your case. A lot of people believe in fighting fire with fire. If your spouse hires a lawyer with a reputation for being overly aggressive, difficult, or unreasonable, then you might be tempted to hire a similar type of attorney. Although this has little effect on the outcome of your case, it will cost you a lot more money. It's better to fight fire with water.

Tip Sometimes when it comes to divorces or lawsuits, it's better to fight fire with . . . water.

Lawyers are Expensive

The main cost in a divorce is legal fees. Lawyers charge by the hour for their work. Depending on where you live, the cost could be anywhere from $150 to over $500 an hour.

Many people look for the lawyer who charges the least per hour, thinking they are getting a bargain. But the higher fees usually mean that the lawyer has more experience and, having handled many cases like yours before, can do it faster than the lawyer with the lower hourly fee. So, you need to think about the overall cost of your case and not just the hourly rate.

How much will a divorce cost you in legal fees? It will cost about the same as a new car. But that new car may be a Hyundai or it may be a Porsche. Even your attorney will be guessing when they give you an estimate of legal fees. That's because there are too many unknowns and too many things that are not within your control, like the judge, your spouse, and your spouse's attorney.

Since the total cost is unknown, divorce attorneys require a retainer, which is an up-front payment. A typical retainer is $5,000. The retainer is placed in the attorney's trust account, and they bill against it at their hourly rate plus the costs mentioned above. If the lawyer is able to resolve your case within the price of the retainer, any balance remaining in the trust will be refunded to you. If your case costs more than $5,000, the attorney will ask you for more money.

Note Your divorce attorney will likely require you to pay an up-front fee called a retainer. Typically, the retainer is $5,000. The lawyer will draw from the retainer to pay your bills until it runs out or the costs are met. Any balance remaining in the trust account will be refunded to you.

It will also pay to get a little perspective on your case. You don't want to spend $5,000 in legal fees fighting over $5,000 in marital assets. The larger the stakes, the more the legal costs can be justified.

The divorce attorney will give you a fee agreement that sets out all this in writing. You both sign the agreement.

It is possible to recoup some of your legal fees and costs from your spouse, either in settlement or at trial. You would either negotiate this with your spouse as part of your settlement agreement or ask the court to award you attorney fees. At trial, the judge considers the resources and needs of each party. However, the court-ordered attorney fees rarely cover the full amount you have advanced.

Additional Litigation Costs

While legal fees will be the most expensive part of your divorce, there are other costs as well. You will have to pay fees to the court for filing your divorce and other pleadings. You will have to hire a process server to serve the divorce papers to your spouse. You will have to pay for transcripts. You will have to pay for mediation. You may need expert witnesses, such as custody evaluators, appraisers, accountants, vocational rehabilitation experts, and so forth. Expert witnesses can cost thousands of dollars.

HIDDEN COSTS

In addition to legal fees and costs, there is an emotional cost to divorce that can have a damaging impact on your finances as well. You may be unable to work and earn a living, or your income may be reduced due to the stress, depression, and time that a divorce involves. You may have to pay for therapy and medications during this time. These are the hidden costs of divorce.

Knowledge

If you do not use a lawyer, you will be expected to know the rules even if you do not. Don't expect your spouse's lawyer or the judge to give you any leeway because you are representing yourself and you are not a lawyer. If the other side finds a way to exploit your lack of knowledge and experience, it will.

Main Consideration: Simple or Complex Divorce?

First, let's discuss the difference between an uncontested divorce and a contested divorce.

Uncontested Divorce

An uncontested divorce means that you and your spouse have agreed on everything and there are no disputes between the two of you for the judge to decide on. In many cases, you can make a signed, written agreement that spells everything out. The court will reference and incorporate this into the divorce order. The uncontested divorce hearing only takes from fifteen to twenty minutes. This is the kind of divorce you want if you can get it. The hardest part is getting the agreement.

You should be able to handle an uncontested divorce yourself, especially if you go to the courthouse and watch a few of them. If you do not have the time, energy, or tolerance for frustration that this may require, then, by all means, hire a lawyer to do it for you.

Tip Get an uncontested divorce if at all possible. The hearing will take all of 15–20 minutes. But you'll have to work hard to get an agreement you and your spouse can both live with.

Contested Divorce

If you cannot reach an agreement with your spouse, then you will have a contested divorce. That's true even if there is only one issue in dispute. In a contested divorce, you have a trial and you present testimony, documents, and witnesses, and the judge decides all the issues for you. This is time consuming and expensive. You want to avoid a contested divorce if you can.

Whether or not you need a lawyer for a contested divorce case depends a lot on how simple or complex your divorce is. You can probably handle a simple divorce without a lawyer. The more complications that you have, the more you need a lawyer.

Simple Divorce

A simple divorce is usually one in which the parties have been married a short time, have no children, and have little or no marital assets or debt to divide, and one in which both make about the same amount of money. This is the sort of case that you can probably handle yourself.

Sometimes people will say to a lawyer they have a simple divorce and they have agreed on everything. But when the lawyer draws up a written agreement for them to sign, it turns out they do not agree on everything. Then things become complicated.

Complications

The following situations will make your divorce more complicated. Each of them will be discussed in more detail later in the book. If any of these issues are present in your case, you should at least think about getting a lawyer.

- **High conflict:** Some couples can't even agree on what day of the week it is. If you spend all your time arguing with your spouse, you may need an attorney to help present your case to a judge.

- **High stakes:** The higher the stakes, the more complicated your divorce becomes, and the more you need a lawyer. The stakes can be property, alimony, or children—the highest stakes of all.

- **Children:** If you have children, you will have to determine legal custody, meaning who makes the long-term parenting decisions like education, medical treatment, and religious upbringing. You will have to determine physical custody, which is where the children live most of the time. You will have to determine an access schedule.

There may be parenting disagreements over routines at each house or how the children are disciplined and so forth. You will have to determine child support, which is based on guidelines that involve alimony, time spent with each parent, both parents' incomes, health costs, day care costs, and other factors. Disputes sometimes arise over each of these factors; for example, it can be difficult to ascertain the income of a business owner who controls which bills get paid and which customer invoices are collected.

- **House:** If you own a house, will you keep it or list it for sale? How will the proceeds be distributed? What if you owe more than the house is worth? Who will pay for it until it's sold?

- **Retirement Funds:** What portion of your retirement account is marital and what portion is nonmarital? How will the marital portion be divided? How much is your retirement account worth? What happens if you are receiving retirement payments over time and you or your spouse dies?

- **Alimony:** Will you need spousal support? Will you have to pay spousal support? How much and for how long? Do you want it to be modifiable by the court if your circumstances change? What circumstances would cause alimony to change or be terminated? What impact will alimony have on taxes and child support?

- **Domestic abuse:** If domestic abuse is involved in the cause of your divorce, you will probably need the advice of an attorney.

- **Business interests and investments:** If you have a lot of assets to divide, or there are one or more businesses, then you should hire an attorney to help you.

- **High-income earner:** An attorney may be able to help you find hidden "perks," which high-income earners sometimes have. If you are a high-income earner, an attorney may be able to help you present your finances to your spouse in a fashion that leads to settlement.

- **Government employees:** Government employees have special retirement accounts, health insurance, and other benefits that are somewhat complicated and often can benefit from the services of an attorney.

- **Military divorce:** There are special rules for military divorces regarding retirement funds and health care.
- **Same-sex divorce:** This is an evolving area of the law, and there are special considerations in same-sex divorces. For example, what happens when a same-sex couple marries in a state that allows them to marry and then they move to a state that does not?
- **Missing spouse:** You will have to make efforts to locate your spouse if they can't be found. Then, you'll need to file a motion for alternative service with the court and attach an affidavit of your efforts. Finally, there will be a default hearing where you alone will testify.
- **Your spouse has a lawyer:** If your spouse has a lawyer, that lawyer is looking out for your spouse's interests, which are likely to be contrary to yours. A lawyer knows the law better than you do and where to place all the tricks and traps for the unwary.

Mediation

A mediator is a neutral third party who tries to help you reach a settlement with your spouse so that you can sign a separation agreement and have an uncontested divorce. The mediator does not represent either side in the negotiations.

Not all states regulate who serves as mediators, so they can be lawyers, or therapists, or anyone else. A good mediator will guide both parties through a series of steps that result in a complete marital settlement agreement.

Mediation takes place with both parties present and the mediator serving in one or more sessions. It is usually done without attorneys present although the parties may have them if they wish.

Why You Should Mediate

Mediation has several advantages:

- **An end to litigation:** If you can settle your case in mediation, you will avoid a trial—and the related time, energy, emotion, and legal fees it involves.
- **Certainty:** A mediated settlement brings certainty to uncertainty. You may not get everything you want, but you control the outcome through negotiation and compromise, instead of letting a judge—a stranger to your case—tell you the outcome.

- **Breaking impasses:** Sometimes spouses are just unable to talk to one another or have a civil conversation. Mediation brings them together in the same room, and the mediator can act as a referee when discussions become heated. Or the mediator can become an interpreter when parties have trouble understanding one another.

- **Level playing field:** Mediation can level the playing field. When one party has a style that is controlling, overpowering, dominant, aggressive, or self-centered, the mediator can help the other party be heard and respected so that a fair agreement can be reached.

- **Options:** Judges are limited by the legislature in terms of how they can decide a case. In mediation, the parties are freer to pursue other options. The court has the power to approve and enforce their agreement even if it contains provisions that the court would not be able to order on its own. The mediator can present various options to the parties for resolving their disputes. And sometimes when the parties are talking, a workable solution falls on the table in the middle of the conversation that no one had thought of before.

- **No appeals:** If your case is settled in mediation, there can be no appeals. There is some evidence that parties who undertake mediated settlements are happier with the outcomes than those who litigate their cases. There are also fewer postdivorce disputes.

- **Cheaper cost:** Lawyers usually charge less than their normal hourly rates when they act as mediators. And that hourly fee is split between the spouses. In addition, you are sitting across the table from the other party, so you can ask questions and get immediate feedback. In traditional negotiation, you would ask your lawyer a question, who would in turn write to your spouse's lawyer, who would then ask your spouse and write back to your lawyer, and so on. Each letter or phone call might cost $25 or $50. So, mediation may be a cost-effective way to reach an agreement.

- **Faster procedure:** It may take a year or longer to complete a contested divorce. There are a lot more cases filed than there are judges to try them. The system counts on a majority of cases being settled. If you try your case, your trial will be set on the next available date on the judge's calendar. But you can make an appointment with a mediator right away.

Why You May Not Want to Mediate

Mediation also has a few disadvantages:

- **No settlement:** There is no guarantee that your case will settle in mediation. So, you could go through the entire mediation process and end up spending money for the mediator with nothing to show for it in the end.

- **Level playing field:** If you are the one who controls all the assets, you may not want a level playing field. You may want to try to use your resources to your advantage in a trial. It's a harsh reality but true: many people don't want to be fair with their soon-to-be ex.

- **Commitment:** In order for mediation to work, both parties have to be committed to it. If you are there because your spouse dragged you, it will be difficult for the mediator to help you resolve your case.

What "No Fault" Means

In order to file for a divorce, you have to have grounds. Grounds refer to reasons for a divorce.

It used to be that you could only get a divorce on fault grounds, such as desertion, adultery, cruelty, imprisonment, or insanity. Then, legislatures started adding no-fault grounds to the original fault grounds. California was first. New York was last. Some states would permit a divorce with no fault if there were "irreconcilable differences." Others permitted a divorce if there was "no hope or expectation of a reconciliation." Some just required a separation for a certain period of time. And now, some states have done away with their fault grounds altogether and have only no-fault divorces.

You should be aware, however, that even in no-fault states, fault may still make a difference. Some states, which have abolished fault as grounds for divorce, may still look at the circumstances surrounding the estrangement of the parties to determine alimony and property division. Those circumstances involve fault. And even in states where fault is not a factor that is considered in alimony and property division, evidence of fault may still persuade a judge to rule one way or the other.

Summary

Deciding whether or not to hire a lawyer or do your own divorce involves considering the costs and benefits as well as the complexity of your case. Mediation may be an attractive alternative for you. No-fault divorce has made a divorce easier to obtain in some cases, but fault may still be a factor in such cases. Next, we'll help you find the right lawyer if you have decided you need one.

CHAPTER 5

Finding a Lawyer

One of the most important things you can do in your divorce is to find the right lawyer. Your divorce lawyer will be the central manager for the facts, the law, the other people involved, the documents and other evidence, the settlement, and the trial of your case. The lawyer will be the quarterback of your team and the general of your army. It is vitally important to select the proper one. If you decide to hire a lawyer, this chapter will tell you where to find and how to select the right one for you.

You Need a Divorce Lawyer

In days past, most lawyers were general practitioners and every lawyer was a divorce lawyer. But as lawyers have become more specialized, divorce law has become more complicated. Divorce lawyers not only need to know divorce law, but also businesses, contracts, bankruptcy, options, intellectual property, partnerships, corporations, and taxes, which can be involved in their cases as well.

Divorce law is based on equity, which means fairness, as opposed to contract law or tax law, which is based on logic. In contract law, the breaching party has to pay damages to the other party. In divorce law, the breaching party may get half the property, alimony, child support, and attorney's fees. You need to find a knowledgeable, experienced family lawyer who devotes most of her practice to divorce law.

Note Keep in mind that fairness is the main criterion for assessing the case in divorce law. In contract or tax law, on the other hand, logic rules the day.

Word of Mouth

Word of mouth is usually the best way to find a good divorce lawyer. Ask your family, friends, neighbors, and coworkers. You probably know many people who have been divorced. Ask them who they used and what their experience was with their lawyer. People love talking about their divorce (once they've had a chance to heal and get over it). You may also ask other professionals who interact with divorce lawyers—like accountants, financial planners, and real estate agents. Actual experience is the best way to gauge how good a lawyer is.

Internet

It used to be that attorneys were prohibited from advertising, so the only way to find one was by word-of-mouth. Now, attorneys are permitted to advertise in the yellow pages, magazines, and newspapers; on radio and television; and even on billboards.

Most law firms and lawyers have Web pages. Many publish blogs. You can use a general search engine like Google to identify divorce lawyers in your location. There are a few specialized Web sites that can help you find the right lawyer for your divorce:

- **www.avvo.com:** Click on "Find a Lawyer," then type in "divorce" as the practice area and enter your location. This site rates lawyers from one to ten (ten being "superb"), reports any ethics problems, has lengthy biographies, and allows you to read reviews by former clients and other attorneys.

- **www.lawyers.com:** Lawyers.com is affiliated with the first and oldest lawyer rating service, Martindale-Hubbell. The ratings are strictly from other lawyers. The highest rating is "av preeminent." The av signifies that the lawyer has been given very high "general ethical standards" and "legal ability" numerical ratings.

- **www.superlawyers.com:** Super Lawyers uses a combination of editorial research and voting by other lawyers to select the top 5 percent of lawyers in different practice areas in each state. Lawyer profiles are included on the site.

Experience Counts

"The reason I called you, Uncle Pete, is that I thought you might be able to refer me to a reasonably priced attorney that can help me with my divorce," the caller says.

"It depends on what you mean by reasonably priced," Pete says to his nephew. "I can refer you to a younger lawyer who charges $150 an hour or I can refer you to a more experienced lawyer who charges $300 an hour but who will do the job in half the time it takes the younger lawyer."

You wouldn't shop around for an inexperienced heart surgeon, and you wouldn't try to get the cheapest brain surgeon in town to operate on you. If the stakes are high, you probably don't want a lawyer who is just out of law school to handle your divorce. Look for a seasoned professional who has been around the block before and knows how to advise you.

Skills

You want to look for a lawyer who is knowledgeable in the family law of your state. Some states certify skilled family lawyers. Other states do not allow lawyers to claim they are an expert in any one area of law, but you can still find out what percentage of practice a lawyer devotes to family law. Many states require continuing legal education for lawyers but some do not.

Some lawyers are very good at memorizing the law and reciting it when called upon to do so. They seem skillful but lack common sense and creativity. Sometimes, a case calls for a creative solution.

When Alexander the Great entered Gordium in the fourth century BC, there was a chariot tied with an intricate knot. It was prophesied that whoever could undo the knot would become king of Asia. Alexander drew his sword and sliced the knot in half. Hence came the phrase "Gordian Knot" to signify a complex problem that defies solutions except for by the most creative and well trained. Look for a lawyer that can cut through the Gordian knots in your case.

A divorce is about money as well as children and the end of the marriage. So, it helps to have a lawyer that is conversant in money issues, such as accounting, pensions, taxes, investments, promissory notes, stock, business valuations, corporations, and real estate.

Trust

The attorney-client relationship is unique. Your attorney is your confessor, champion, and advisor. You must find an attorney you trust.

You are going to be telling your attorney personal information, confidential secrets, and sometimes embarrassing things. You are going to be sharing all your financial information with your attorney, the history of your marriage, and the details of why you are getting a divorce.

You can get a feeling for how much you trust an attorney in your initial telephone conference or meeting. Does the attorney answer your questions directly, honestly, and in plain English? Do you feel comfortable talking with this person?

Attorneys are usually busy people, especially divorce attorneys. So, don't expect to get one on the phone the first time you call. But it is important for you to note how long the attorney takes to return your call. Is this attorney prompt, reliable, and accessible or is he too busy to give your case the attention it deserves?

Style

Divorce attorneys come in a number of flavors. Let's take a look at a few:

- **The shark:** There seems to be at least one lawyer in every town that has a reputation for being tough. This lawyer is described as one who eats nails for breakfast. One lawyer advertised that while other lawyers wrote their agreements in ink, he wrote his in blood. Why would you hire such a lawyer? Because you've watched too much TV and believe that projecting strength and intimidation are effective tools in the practice of law. A mean-spirited lawyer is not a good lawyer.

> **Tip** A mean-spirited lawyer is usually not a good lawyer. Look for those with quiet confidence and experience.

The new traffic cop on the corner flaps his arms, blows his whistle loudly, and gestures wildly to get the cars to go where he wants. The veteran traffic cop lifts an eyebrow, wiggles a finger, and gets the cars to go where he wants with small gestures.

So, it is in the practice of law. All that shouting and flapping does not move your case forward. If anything, they will delay resolution of your case and increase your expenses. These types of lawyers are in it for the show. They, at worst, have personality defects or, at best, use their personalities as marketing techniques to sell you the sizzle without the steak.

Don't get taken in by the shark. If your spouse hires a shark, don't fight fire with fire. That only leads to more fire. Divorce is a fight, but it is a formal and civilized fight, with rules of engagement. Good attorneys can argue the facts and the law vigorously and still be polite to the parties and opposing counsel. The more rude and obnoxious the shark becomes, the calmer and quieter your attorney should become. That highlights the shark's behavior to the court.

- **The pushover:** On the other hand, you don't want an attorney who is truly weak in defending your interests and prosecuting your case. Your attorney needs to have self-confidence and a quiet strength. You don't want your attorney to cave in on every issue. You need someone who can confront disputes head on and say the hard things that have to be said, both to the other side and sometimes to you.

- **The technician:** This is the type of lawyer you are looking for. She moves your case forward, solves problems, returns your calls, and meets deadlines, and completes the work in an organized, efficient, economical, and timely fashion. She minimizes conflict and disputes over small issues. She helps you identify and prioritize your goals and objectives.

- **The zen lawyer:** Finally, there is the kind of lawyer that brings enlightenment to your case. This lawyer helps you rise above issues of squabbling over money. Instead, he helps you to focus on long-term issues like preserving the relationship of the children with each parent and keeping a civil relationship with your ex so that you are able to coparent.

Note A really good lawyer will help each spouse preserve their relationships with your children—and with each other—for the long term.

People spend hundreds of thousands of dollars fighting over their money in a divorce. After all, it is hard to work, sacrifice, and save for years to build up an estate only to watch helplessly as it is destroyed almost instantly in a divorce. It is tough to let go of money. Yet, that counterintuitive step is the secret of what

I call the zen divorce. Walk away from the fight. Value your happiness more than the money. The attitude is summed up nicely by this poem:

> *Oh me, oh my,*
>
> *A fortune in gold and silver had I.*
>
> *But I spent it all in town last night,*
>
> *In case tomorrow I might die.*

—Unknown

Male or Female Attorney?

Does it matter which gender you choose in deciding to hire a divorce attorney? If you are a woman, do you want a male or female attorney, and vice versa? Does it make a difference if the judge in your case is male or female? It is more important to get a good lawyer, regardless of gender. Some good lawyers are men and some are women.

Litigator or Negotiator

One law firm runs an ad that says, "When you've absolutely decided not to settle, call us." Obviously, this firm likes to litigate.

A negotiated settlement in a divorce case is usually preferable to litigation. Some lawyers are better at settlement negotiations than others. They work better with people and have an agreeable personal style. Some lawyers are better at litigation and feel more comfortable making presentations in the courtroom.

Note   A negotiated settlement in a divorce case is usually preferable to litigation.

Ideally, you would like to have a lawyer that is good at settling cases but is not afraid to go to trial if a settlement cannot be reached. An alternative is to find a firm that has both litigators and negotiators.

A mismatch can occur if your philosophy clashes with your lawyer's. Some people like to fight. Others like to try to reach agreement in a cooperative fashion. Lawyers have different approaches, too. Some will say, "Let's take her to the cleaners." Others will say, "Let's see if we can settle first." Ask your lawyer about his philosophy in this regard. If you want to settle, don't hire the attorney who would rather file suit first and talk later. You will be at cross-purposes.

Phone Calls and E-mails

When a divorce lawyer gets a message that you've called, it's likely to be one of a dozen or more messages on his desk. A divorce lawyer spends a lot of time on the phone. It's a routine part of the job.

But it's probably not the same for you. You are calling about money, or children, or the house, or some other important matter that you need to discuss now.

Find a lawyer that's accessible to you when you need to talk to him. There are lawyers who promptly respond to voice mails and e-mails. There are also lawyers that you can never reach. Nothing is more frustrating than a lawyer who won't call you back.

Fees and Retainers

Attorneys are not permitted to take divorce cases for a percentage of the money received by a spouse or the money saved by a spouse. Also, flat fees are rare except in the simplest of cases because the amount of work involved is unknowable at the outset.

For that reason, divorce lawyers charge by the hour. Rates can be anywhere from about $100 an hour to over $600 an hour. The rate will vary according to their experience and the amount of demand for the lawyer's time by other clients as well as where you live. City lawyers charge more than country lawyers because the rent is higher in the city. And for the same reasons, the bigger the city, the higher the hourly fee.

Divorce lawyers also require a retainer, which is an up-front payment and is typically $5,000 to $10,000. They are required by law to place this money in a separate trust account that is used to pay their bills as they work. Transfers from the trust account are usually made once a month after the hours are tallied and a bill is prepared. If there is any money left over at the end of the case, it belongs to you. If the lawyers exceed the money in the trust, they will request that you pay additional retainers if you want them to continue working for you.

How to Save Money

Here's a laundry list of tips you can use to save on legal fees:

- **Discuss your emotions with your therapist, not your lawyer:** Your lawyer is not your therapist. Your lawyer charges you by the hour whether you are calling to ask a legal question about your case, complain about your spouse, or talk about the weather. Emotional stress is part of every divorce, but try to separate your emotions from the legal issues. Instead, talk to your counselor, religious advisor, friends, or family about your emotions. Talk to your lawyer about legal and financial matters. By the way, if you are finding it difficult to control your emotions, getting some counseling may help you obtain a more successful outcome in your divorce in the long run.

- **Do some research:** Knowledge is power in a divorce. It used to be that only lawyers had access to the law. Now, it is freely available on the Internet. You can also use search engines to do legal research and check up on your spouse. Check the computer, desk drawers, phone and credit card bills, checkbook, and even the trash can for information you can use in your divorce.

- **Prepare a financial statement:** Use the court financial forms. These will help you and your attorney organize your income and expenses and your assets and debts so that you can present them in settlement negotiations, mediation, or trial. They will also help determine what you will need in the way of finances going forward.

- **Determine the value of your house:** You will need to know this in your negotiations. You can check one of the online sites like www.zillow.com or you can ask a real estate agent her assessment. For a more formal valuation, you can hire an appraiser to give you a written report for around $400. If you can get your spouse to pay half or pay for it from a marital account, even better.

- **Determine the value of your business:** If you or your spouse own a business, you will need to ascertain its value. Your accountant can probably give you a rough idea. If you need a formal appraisal for trial, that may cost around $5,000 to $10,000.

- **Estimate alimony and child support:** Alimony is within the judge's discretion in most states, but child-support is determined by the state's guidelines.
- **Do your divorce yourself:** If your case involves no children, a short marriage, and few assets or other complications, you may be able to do it yourself. Some courts are more user friendly than others, and they will help you with forms and information.
- **Talk to your lawyer's staff:** Usually, a lawyer's secretary, receptionist, and bookkeeper do not charge for their time. Paralegals do charge for their time but at lower rates than lawyers. If you are calling with a simple question, like "Did my pleading get filed yet?" it is cheaper to talk to the secretary than it is to talk to your lawyer.
- **Make your own copies or buy a printer:** There is a lot of paperwork involved in a divorce. Many lawyers charge you for the time the staff spends making copies. When you are asked to produce documents, go to a copy center and make a copy for your lawyer and a copy for the opposing party. You may also be able to save money by scanning documents to a computer disc or thumb drive. Check with your attorney first to see if she will accept electronic documents or wants paper documents.
- **Try mediation or another form of alternative dispute resolution:** In mediation, you and your spouse work with a neutral third party to try to reach an agreement using a problem-solving approach rather than an adversarial one.
- **Try collaborative law:** This type of approach uses another approach to reaching an agreement. You and your spouse meet with two specially trained attorneys in four-way meetings. The attorneys are hired only to settle your case. If you fail to reach an agreement, you must hire new attorneys to litigate.
- **Make the best use of your time with your lawyer:** Write down your questions before your initial consultation. Stay focused and on topic. Understand how attorneys bill their time. If you call every time you have a question, you will be billed $50 to $100 for every phone call.

That adds up quickly. It is more expensive to call your lawyer to say your spouse took the rake out of the garage than it is to buy a new rake. So, organize your questions and your time with your attorney. E-mail may also be an efficient way to communicate with your attorney.

- **Let your spouse be the one to file for divorce:** If your spouse files the suit, he has to pay the filing fee. There might be strategic legal reasons for you to file first, but usually it doesn't matter who files first.

- **Don't try to hang on to the house:** Sell your house and split the proceeds if there is any equity in it. Otherwise, you will be stuck with the mortgage payment, taxes, repairs, utilities, and insurance expenses. You may also have to pay to refinance it in order to get your spouse off the mortgage. And when you sell, you'll have selling expenses and possibly capital gains taxes to pay. Sell before the divorce and split the selling costs and you'll get a bigger deduction for capital gains.

- **Don't overlook the pension plans:** These plans have present value even if not vested or only partially vested. The value of IRAs and 401(k) plans are indicated on your monthly statements. But some other plans need to be valued by an actuary.

- **Choose the right lawyer:** A good lawyer can guide you through the divorce process successfully. The wrong lawyer can increase the difficulty and cost of your divorce.

- **Make a budget for your expenses after the divorce:** Look at your spending over the past year to help you get started. Are there any expenses that you can reduce if you do not have enough income?

- **Try to agree on a settlement with your spouse:** Fighting only increases the time and expense required to settle your case. The more money you spend on lawyers, the less money you will have to divide. Don't cave in if your spouse is being a bully or unreasonable. But two adult, civilized people ought to be able to sit down at the kitchen table and work out how to divide the property they have accumulated during the marriage.

- **Work out a custody plan with your spouse:** A custody battle over children will double the cost of your divorce. If you are fighting over whether the children should be with dad on Tuesday night or Wednesday night, you are spending your children's college money on that of the lawyer's children. If you really can't agree on a parenting plan or shared visitation schedule, ask a mediator, a custody evaluator, or a parenting coordinator to help you out.

- **Listen to your lawyer:** You are paying hundreds of dollars for your lawyer's advice. So listen to it carefully. Your lawyer has done this more times than you have. Whenever you hear your lawyer say, "I wouldn't do that, but you're the client and I'm just the lawyer," it means you are not listening and you will probably be sorry later.

- **Divide your stuff:** You don't want lawyers and judges fighting over your pots and pans. The furniture, furnishings, clothing, jewelry, and miscellaneous other things are usually less than 10 percent of the total marital estate. When dividing the furniture, remember what once was Ethan Allen is now just Sticks and Stones. Make list of your things and find a way to divide them, even if it's just by flipping a coin. Make copies of family photos.

Tip If you get stuck on dividing things in your divorce, ask yourself if the thing you are stuck on is symbolic and what you are really trying to hang onto is your marriage. Maybe it is time to let go of both.

Summary

In this chapter, we've given you some ideas on where and how to find a good divorce lawyer for your case, focusing on skills, experience, trust, and style. We've also discussed how you can avoid the wrong lawyer. And we've given you a few tips on how to save on legal fees. Once you've narrowed down your search for a lawyer, you will want to set up a consultation. The next chapter explains what you can expect at that first meeting with a lawyer.

CHAPTER 6

First Meeting with Lawyer and Beyond

You've asked around and done your research to find a great divorce lawyer. The next step is to call or e-mail him and set up an initial meeting. This chapter will tell you what you can expect from the first meeting with your divorce lawyer.

Before the Meeting

Usually, you will set up an appointment to go to the attorney's office and meet her face to face. Make the call to set up the meeting. Your call will be kept confidential. You can give your name and answer questions over the telephone.

Many divorce lawyers are too busy to talk to you on the first phone call. They have the receptionist or paralegal speak with you instead. They will probably ask you your spouse's name so they can make sure they do not already represent your spouse, which would be a conflict of interest. If someone needs to call you back, make sure you give them a "safe" number and time to call you. You can also set up an appointment by e-mail. Just be sure to use an e-mail account that your spouse cannot access.

A few attorneys like to have a fairly long telephone conversation before the first meeting. That way, they can find out if there are any legal emergencies, get to know a little bit about the case and you, and put you more at ease for the first meeting.

When you make the appointment, get directions to the lawyer's office and ask about parking. Ask if there is a fee for the consultation. Some divorce lawyers offer free consultations. Others charge for all of their time and advice. Ask what you should bring to the meeting. Ask what credit cards they accept.

Try to relax. Most people are nervous about the first meeting with the lawyer. They are in an uncomfortable predicament. You may be anxious or worried. You may be fearful for the future or tearful over the past. Realize, though, that your lawyer is in the business of solving problems like yours. The lawyer will know what to do and will probably start by asking you some questions.

Think about what you want. Many clients start by asking, "What are my rights?" or "What am I entitled to?" The answer to those questions is the lawyer's favorite answer, "It depends." Rather than ask, tell the lawyer what you want and see if it's possible or likely with the facts and law in your case. You can make a list or an outline of the top-ten things you want. That will help you and your lawyer make a plan to achieve some reasonable objectives.

Copy any financial information you are able to find. Also, copy any letters or pleadings you have received from your spouse or your spouse's lawyer.

Write down your personal facts. The lawyer will need the names of you and your spouse, your ages, your current address, the date and place of your marriage, and the date of separation. Also, provide the names, the ages, and the birth dates for your children.

Prepare a marital history. This is helpful for the lawyer to understand the timeline and background facts as well as the difficulties involved in your marriage.

Write down your questions. The first meeting will be a time for answering them. You probably have plenty, like the following examples: What about the house? How much support will I get or have to pay? What will it cost? How long will it take?

Tip Write down all the questions you can think of before you meet the lawyer. It will save you money.

What to Bring to the First Meeting

You really don't have to bring anything to the first meeting. In fact, most people don't. Your lawyer can get the information from you later or in discovery once a divorce is filed. But you can save some time at the first meeting and help move your case forward by bringing copies of the following to your first meeting:

1. **Legal documents**
   - **Agreements:** Bring any prenuptial or postnuptial agreements in writing.
   - **Pleadings:** Collect legal pleadings received from your spouse or your spouse's attorney. Also, bring any judgments, garnishments, bankruptcy pleadings, foreclosures, or any pleadings from other pending lawsuits.
   - **Correspondence:** Take any letters sent by your spouse's attorney.
2. **Evidence of income**
   - **Pay statements:** Bring the last three pay statements for you and your spouse, which will show salary, bonus, commissions, overtime, expense reimbursement, health insurance, tax deductions, and pension plan contributions.
   - **Tax returns:** Gather tax returns for the last three years, including W-2s, 1099s, and other related documents. Tax returns will reveal income and as well as investments. They will give the lawyer an overview of your financial situation. Finances are a big part of divorce. In the process of divorce, assets and debts are divided and income and expenses determine future support for children and spouses.
   - **Court financial statement:** Many courts have a form for each party to fill out for uniformity so the judge can get a quick view of both of their finances. Your attorney will probably give this to you at your first meeting. Sometimes these forms are published on the Internet. If you can find one for your jurisdiction and complete it before the meeting, you will be one step ahead.
3. **Bank and stock accounts**
   - **Bank statements:** Bring the most recent statements for checking and savings accounts or certificates of deposit for both spouses so that your lawyer has current balances and loan information.
   - **Stocks and bonds:** Take along the most recent statement for any brokerage accounts you and your spouse have.

4. **Real estate**
   - **Deeds:** Deeds will show how the title to real estate is held by you and your spouse.
   - **Mortgage:** The current mortgage statements will show the monthly payment and the total balance due on the property. Also, bring any statements from any other loan for which real estate is collateral, such as a second mortgage or home equity line of credit.
   - **Tax assessments:** Real estate tax assessments can give an indication of approximate fair market value.
   - **Closing documents:** If you want to claim a premarital interest in real estate, bring copies of the closing documents and canceled checks for the down payment and closing costs.
   - **Leases:** If you own rental property, retrieve a copy of the lease(s).

5. **Retirement Funds**
   - **IRA, 401(k), or other retirement and pension plans:** Bring current retirement and pension statements for you and your spouse.
   - **Social security:** Find copies of the latest annual report for each spouse showing the earnings history.

6. **Miscellaneous Items**
   - **Business statements:** Locate copies of organizational documents and ledgers and record books of sole proprietorships, partnerships, or corporations.
   - **Intellectual property:** Bring documents related to intellectual property, including licensing or royalty agreements and accountings.
   - **Vehicles:** Collect copies of automobile and other vehicle titles and related loan documents.
   - **Life insurance:** Take with you copies of life insurance policies.
   - **Frequent-flyer miles or reward points:** Bring copies of documents showing total airline-mile awards or credit-card reward points.

- **Time shares:** Retrieve documents related to any time shares you or your spouse own.
- **Country club memberships:** Pull out documentation related to any country club memberships or dues.
- **Pets:** Write down who will get which pets.
- **Photographs:** *Take* photograph or videos of furniture, furnishings, or any collections of value.
- **Budget:** Prepare a budget of your living expenses.
- **Separate property list:** Make a list of items each of you claims you owned before the marriage, inherited, or was a gift from a third person. Also, list any debts that still exist and were incurred before the marriage.

7. **Debts**
   - **Credit cards:** Bring the most recent statements from your credit card accounts.
   - **Promissory notes:** Take with you copies of any promissory notes you have signed for student loans, loans from banks, credit unions, pension plans, or friends and relatives.
   - **Loan applications:** Gather copies of any financial statements prepared for loan applications made in the past three years.

8. **Nonfinancial Items**
   - **Evidence:** Procure anything you might want to introduce at trial to prove a claim, like adultery or cruelty. This includes photographs, videos, sound recordings, letters, texts, and e-mails.
   - **Family photographs:** Take photos of the children and you together if custody is an issue.
   - **Questions:** Produce a list of questions you want the attorney to answer.
   - **History:** Provide information on previous marriages and a brief outline of the history of your current marriage including any marital counseling that has taken place. Prepare the outline in chronological order so the lawyer can see the timeline of important events in your marriage and determine if you have grounds for a divorce.

- **Goals:** Write down what you expect out of your divorce.
- **Payment:** Bring your checkbook, cash, or a credit card in case your lawyer charges for the initial consultation.

What You Can Expect When You Get to the Lawyer's Office

Divorce lawyers are usually sensitive to the client's need for privacy. You will probably not have to sign in or sit in a waiting room full of people as you would in a doctor's office. No one will come out from an inner office and announce your name and say "the lawyer will see you now." You probably won't have to wait more than a few minutes. Divorce lawyers tend to schedule client appointments far enough apart that you won't see someone you know when entering or leaving the lawyers office.

Marshaling the Facts

The attorney's goal at the initial consultation is to obtain information from you about your case. Before he can answer your questions, the attorney must first get the facts. So, he will usually begin by asking you some simple questions like your name, age, name of your spouse, date of marriage, and so forth. He is not only getting to know you but marshaling the facts in your case.

If you have written this information down ahead of time, you can give the attorney a copy of the information you have compiled now and go over it with him. He will use the personal data he collects about you and your family both in a settlement agreement and in a divorce complaint if settlement efforts should fail.

Everything you say to your attorney is confidential even in the first phone call or e-mail and the first meeting. Providing information can be uncomfortable for you since you are telling a stranger very personal details about your life, but the more information the attorney has, the more the he can help you. Each divorce is unique and has its own set of facts, circumstances, and legal issues.

Note Expect to tell your attorney personal, even embarrassing, facts. It will remain confidential, and it will help the lawyer craft a compelling strategy.

The Proceedings

If you have already received a complaint or a letter from your spouse's attorney, the lawyer will want to see those documents. If your spouse has an attorney, your lawyer will want to know who it is. Some couples have talked about divorce or separation already and are committed to settling their differences as quickly and inexpensively as possible without litigation. Others have already been served with a complaint. Some may be surprised that their spouse wants a divorce. Some may have spouses who do not even know they are meeting with a lawyer. And some may not yet be sure they want a divorce but want to find out what happens if they do decide to get one. Your lawyer will want to know your present situation.

The Marriage

Some of the questions your lawyer will ask you will be about the history of your marriage and courtship. Others will be about your separation. They often include: What are the problems in your marriage? Who did what to whom? How long have you had these problems? Have you tried marital counseling? Has there been any physical violence? Is there another love interest in your life? It is important that you tell the lawyer everything. If you cheated, tell the lawyer. That is the only way the lawyer can help you with your case.

The Children

The lawyer will also ask you questions about the children, such as, Do you think that you and your spouse can coparent together? Where do you want the children to live most of the time? What is the access schedule with your spouse? What are the kids' names, ages, and dates of birth, and where have they lived for the last five years? Do they have any special needs? Where do they go to school? Are there any emotional or educational problems? What do you think of your spouse's parenting skills?

The Finances

The lawyer will need to know about financial matters in order to advise you about property division, child support, and spousal support. She might ask questions like: What bank accounts, brokerage accounts, real estate, investments, retirement funds, and other assets do you own? Whose name is each asset in? What debts do you have? What are and your spouse's incomes? What are your and your spouse's educational backgrounds and work experience? Are there any medical reasons you cannot work full time? If unemployed or underemployed, what efforts have you made to find full-time employment? What is the standard of living you have enjoyed during the marriage?

Once the lawyer has marshaled the facts of your case, he will be able to sort out the legal issues and answer any questions that you have. Don't worry if you cannot produce all of this information at the first meeting. The lawyer will know how to get additional information.

Asking the Lawyer Your Questions

The first meeting is also a time for you to ask the lawyer questions about your case. If you write down your questions ahead of time, you will not forget any of them.

Parents will want to know about the children: Are they going to be taken away from them? How will custody and access be determined? How much child support will be received or owed?

You will also want to know about alimony: How much will you receive or have to pay? How long will it last? Will it be modifiable or nonmodifiable in the future?

Here are some other typical questions:

- What about getting health insurance for yourself and the children? What about life insurance?
- What will happen with the house? Who will pay the bills?
- How will the property be divided?
- What is the process for getting divorced? How long does it take? How much does it cost?

Know What You Want: Goals, Objectives, and Priorities

Knowing what you want is half the battle. You will probably come out as the one who is most successful in negotiations if you go in knowing what you want. At the same time, you must be willing to compromise if you want to reach a settlement. Your lawyer will be able to tell you whether what you want is achievable or not and help you develop some reasonable goals and objectives.

Tip Know what you want out of the divorce. The more you know, the better the chance that the negotiations will work out in your favor.

Knowing what you want will also allow you to recognize success when you get it. Believe it or not, some clients say no even after their spouse offers to settle for everything they could get by trying their case before a judge. Some people want a judge to place blame on their spouse for the end of the marriage. This rarely happens and is probably not a reasonable objective.

The issues to be decided in a divorce are custody of the children and an access schedule, child support, alimony and property division. Each of these can have subissues, for example the house and retirement plan would be subissues under property division.

One way to figure out what you want is to list all the issues on a piece of paper and then make three columns: best case, worst case, and middle. Best case is what you ultimately want. Worst case is the minimum you could accept without walking out of settlement negotiations.

Then, to determine your priorities, go down the list and number the issues in their order of importance to you. In most cases, what is important to one party is not that important to the other. If you find this to be true in your case, it will allow you to make trades in negotiation.

Legal Advice and Counsel

After you and your lawyer have exchanged questions, the lawyer can then advise you about what to expect with regard to custody of the children and sharing time with them. Many parents are afraid the children will be taken away from them. Unless you are an unfit parent, as your lawyer will probably assure you, the courts favor the maximum amount of time possible and practical with each parent.

Child support is calculated from guidelines in most cases, and your lawyer can run through these and give you a good estimate of the amount of child support to be paid at your first meeting.

Alimony is a little harder to determine, but as your lawyer will probably also tell you, you won't go broke paying it or become destitute receiving it.

At the first meeting, the lawyer can give you a rough idea of how the property is likely to be divided if you go to trial and alternatives you can work with if you settle.

First Consultation Free! After That ...

Some, but not all, divorce lawyers offer the first consultation for free. At that meeting, the lawyer will discuss legal fees for going forward with your case.

The lawyer will tell you about hourly rates and retainers. He will also give you a written agreement setting forth charges and costs in detail. But although he may give you an estimate of what your case will cost, that is just a guess, not a guarantee.

If you decide to hire the lawyer, after the first meeting you will be charged for any time he works on your case, including telephone calls and e-mails.

The lawyer should keep you informed of each step in your case so that you can actively participate. You should also receive copies of all pleadings, letters, e-mails, and discovery documents.

Don't Let Them Switch Lawyers on You

Most divorce lawyers practice on their own and not in a firm. But a firm that has several lawyers is able to assign work to different lawyers in the firm. Frequently, a partner who conducts the first meeting then assigns the case to an associate lawyer. This is not necessarily bad as long as you are satisfied with the associate and it doesn't come as a surprise that you are being referred to her.

At the first meeting, you will want to ask who will be working on your case, who will be supervising the work, which lawyer will be your contact with the firm, and who will be the attorney responsible for the case. Most law firms will honor a client's request to work with a specific lawyer.

Heed Your Intuition: Fire a Bad Lawyer Fast

Just like in every other profession, there are good lawyers and bad lawyers. Some lawyers will procrastinate. Others are hopelessly overworked and cannot give your case their full and prompt attention. Some will not return your phone calls or answer your e-mails.

No lawyer is perfect. But if he makes a mistake, he should stand behind his work and correct it immediately at no cost to you.

If you have doubts about your lawyer, listen to your intuition. Get a second or third opinion about your case from other lawyers. It is easier to change lawyers early in your case than later. If you wait until just before the trial to change lawyers, the new lawyer will not have had a chance to prepare your case, conduct depositions, or interview witnesses.

Summary

Now you know what to expect from your first meeting with the lawyer. It is time to begin your education about the important issues in your divorce. First, we'll discuss issues pertaining to children. If you don't have any children, you can skip to Chapter 10 on alimony.

CHAPTER 7

Custody in General
Legal Custody in Particular

John looks anxious and rumpled as he talked to his lawyer, Alicia, in her office. "These are my children and I'm their father. I have a father's rights. No judge is going to tell me how to raise my kids."

"It's true that parents have the right to raise their children as they see fit," Alicia says in a calming voice. "The courts have said this right is one of those included in the right to pursue happiness, which is guaranteed by the Bill of Rights of the United States Constitution."

"There you go," remarks John. "I'm standing firm on my constitutional rights."

"However," adds Alicia, "the right is not unlimited."

"The doctrine of *parens patriae* means father of a country or, more figuratively, the government acting as a father. Under this doctrine, the courts are allowed to decide custody and override parents' rights in order to protect children."

"I want joint custody of my children!" John says.

Alicia stirred a cup of Jasmine tea as she spoke. "That's easy," she tells him. "You already have joint custody under the common law."

"I do?"

"Yes. And avoid saying, 'My children.' Judges don't like that. Make a habit of saying, 'Our children.' They belong to both of you."

> **■ Tip** Keep in mind that you already have joint custody of minor children until and unless a court orders otherwise.

"OK," John goes on. "What else do I need to know about custody?"

"Custody means the care and control of a child," Alicia explains. "First, let me tell you about custody in general. Then, I will break it down into its two components, which are called legal custody and physical custody."

How Is Custody Decided?

"So how does the judge decide who gets custody of our children?" John asks Alicia. "Does the mother automatically win?"

"No," Alicia replies. She then gives John the following explanation of how custody is decided by the court.

Historically, children were viewed by the law as property. They were "owned" by their parents. Since men controlled most property, they were considered to be the primary owners of children in the case of a divorce.

The Tender Years Doctrine

When the Industrial Revolution came, husbands went to work in the factories, and wives stayed at home and took care of the children. That caused the courts to develop what became the "tender years doctrine."

Under the tender years doctrine, mothers were awarded custody in most cases and especially for young children. The theory behind it was that mothers knew best how to take care of young children. According to the thinking of the time, mothers also had a special bond with their children. The court considered the most important factors to be the age and sex of the child. Fathers could win custody only by showing that the mother was either abusing or neglecting the children or was an unfit parent for some reason.

When women started to enter the workforce, men started to take a more active role in parenting and caregiving for the children. Congress passed the Equal Rights Amendment, which was ratified by all but fifteen states. The Fourteenth Amendment requires equal protection under the law, requiring that the law be applied equally without regard to gender. The tender years doctrine was abolished. Mothers no longer gained preference in custody decisions.

The Best Interests Doctrine

Nowadays, the tender years doctrine has been replaced by a consideration for the "best interests of the child." This means that the judge considers several different factors to determine what custody arrangement is in the best interests of the child.

There are also presumptions that differ from state to state. In some states, there is a presumption in favor of joint custody except when there is domestic violence. This entails that joint custody is presumed by the court to be the best arrangement unless one party overrides the presumption by proving that it would not be in the child's best interests.

"What does the best interests of the child mean?" John asks his lawyer.

"It means whatever the judge decides," Alicia replies. "Every judge sees it differently. At best, it is an educated guess. The judge has to weigh ambiguous factors and predict the future."

"So, custody is a guess?" asked John.

Alicia adjusts her reading glasses and says to John, "Let me read you a quote to you from a case, *Montgomery County v. Sanders*."

"There is no litmus paper test that provides a quick and relatively easy answer to custody matters. Present methods for determining a child's best interests are time consuming and involve a multitude of intangible factors that ofttimes are ambiguous. The fact finder is called upon to evaluate the child's life chances in each of the homes competing for custody and then to predict with whom the child will be better off in the future. At the bottom line, what is in the child's best interests equals the fact finder's best guess."

Note Custody is the judge's best guess as to what will be in the best interests of the child.

Custody Factors

To help the judge decide what is in the best interests of the child, each state has developed, through legislation or cases, certain factors to take into account. While the factors are different in each jurisdiction, they can be summarized as follows:

1. **Fitness of the parents:** There is a presumption that parents are the best caretakers for the children. So parents almost always win in custody disputes with grandparents, stepparents, adult siblings, and other third parties. The court can consider the character and reputation of the parents and any agreements between them.

2. **Preference of the child:** A judge will consider which parent the child wants to live with, but this is not binding on the court. The judge will take into account the age and maturity of the child. Children are usually interviewed privately by the judge in chambers or by an attorney appointed to represent them or by a custody evaluator.

3. **Routine:** The court considers routine, continuity, and stability to be good for children. So, if the children are doing well, there is a certain judicial inertia at work. A judge doesn't want to change things, because a change may make things worse.

4. **Other factors:** A judge will also consider other factors, including each parent's health, age, income, resources, residence, religion, and conduct. The judge can order psychological tests of one or both parents. She can also consider school performance, where siblings live, or any other factor she thinks is important.

What Are My Chances of Getting Custody?

"Consider this," Alicia tells John, "before you submit the future of your child to a judge. Judges are not trained for this. Judges are usually not psychiatrists, psychologists, therapists, social workers, or any other kind of mental health professional. Judges are lawyers. And the legal system is based on logic and the adversarial system. It works fine for contracts and torts. But using it to make family decisions is forcing a round peg into a square hole."

"Based on all that, what are my chances of getting joint custody?" asks John.

"I can't tell you that," replies Alicia. "Custody is decided on a case-by-case basis. The judge has to consider all the unique facts and circumstances of each case."

"My wife and I argue all the time," explains John. "We can't agree that today is Tuesday."

"That doesn't worry me," Alicia says. "The courts realize that parents are not always on the best of terms when they come to court for a divorce. So a judge will not necessarily deny joint custody just because the parties are arguing at the moment. They will look at past history to see if the couple has been successful in raising the child together so far. If so, the courts tend to favor joint legal custody."

Employing a Custody Notebook

"Even if we get joint custody, how do we communicate with each other? Whenever I talk to her, it always breaks down into a shouting match," John said.

"Here's an idea I got from the courts in Missouri where I went to law school," Alicia tells him. "Take a three-ring binder and make a custody notebook. The parents will pass the custody notebook back and forth as they alternate caretaking in joint custody. You communicate with each other about parenting decisions, schedules, homework, and so forth by inserting messages into the notebook."

Alicia pauses and then continues: "Place a copy of all the children's medical records and bills in the notebook. Also put in copies of reimbursement requests for uncovered medical expenses or extracurricular activities and the reimbursement checks."

"I think we could do that," says John.

Tip Use a legal custody notebook if you and your ex have trouble communicating.

Future Custody

"Can I ask the court to give the mother custody until completion of the fifth grade, then switch custody back to me?" asks John.

"The short answer is, No," says Alicia. "The court has to determine the best interests of the child based on the facts and circumstances that exist at the time of the change in custody. It is hard enough to determine custody at the time of the custody trial. But to try to divine what the facts will be years in the future is not something a judge would try to do."

What Is Legal Custody?

Until now, I've been talking about custody in general terms. But there is a further distinction that can be made: There is physical custody, which is what most people mean when using the word custody. Then there is legal custody. This involves long-term parenting decisions, such as education, medical treatment, discipline, housing, and religious decisions. Other legal custody decisions include the right to permit a child to marry, join the armed services, or hire an attorney to represent a child.

Now, let's further break down legal custody into two separate categories: You can have joint legal custody or sole legal custody.

Joint Legal Custody

Every parent starts out with joint legal custody. The court can change that, but until there is a court order, you have joint legal custody of your children. Joint legal custody means that two parents make decisions about their children together. One parent cannot make final decisions alone. If the parents can agree and share the responsibilities of raising children, then joint legal custody is the best solution.

When parents can raise children in harmony, even though they are divorced or separated, the children ultimately benefit. They benefit because parents have different personalities and skills that they combine when raising the children. Each parent can participate in decisions, and neither is burdened with full responsibility for the children's care. When parents share decision making, they can both actively participate in their children's future.

Sole Legal Custody

When one parent is given the right to make all the long-term parenting decisions, that person is said to have sole legal custody. He is called the legal custodian of the children. That parent can decide where the children will live, where they will go to school, what physicians they will see, and what religion they will be brought up as.

The legal custodian can decide on public or private school. He can also decide on orthodonture, medication, mental health professionals, and cosmetic surgery. He has the right to give consent for their minor children to enter the military or get married. He can select a lawyer to represent the child in the event of a car accident or other legal matter.

This can have a practical effect on child support. The noncustodial parent has the obligation to contribute to uncovered medical expenses like orthodonture, therapy, or cosmetic surgery even if she doesn't agree they are necessary. The same goes for private-school tuition.

Summary

You have your emotions under control, you have decided to get divorced, you have selected a good divorce attorney. Now, it is important to think long and hard about whether you want to become involved in a bitter child-custody battle. Your legal fees will easily double. Your stress level will soar. You will spend your time in court. The judge will make a guess about the future of your child. If you can instead agree on joint legal custody, even though you and your ex will be living apart, you will both be able to participate in the business of raising your children. In the next two chapters, we will focus on physical custody and access, which concerns where the children will live and the amount of time they will spend with each parent.

PART II

Children

Children are precious gifts to a parent. They are the highest of high stakes in a divorce. Some people will do anything to win a custody fight. They are losing their identify as part of a married couple, so they work that much harder to save their identity as a good parent. Custody battles are the hardest part of divorce. In this part, we will examine issues affecting the children, namely custody, timesharing, and child support. If you have no minor children, you can skip to Chapter 11.

CHAPTER 8

Physical Custody

Physical custody means having care and control of children on a daily basis. It involves all the daily short-term decisions, like homework, meals, and bedtimes, rather than the long-term decisions involved in legal custody. Physical custody is residential custody. It refers to where the child lives most of the time.

Three Types of Physical Custody
Physical custody may be shared, sole, or split.

Shared Physical Custody
Shared physical custody means that both parents spend substantial time with the children. Both parents start out having this right. Even if the parents have separated and the children are living with one of them, under the law both parents have shared physical custody until and unless one of them obtains a court order that changes it to sole physical custody.

A simple way to share physical custody is to have the child alternate weeks between the mother's home and the father's home. She might spend a week at each place. This arrangement minimizes the transfers. The change can take place on Fridays, Mondays, the weekend, or any other agreed-upon time.

Another way to divide time in shared physical custody is that the child spends schooldays with one parent and weekends with the other. The weekend parent also has the child for holidays and summer vacation. This disadvantage of this arrangement, however, is that one parent has the fun time and the other has the homework time.

Sometimes, the children stay in the family home, and it is the parents who move in and out. This is known as a "nesting arrangement." When there are enough resources to do this, the advantage is that the children keep continuity and routine instead of shuttling back and forth between homes. And all their clothes, toys, and pets stay at one place.

There are as many ways to arrange shared time spent with the children as you can think of. One parent can have the children four days a week and the other for three days a week. Then, they switch on the following week. These are just some of the creative ways parents have maximized the children's time with each parent.

Sole Physical Custody

Sole physical custody means the children live mostly with one parent. The person is called the custodial parent. The other is called the noncustodial parent. The noncustodial parent has visitation with the children, which will be discussed in the next chapter.

Split Physical Custody

Split physical custody refers to a situation where the homes of the siblings are split between parents; for example, one child lives in the mother's household and the other child lives in the father's. Custody is divided. Courts do not favor this type of arrangement, and try to keep brothers and sisters together whenever possible.

> **Note**   Courts do not like split physical custody. They like to keep siblings together.

Custody Evaluation

The court on its own determination may order a "custody evaluation" in a contested custody case or either party may ask for one. The evaluator is an independent agent of the court. The parties may also hire their own private custody evaluators.

The evaluator will visit the homes of each parent while the children are there and do interviews the parents and children. He may also interview with neighbors, relatives, teachers, coaches, and therapists who have seen the lives of the children. He then makes a report to the court and recommends custody arrangements.

Typically, he is a trained mental health professional like a social worker. The evaluator will make a report to the court on each parent's parenting skills and other observations. He will make a recommendation about physical custody and sharing time between parents. The judge does not have to follow the evaluator's recommendations. But in most cases, the judge will give great weight to those recommendations.

Case Study: Custody Evaluation

"Belval!" exclaims Jeff as he answers the phone in his law office on the second ring. He is answering his own phone because he hates trying to get through voicemail and the receptionists at other law offices. He tries to put as much energy and enthusiasm into his voice as he can after a week-long trial.

"It's Jane Key," says the voice on the other end of the phone. The Keys were fighting a fierce custody battle over their two minor children and Jeff was representing Mrs. Key. "The evaluator called and scheduled an appointment at my house for next Tuesday. What should I do?"

"First thing's first," Jeff tells her. "The evaluator will report on the condition of your house and the sleeping arrangements for the children. Make sure the house is clean, orderly, and safe."

"What do I tell the kids?" asks Jane.

"Don't tell them what to say," Jeff answers. "Evaluators are keen to pick up on coaching, so don't do it. Just tell them that someone is coming to talk to them, and it's OK to answer questions truthfully."

"Fine," says Jane. "And what do I say to the evaluator when I'm interviewed?"

"Keep a big neon sign flashing in the back of your head." says Jeff. "The sign says, 'It's All About the Children.' That will help you stay on track. Answer all the questions with that theme in mind. Instead of saying something negative about your spouse, turn the answer into something positive about yourself. Wrong: 'He lets the children do whatever they want. He lets them watch way too much TV and stay up past their bedtime.' Right: 'I feel that the children do better with the structure, routine, and discipline that I provide.'"

"Got it." Jane says. "Anything else I should remember?"

"No distractions," says Jeff. "Turn off the TV and video games. If you are a smoker, it's time to quit."

Tip Focus on the children and avoid distractions during the custody evaluation interview.

"Best Interest Attorney"

The court can appoint a "best interest attorney" for the children if one of the parties requests it. The best interest attorney will be the children's lawyer and represent them in court. This lawyer will talk to the children and the parents and inform the court what the children want with regard to custody and what the attorney thinks is best for them. The best interest attorney may also be called upon to decide whether or not to allow a therapist to testify in court for the children.

The custody evaluator and the best interest attorney can be of great help to you. Or they can work against you. So if you have the choice of making them friends or enemies, it is better to make them friends. Working against them is an uphill battle.

Tip It's better to be friends than enemies with the custody evaluator and best interest attorney.

Custody Modification

Otis Sloan divorced April Bently 12 years ago. They had two daughters: Cathy, 12, and Joan, 14. They had joint legal custody and the mother had primary physical custody by agreement. Otis had visitation every other weekend.

Otis remarried. He was a fireman. When he received a promotion, his work hours changed from five days a week to three-and-a-half days a week.

Otis asked his former wife if he could change the custody arrangement so that he could spend equal time with the children. She responded by filing a petition with the court asking it to give her sole legal custody and reduce his time with the children.

The court appointed a best interest attorney, who determined that the daughters loved both parents and wanted to spend as much time with each as possible. On the day of trial, attorneys for both parents met with the best interest attorney and worked out a new custody arrangement that gave the father more, but not equal, time.

The court always maintains jurisdiction over modifying child custody. But one parent has to ask it to do so and show that a change in circumstances has taken place since the last agreement or order. A change in circumstances can be falling grades, emotional problems, or a relocation. It cannot be something that could have been anticipated like, "The children are older now."

Tip The court can always modify custody if circumstances change.

Relocation Cases

When Paul Kettering, an electrical engineer, and Angela Silvers, an army medical technician, divorced, the judge gave custody of their five-year-old son, Kevin, to Angela. Paul loved Kevin very much, and he continued to be a very involved father.

Paul was unhappy when Angela started seeing a new man, Steven, but he was shocked when she told him she had applied for military reassignment to Georgia. Unable to talk her out of it, he filed a petition with the court to modify custody.

He asked the court for a custody evaluation, and he hired his own private custody evaluator as well. Both recommended that custody be changed to Paul.

At the court-ordered mediation, the parties almost reached an agreement that would allow Angela to move to Georgia with Kevin in exchange for his spending more time with Paul in the summer. However, Angela would not agree that custody could be changed to Paul if she were assigned overseas. Mediation failed and the parties tried their case. Judge Ogens denied Paul's petition to change custody.

Another judge might have ruled differently. Relocation will get you into court because it is a change of circumstances. A relocation case is basically the same as a custody case. The same standard applies—namely, what is in the best interests of the children. You can file before a threatened move or after the move and ask that the children be returned. Some states will permit relocation of the children, others will not. Some decide case by case.

If you are trying to stop a move, you will want to show that the children are attached to their home, school, neighborhood, friends, and family. Their doctors and dentists are all there. So are their teachers and coaches. You can also compare the two locations to show that educational, social, economic, and cultural opportunities are better where the children are now.

If you are the one that wants to move, you need to show that you are not moving in order to make visitation more difficult for the other parent. It is best to have an explanation for the move such as a higher-paying job. You will also want to show that the range of opportunities for the children are better at the new location.

Tip For relocation cases, research the differences between the two locations.

Third-Party Custody

Can third parties (nonparents) sometimes gain custody of a child? Let's take a look.

Sandy Patterson is having a muffin and a coffee in the diner next to the courthouse where most lawyers start their day when he spots Earl Wymer, the best divorce lawyer in town.

"Earl," calls Sandy. "I'll buy you a cup of coffee if I can have a moment of your time."

"Deal," says Earl as he sat down at Sandy's table.

"My client was the dad's girlfriend," says Sandy. "Mom died and Dad left their one-year-old with Girlfriend for the last five years. They broke up, and Dad is now marrying another woman. With me so far?"

"Yep," says Earl. "It sounds complicated."

"It is. That's why I'm buying the coffee."

"OK. So what's the problem?"

"Dad wants to pick up the kid. Does my client have a chance of keeping the child?" asks Sandy.

"The general rule is that biological parents are favored over third parties in custody disputes. That includes grandparents, stepparents, and former girlfriends," Earl tells him.

"In law school, I learned that general rules were on the left side of the law library, and exceptions were on the right side." says Sandy. "I have a feeling you're about to tell me the exception."

"That's right," agrees Earl. "There is an exception for unfit parents. And the Dad in your case might be an unfit parent if he abandoned the child."

"Well, I guess you've earned your pay. Here's the waitress with the coffee just in time."

Tip Biological parents win custody disputes against third parties unless the parents are unfit.

Practical Considerations

People often get hung up on the word *custody*, which has strong emotional connotations. But it is possible that a legal document is titled a "joint custody agreement" and then, in the body of the document, one party is given all the decision-making authority.

It is also possible that although one sentence of an agreement says that the parties shall have joint legal custody, another sentence will give tie-breaking authority to one parent or the other.

Custody is a convenient label to use to explain the concepts of care and control of children. But you should look beyond the label to the real essence of what is being described. That means you should focus on how parenting decisions will be made and what quality time you will be spending with your children.

Remember, in the legal world, joint legal custody means joint decision making regarding the children. But in the real world, the party with primary physical custody usually makes all the decisions. If the custodial parent selects a pediatrician without consulting the other parent as they should, is the other parent really going to hire a lawyer and go to court over it? Not likely.

Note Having primary physical custody is almost as good as having sole legal custody for all practical purposes.

Summary

In the last chapter, we discussed legal custody of children and how long-term parenting decisions are made. In this chapter, we explored physical custody, day-to-day decisions, and where the children live. In the next chapter, we will talk about various schedules for sharing time between parents.

CHAPTER 9

Timesharing

The loud clock on the courtroom wall said, "8:55 a.m.," which was five minutes before the custody trial was set to begin. Judge Claven had not yet taken the bench. His law clerk picked up the telephone and said, "We're ready." He listened for a second and then announced, "The judge wants to see counsel in chambers."

The clerk led the lawyers to the judge's office behind the courtroom. "This case ought to be settled," the judge said. "What's the problem?"

"Your Honor, we are very close." said Michael Sloan, the father's lawyer.

"How close?" asked the judge, raising his bushy white eyebrows.

"We only differ on where the child spends one day out of the whole year, Judge." said Julie Bomgarten, the mother's attorney.

"Oh, for crying out loud," said Judge Claven. "Why don't you just go out in the hall and flip a coin?"

The parties eventually settled by alternating spending the extra day with their child every other year and splitting leap years equally.

This shows how important time with their children is to parents and to what lengths they will go to fight for it.

Traditionally, when one parent has physical custody, the other parent has visitation. Visitation means time the children spend with the noncustodial parent. However, the word visitation carries with it an emotional connotation. It doesn't sound right that you have to visit with your own children. So, modern lawyers and judges use words like "access" and "timesharing" in place of visitation.

Abbreviated Custody

When the noncustodial parent has a joint agreement for timesharing, the children are in that parent's control or custody for a brief time. So, timesharing is, essentially, abbreviated custody.

Tanya Seals won physical custody of her two daughters, Kim, 14, and Sue, 12, in her divorce. She objected when her ex, Sam Seals, sometimes left them in the care of his new wife during his scheduled timesharing.

Tanya complained to her lawyer, who wrote to Sam and requested that Tanya be the preferred caretaker when Sam was not available for timesharing with the children.

Sam's lawyer wrote back that when it was Sam's turn for timesharing, he had care and custody of the children. It was Sam's choice whom he selected as a third-party caretaker and that Tanya was overreaching by trying to control the children and Sam when they were in his custody.

■ **Tip**   Timesharing is a form of abbreviated custody.

Timesharing Schedules

Some parents are able to agree on parenting issues and scheduling. It is possible to agree on a timesharing provision that says the noncustodial parent will have timesharing on a reasonable and liberal basis. They manage to do fine with that language. If they do run into difficulties, they can add a more detailed schedule later on or ask the court to establish one for them if they cannot agree on one.

Others, however, need more detail in their timesharing schedules. Or both can be combined, with a provision that provides for liberal timesharing but involving not less than the following of a detailed schedule.

In preparing a schedule, first you need to look at the basic routine weekly schedule. Here are some options:

- One common arrangement is timesharing where the noncustodial parent gets to see the child every other weekend and for Wednesday dinner. The Wednesday dinner is so the child and parent don't have to go two weeks without seeing one another. The reason that the noncustodial does not get every weekend is that it allows each parent to get to have some weekend time with the children. This is sometimes called a "standard" schedule, but there is no such thing. The schedule can be as varied as your imagination. Each case is unique and people have different work schedules and social schedules to coordinate with the timesharing schedule.

- Another popular weekly schedule is week-on/week-off timesharing. The children spend one week with Mom and the next week with Dad. You can also insert a Wednesday dinner with the other parent into this schedule if you want. The great thing about this schedule is that it maximizes the amount of time the children get to spend with each parent and minimizes the number of transfers.

- Alternatively, the parties could alternate weekends where they spend from Friday night to Monday morning with the children, and the kids would also be with one parent every Monday and Tuesday and with the other parent every Wednesday and Thursday.

- Or one week the father could have Monday and Tuesday and the mother could have Wednesday, Thursday, and Friday. The second week it would reverse. Weekends would alternate.

- Another schedule gives the father timesharing every fourth week of the month from Friday to the second Sunday following and a weekend in between.

- In some cases, one parent wants to have the children primarily during the school year and the other parent prefers spending more time with them in the summer. In that case, you could have one parent with custody all the weekdays during the school year and the other parent with timesharing every other weekend. Then, during the summer, physical custody would switch and the other parent would get every other weekend.

Other details to consider and include are specific pickup and drop-off times and places, and who will do the transportation to school and extracurricular events. Travel expenses should be considered. It helps to be a little flexible, because in real life there are emergencies and work schedules to contend with.

Tip There is no such thing as a standard timesharing schedule. It can be as varied and creative as you wish.

Holidays

Clay Walker sent his ex an e-mail: "I will pick up Darian at 7:00 a.m. on Thanksgiving."

Sheila Walker wrote back, "Oh, no, you had him last year, so it is my turn this year. The agreement says we alternate holidays."

"I didn't have him last year," replied Clay.

"Yes, you did."

Sheila kept Darian at her house until 5 p.m., when she allowed him to go to Clay's house. Clay had to reschedule his Thanksgiving meal with relatives and guests from 3:00 p.m. to 6:00 p.m.

Clay filed a petition for contempt with the court, and the parties finally settled by putting their timesharing dates down on a multiyear calendar. The parties could have avoided this dispute with a little careful drafting of their alternating holiday schedule so there would be not mistakes or confusion.

Holiday Schedule

Sheila and Clay's holiday schedule looked like this (though you may have other religious holidays in your schedule):

In even-numbered years, Sheila will have timesharing with Darian:

Memorial Day

Labor Day

Halloween

Christmas Eve and Christmas Day until noon during the Winter School Break

In even-numbered years, Clay will have timesharing with Darian:

President's Day

Easter (Spring Break)

Fourth of July

Thanksgiving

Christmas Day from noon through New Year's Day during the Winter Break

The schedule is reversed in odd-numbered years.

Other Special Days

Clay will have timesharing with Darian on Clay's birthday and Father's Day.

Sheila will have timesharing with Darian on Sheila's birthday and Mother's Day.

Darian will alternate timesharing on his birthday between each parent. Sheila will have the even-numbered years and Clay will have the odd-numbered years.

Holidays have priority over the basic weekly schedule, which will resume after the holiday.

Tip Spend a little extra time to carefully detail your timesharing schedule to help you avoid disputes later.

Summers

There are about ten weeks of school vacation for children in the summer. Usually, each parent will want to take a vacation with the children during the summer. To avoid disputes and conflicts with summer camps, you can agree to establish the exact summer vacation schedule in the spring of each year, with one parent having first choice in odd-numbered years and the other parent having first choice in even-numbered years. The summer schedule will supersede the basic weekly schedule and the holiday schedule.

Timesharing and Child Support

A lot of states make the time a child spends with each parent part of the child support calculation. After all, the more time the child spends with you, the more it costs in food, clothes, haircuts, transportation and the like. So a dispute over timesharing may actually be a dispute over child support.

However, you cannot stop paying child support because the other parent is denying you timesharing with the children. Likewise, you cannot legally deny timesharing to a parent because they are not paying child support. The court views timesharing and child support as two separate and independent issues although the parties may view them as interconnected.

When a Child Does Not Want Timesharing with a Parent

It is up to the adults to comply with the timesharing schedule and not the children. But children can make things difficult. Trying to pull a reluctant child out of the car for visitation is no picnic, and it can lead to resentment and even charges of child abuse.

As one judge put it, "I can't order a crane to pick up the child from one house and deliver him to the other house."

Counseling may be the only way to deal with this situation. It will help identify the problem and find a solution. But that requires time, patience and money.

Third-Party Timesharing

Gordon Fox had made a fortune when he sold his software company. He loved his granddaughters, ages 9 and 13, more than anything. He loved picking them up in the morning and talking with them as he drove them to school.

But when Gordon's son divorced, the son's ex-wife said she would start driving the girls to school. In addition, the girls could not go on their annual vacation to Gordon's country estate with horses and a lake. And Gordon had arranged for them to ride in the town parade as princesses on a float but their mother would not let them go.

Gordon called his lawyer immediately. His lawyer told him that the courts will grant timesharing to a third party like a stepparent or a grandparent. But the U.S. Supreme Court has ruled that a parent's suggested timesharing schedule is presumed to be whatever is in the best interests of the child. And in the case of a conflict between the parent's schedule and the grandparent's schedule, the parent usually wins. You can try to rebut the presumption, but it's an uphill battle. Your chances improve if the mother is refusing any timesharing.

Supervised Timesharing

In most cases, timesharing will include spending the day and night with the noncustodial parent and it will be unsupervised. Sometimes timesharing might not include overnights—for example, if a child has not seen a parent for a while, there may be an adjustment period without overnights to start. Or perhaps one parent does not yet have suitable living space to have overnights. In cases where a parent may harm or neglect a child, the parties can agree upon, or the court may order, supervised visitation and require a third party to be present at all times during timesharing with that parent.

Changes in Timesharing

You can try to anticipate some foreseeable events and build some changes into your timesharing schedule. When children are very young, they need regular and consistent schedules. Then, they enter the school system with its schedules and activities. Teens usually want to spend more time with their friends and have more activities outside of the home.

Or in the event of a relocation, the timesharing schedule may no longer work. You can provide an alternative schedule in your parenting plan for that eventuality or you may decide that you will revise your plan in the future if there is a relocation.

Because work, social, and educational schedules often conflict, it is a good idea to build in some flexibility to timesharing schedules with plenty of notice to the other parent and makeup time.

Introducing the Children to Others

After the divorce, chances are good that both parents will have a social and dating life. Third parties should be introduced to children on a gradual basis. The children and both parents will need to be comfortable with the concept before a new person is introduced into their lives. You may want to include some provisions in your parenting plan about how that will be done.

Other Timesharing Provisions

Timesharing covers a lot of ground. Here are some other decisions you'll need to consider:

- In addition to actual timesharing, you will want to make sure your parenting agreement includes the ability to send mail to the child and that the other parent will not open or censor it.

- You will want to be able to speak with the child by telephone when the child is with the other parent.

- You will want to be able to receive notice of your child's extracurricular events and be able to participate in them.

- You are entitled to receive your child's school and medical records and prompt notice of hospitalization and major illness.
- If a parent leaves the state with the child, the other parent should be given an itinerary and contact information.
- Finally, it doesn't hurt to have a provision that neither parent will speak ill of the other in front of the child.

Summary

We have covered legal custody, physical custody, and timesharing. Now, it's time to explore child support.

CHAPTER 10

Child Support

When Clarence got to his law office this morning, he was already in a bad mood. There were several e-mails for him and the red light was blinking on his telephone that told him there were messages. He reached for the aspirin on his desk, swallowed the pills with his coffee, and stabbed the blinking voicemail button on the phone.

The first message was from a man named Tom Paris, a medical doctor, whose wife was divorcing him. New clients always come first, so Clarence called him back.

Tom said to Clarence, "My most pressing concern is our three children. Tell me everything I need to know about child support."

"The cost of raising a child to age 18 can be well over $200,000," said Clarence. "The law requires both parents to pay for their children's food, clothing, shelter, transportation, and the like."

Who Pays?

"When you say both parents pay for their children, that sounds like she will be helping me pay." Tom asked, "How are the costs divided?"

"Our state uses the 'income shares' model of child support, as do most states," Clarence said. "The concept is that one parent pays providers of goods and services for the child directly and the other parent pays them indirectly."

Direct Payments

"OK, which parent pays directly and just what does 'directly' mean?" asked Tom.

"The custodial parent—that is, the parent the child lives with most of the time—pays child support directly," said Clarence. "That means they pay suppliers of food, shelter, transportation, clothing, and the like for the child. So when the custodial parent pays the rent, the telephone bill, or buys groceries, a portion of that payment is considered to be for the child."

Indirect Payments

"Let me guess," said Tom. "The other parent pays child support indirectly."

"That's right," said Clarence.

"So what does 'indirectly' mean?"

"The other parent pays his share of these expenses indirectly through the custodial parent in the form of child support," said Clarence. "Here, let me give you an example of how it works: If the cost of raising a child is $1,000 a month, and the custodial parent makes 40 percent of the total income of the family, that parent is presumed to spend $400 on the child when she pays the rent, telephone bill, and other family expenses. The other parent, the noncustodial parent, would have to pay their share, $600 a month, to the custodial parent."

"Where does the $1,000 a month figure come from?" asked Tom.

"Ah!" said Clarence. "That number comes from the tables that are in law books commemorating the collective wisdom of our state legislators." By now, the aspirin and the coffee were doing their job. Clarence's headache was receding, his mood was improving, and he was becoming more expansive in his gestures and eloquent in his explanation.

Tip The noncustodial parent pays child support to the custodial parent as a contribution to the costs of raising a child.

What Does Child Support Cover?

"I've got more questions," Tom said.

Clarence hooked his thumb in his suspenders and leaned back in his leather chair. "Fire away," he said.

"What is child support supposed to cover?"

"Shelter and clothing, food, transportation, doctors, school, extracurricular activities, and all other expenses related to the child," said Clarence.

"If I make my child support payments of so many dollars a month, do I have to pay anything else for the kids?" asked Tom.

"You'll have to take care of them when they are with you, including food, shelter, transportation, and other expenses. You can always pay more than the child support amount voluntarily, but you cannot be compelled to do so," Clarence replied.

Accounting for How Child Support Is Spent

"How can I make sure she spends the money I give her on the children? Can I have her give me an accounting each month of how much is spent on the children?" asked Tom.

"No," replied Clarence. "The court will not let you micromanage how your child support payments are spent as long as she is not neglecting the children."

How Much Child Support Do I Pay?

"OK," said Tom. "Now for the bottom line. How much?"

Clarence leaned forward, put his elbow on the desk and made a steeple with his fingers. He then launched into the lecture he gives at the local law school about how child support is calculated.

This is what he said: "Before 1988, child support was left up to the judge to decide. So the results were all over the ballpark, even in similar cases. Congress passed a law requiring states to adopt child support guidelines if they wanted to keep their federal funding. The goals and purpose of state child support guidelines were: first, increased compliance through perceived fairness of a child support award; then, consistency and predictability of child support awards; next, ease of administration of child support cases; and finally, an increased adequacy of awards. All the states complied. Most have adopted the 'income shares' model, a few adopted the 'percentage of income model,' and a few have adopted what is called the Melson model."

Income Shares

The income-shares model starts with the idea that the money spent on raising a child should not change due to the parents' divorce. In intact families, the income of both parents is usually pooled, and family expenses are paid from that income.

So, the income-shares method uses the income of both parents to determine what total child support should be. Then, the total child support is divided between the parents according to their percentage of income contributed. Income is defined differently in different states. When you have two wage earners, it is fairly easy to determine, but when you have a business owner, it gets trickier. There are lots of ways a business owner can manipulate income.

The court can also impute income to a parent who is voluntarily unemployed or underemployed to avoid paying child support. In other words, the court uses the income that that parent could be making rather than what they are actually making to determine child support.

Using the income of each parent and the number of children, you look up the amount of child support on the child support guidelines. Then, adjustments are made for certain items like health care, health insurance, and day care.

Note Most states use the income-shares method except for those listed in the next two sections.

Percentage of Income

The percentage-of-income method of calculating child support uses the income of the noncustodial parent only. A percentage of his income shows the amount of child support to be paid. Some jurisdictions use a flat percentage and others use a variable percentage. The custodial parent's income is not used. Alaska, Arkansas, the District of Columbia, Illinois, Mississippi, Nevada, New York, North Dakota, Texas, and Wisconsin use the percentage-of-income model.

Melson

The Melson model, named after a Delaware family law judge, allows each parent an amount of income to be devoted to his own necessities and basic needs. There is a basic child support amount allotted for the children's basic needs. The children get an additional percentage for any excess income of the parent above the amount spent on basic needs, which is considered to be a "standard-of-living allowance." Delaware, Hawaii, and Montana use the Melson model.

The Calculations

In all three models, the details of the calculations are found in laws, rules, or cases. They take the form of a formula or tables. Worksheets have been developed to calculate the guideline amount by hand. But the modern-day and easier way of calculating child support is by computer, and there are calculators available for couples divorcing at Web sites like www.alllaw.com and www.dadsdivorce.com.

While it should be easy to calculate child support, there are frequent disagreements over the correct income and expenses to use, as well as variations due to timesharing schedules and alimony.

Tip Use the child support calculators at www.alllaw.com or www.dadsdivorce.com on the Internet to determine how much the amount of your child support will be.

Above-Guidelines Cases

Some parents are so wealthy that the guidelines do not cover them. In those cases, the court still looks after the children. The theory is that children with wealthy parents should not have to suffer financially because of the divorce. So, the courts will extrapolate above the financial limit of the guidelines or look at the actual expenses for the children to determine child support that is financially above the guidelines.

Adjustments to Child Support Guidelines

Depending on which state you live in, there are various adjustments to the child support guidelines to take into account. Your state may allow adjustments for other child support orders, new children, time spent with the children, child care, and medical and education costs including insurance premiums. Let's look at a few:

- Child support under a previous court order for children from a prior relationship will reduce the amount of income of the payer used in the child support calculations.

- If someone is paying child support and decides to have a child in a subsequent relationship, should child support to the first child be reduced? Some states say, Yes; some say, No; and some let the judge decide.

- Child care whose necessity is work related is an adjustment in some states.

- Medical expenses, including health insurance premiums, are allowed as adjustments in some states.

- Many states take into account the time that a child spends with the parents in calculating child support. After all, the more time a child spends with you, the more money you have to spend for transportation, food, shelter, and the rest. Some states only count overnights. Because of quirks in the child support guidelines, one day a year can make a big difference in the child support.

- In split custody cases, one parent has custody of one child and the other parent has custody of another child. You calculate child support for each parent and net the amounts against each other.

Tip A small difference in your timesharing schedule can make a big difference in child support.

Deviations from Child Support Guidelines

The amount of child support recommended by the guidelines is presumed to be correct. The judge will order that amount to be paid unless the parties have agreed on a higher amount. But you may also ask the judge to award a lower amount in certain circumstances. One example is when the parties agree that one of the spouses will get the house or more than 50 percent of the marital assets to make up for paying a lower amount of child support.

Private Schools

The decision on whether a child goes to public or private school is made by the parent with legal custody or by both parents in the case of joint legal custody. That means that the noncustodial parent may have no choice in the matter, but they still have to pay a portion of the tuition if the custodial parent enrolls the child in private school. In deciding whether to make a parent pay for the cost of private schooling, a judge will usually look at what the parents have agreed to in the past. If a child has been in private school in the past, the judge will probably allow the child to stay in private school.

College

Many states provide for child support through the age of 18. Or if the child is still in high school and living at home at age 18, then they provide it up until the child's 19th birthday or graduation from high school, whichever comes first. In those states, the court is powerless to order a parent to contribute to college expenses.

However, the parties can agree on how to pay for college in a marital settlement agreement. If they do that, then the court can enforce the agreement even though it didn't have authority to order it in the first place.

There are several ways to handle college costs in an agreement: You and your spouse can not mention them at all and figure out how to pay for them when they arise. You can both agree that your present intent is to pay them to the best of your ability based on available financial resources at the time they arise. Or you can legally bind yourselves now to pay in the future.

You will want to define what college costs include. Some parties decide to limit their obligation to pay to the cost of in-state tuition at a state college. The parties can agree to pay pro-rata to income, equally or in any other fashion they can agree on. You both can provide for funding your children's' college expenses monthly through college fund deposits and agree that these funds will be used first for college. You and the other party may also want to have a provision about how these funds will be disbursed if your children do not go to college.

Tip Many states will not allow judges to order parents to pay for college costs unless you put it in your agreement.

When Child Support Starts

If you enter into an agreement on child support, it will commence on an agreed-upon date; for example, the first day of the first month after the agreement is signed. If you try your case and let the court decide, the court may be able to look back and award child support from the child's date of birth or the date a complaint was filed with the court. In that case, there will be an amount already owing on the date of the trial. That amount is called a child-support arrearage. The court will sometimes allow an arrearage to be paid over time. In those cases, the arrearage payment is added to the amount of child support due each month.

When Does Child Support Stop?

Child support is paid until the child is no longer a minor and becomes an adult. This is called the *age of majority* or *the age of emancipation*. In some states, it is 21.

Child support will stop if the child otherwise becomes emancipated, by becoming self-supporting, getting married, or joining the armed forces.

Child support will also stop upon the death of a child. If the person receiving child support dies, the other parent becomes the child's guardian and begins paying the child's expenses directly to providers. Life insurance may provide security for child support payments if the parent paying child support dies. Otherwise, a claim may be made against the estate.

Child support will stop if the court issues an order terminating parental rights. This happens as a result of adoptions and in cases of neglect and abuse. It is not possible to surrender or give up parental rights to avoid child support. You cannot withhold child support because your spouse is interfering with timesharing. And the parties cannot agree to waive child support. The courts have determined that child support belongs to the child and cannot be waived by either parent.

Child support will not stop automatically if the person paying it becomes unemployed, is disabled by injury or illness, or goes to jail. It will continue to accrue under the latest order until that person petitions the court to modify it.

Child Support Modification

As with custody and timesharing, the court has continuing power to modify child support in the event of a material change in circumstances. A material change in circumstances means that the change was significant and unforeseen. Examples are when custody changes from one parent to another or when one parent's income increases or decreases. Federal law prohibits the court from making any changes to past child support orders. The court can only modify future child support payments.

Child support is an obligation of parents but not stepparents. So, it is not a material change in circumstances if a custodial parent remarries someone who is rich. Only the income of the parents counts in determining child support.

Enforcement of Child Support Orders

By federal law, every state is required to have a child support enforcement agency that will try to collect child support for a nominal fee. The agency will have one of its lawyers file a petition to hold the payor in contempt for failing to comply with the court's order to pay child support. If the court finds the payor could pay but didn't, the court can take away driver's licenses or professional licenses until payment is made or even send the payor to jail. In addition, a parent who is owed child support can have money withheld by the payor's employer and seize bank accounts, retirement funds, automobiles, and other assets. A payor cannot avoid child support by declaring bankruptcy. The obligation to pay child support is not dischargeable in bankruptcy.

Tax Considerations

Child support is tax-free income for the parent who receives it and nondeductible income to the payor. As a result, some people are tempted to try to disguise child support as alimony so they can have an alimony deduction. The IRS has rules to prevent this and to allow it to recharacterize certain payments as child support, such as those terminating around the age of majority of a child.

You can claim an exemption for a dependent if you pay more than half of her living expenses. In the case of a divorce, the party who has the most time during the year with the child is considered to be the one who pays more than half of the living expenses. This exemption may be switched by agreement if the custodial parent signs IRS form 8332 and files it with their tax return. The exemption also entitles you to the Child Tax Credit, the Child and Dependent Care Credit, and Educational Credits if you meet the qualifications.

When the Parties Live in Different States

If the parties lived in different states, the custodial parent used to have to go to the payor's state to sue for child support. In 1950, the Uniform Reciprocal Enforcement of Support Act (URESA) was conceived to allow a parent to file for child support where he lives. The order was then sent to the payor's state for enforcement. This act was revised in 1968 as the Revised Uniform Reciprocal Enforcement of Support Act (RURESA). Some form of URESA or RURESA was adopted by every state.

Both acts had some flaws, which led to conflicting orders from different states, however, and so the Uniform Interstate Family Support Act (UIFSA) was created in 1992 to replace them. Under UIFSA, which more than 50 percent of states have adopted, the first state that establishes a child support order has continuing exclusive jurisdiction over the case. The parties have to go to that court to modify child support for as long as one of the parties or the child lives in that state. No other state can modify the order unless the parties agree to transfer jurisdiction to another state. UIFSA also has some enforcement mechanisms, such as allowing a custodial parent to send an earnings withholding order directly to an employer in another state without having to go through the courts of the second state.

Life Insurance

Child support may be secured by life insurance so that it will continue even if the payor dies. It may also make sense to have life insurance for the parent receiving child support to cover caretaking expenses in the event of that person's death.

Health Insurance

Children may be covered on a parent's group health insurance policy until age 26. The court can issue a special order, upon a parent's request, to the health insurance company that gives the child and the child's custodial parent the right to communicate directly with the insurance company so they do not have to go through the insured parent first. This is called a Qualified Medical Child Support Order (or QMCSO).

*　　*　　*

"Any questions?" Clarence asked as he leaned back in his chair.

"No, I think you've covered everything," answered Tom.

"Good, that will be $450," said Clarence.

"A bargain for all the information you gave me!" said Tom as he wrote out the check.

Clarence felt a lot better now and he thought it might turn out to be a good day after all.

Summary

Once custody and timesharing have been determined, child support may be calculated using the child support guidelines. After issues involving the children have been addressed, it is time to look at other financial matters in a divorce, such as alimony and the property distribution.

Finances

Two may be able to lives as cheaply as one when they are living together. But when they separate, there are two households to support with the income that used to support one. This part is all about the money.

# CHAPTER 11

Alimony

The word *alimony* is derived from the Latin verb *alere*, which means "to nourish." The noun form is *alimonia*, which means nourishment or sustenance. Traditionally, it was a duty of support owed by a husband to a wife in addition to child support.

Historically, divorce was only possible when there was marital misconduct or fault involved. If the fault was the husband's, the wife was awarded alimony on the theory that the marriage and her support would have continued if the husband had not been at fault. Conversely, if the wife was at fault, she would receive no alimony.

When states began adopting no-fault divorce, alimony changed as well. Rather than alimony being a right, its purpose changed to helping a dependent spouse become self-supporting or live with the same standard of living as she did during the marriage. Fault became one of several factors to be considered in alimony awards, and in some cases fault was not considered at all.

The Equal Protection Clause of the U.S. Constitution and the U.S. Supreme Court both say there can be no gender bias in alimony awards. Men and women are supposed to be treated equally, but women still get more alimony awards than men. However, the change in family roles, such as the advent of stay-at-home dads, working wives, and working couples, has had some effect on alimony awards for men. In working-couple marriages, 28% of women now earn more than their husbands.

How Long Does Alimony Last?

There are basically three types of alimony—temporary alimony, rehabilitative alimony, and permanent alimony.

Temporary Alimony (*Pendente Lite*)

Pendente lite is Latin for "pending the litigation." It means a court can order alimony to be paid until the trial. This is usually done to maintain the status quo, so that a spouse who controls all the family income does not get an advantage. Temporary support is for necessary living expenses, legal fees, and expert witness costs for the litigation. The test is one spouse's need and the other spouse's ability to pay. This is not the same test that is used for permanent postmarital alimony.

Rehabilitative Alimony

Rehabilitative alimony is for a fixed term—a definite period of time. Its purpose is to help a spouse to obtain a job and become self-supporting.

Permanent Alimony

Permanent alimony does not have a definite end date. For that reason, it is sometimes called indefinite alimony or lifetime alimony. It runs until one party dies or the person receiving alimony remarries. Some states also include cohabitation as a termination event for alimony.

A court might award permanent alimony when rehabilitative alimony won't enable a spouse to become self-supporting—for example, in the case of a spouse with a disability that limits or prevents work. Sometimes, permanent alimony is granted when one spouse makes a significant amount of more money than the other spouse.

A court may have the authority to award both rehabilitative and permanent alimony to the same person. An alimony award may also be in steps, such as $2,000 a month for two years and $1,000 a month for three years.

How Much Alimony Will I Get (or Have to Pay)?

Alimony is determined by state law and varies widely from state to state. Some states have guidelines on amounts and durations. Others give alimony for marriages of ten years or longer. Still others leave it up to the judge to determine based on various factors, such as duration of the marriage, income-earning ability of the parties, health, age, education, standard of living, and circumstances that ended the marriage.

For an example of the wide variety in state laws governing alimony, in Mississippi judges cannot put an end date on alimony, while in Massachusetts lifetime alimony has been eliminated entirely.

Alimony, like child support, is not dischargeable in bankruptcy. If someone owes back alimony payments, they can be collected by attachment of assets or garnishment of wages. The payor may also be found in contempt of court and be sent to jail until the obligation is paid.

Alimony, unlike child support, is taxable income to the person receiving it and deductible by the person paying it. The parties can reverse this by a written agreement.

It is important to note that you must ask the court to determine postmarital alimony at the time of the divorce trial. If you don't, you have waived alimony forever and cannot get it later.

A payee can ask the court to enter an Earnings Withholding Order, which requires alimony be deducted from the payor's paycheck and mailed to the payee by an employer.

Tip If you don't get alimony at the divorce trial, you cannot go back and ask for it later. So be sure to make it part of your request to the divorce court in your complaint.

Alimony Factors

If you are in one of the states that leave alimony up to the judge's discretion after consideration of various factors, here are descriptions of some of the factors judges will probably take into consideration:

Age. Young people have more time to restart their career after a divorce and more time to earn money than older people getting divorced. The court is likely to give young people shorter periods of support.

Health. People in good health are able to find work. Poor health might lead to limited ability to earn money or to complete disability. The courts will be more likely to award alimony to spouses who cannot find work through no fault of their own.

Income. The court will look at the income of each party and his or her ability to support themselves on that income. The court may use alimony to adjust disparate incomes so they are not so out of balance.

Earning Ability. The court can consider evidence of the future income earning ability of the parties, such as a wife who has been out of the job market for a while or a military doctor about to enter private practice.

Lifestyle. The court can consider the lifestyle the parties enjoyed during their marriage in determining alimony. If they took expensive vacations, lived in a luxurious house, and drove new automobiles, the court may try to adjust incomes so that both parties will be able to enjoy approximately that lifestyle after the divorce.

Length of the Marriage. The longer the marriage, the more the court will be inclined to grant a longer period of alimony.

Fault. In some states, if fault of the person claiming alimony caused the termination of the marriage, such as in the case of adultery, desertion, or cruelty, alimony can be reduced or even barred.

Tip Many states leave alimony up to the discretion of the judge after considering various factors.

Job Status Issues

Since alimony is used to make a dependent spouse self-supporting, employment or employability is a key issue in many alimony disputes. If you are unemployed, you will want to show the court the efforts you have taken to find employment, such as copies of the letters you have sent looking for work. Unless you are unable to work because of illness or injury, or have a small infant at home, the court will hold it against you if you really don't want to work. In such a case, the judge can use your income earning ability as your income for child support and alimony determinations.

On the other hand, if you are trying to show that your spouse is unemployed on purpose, either to avoid paying alimony or to get more alimony, you usually do this with a vocational rehabilitation expert who can testify about your spouse's qualifications and the jobs available in your location.

Changes to Alimony

When the court orders alimony, it always has the power to modify it upon request of one of the parties if circumstances change significantly. A change in circumstances might be an increase or decrease in the income of one or both of the parties.

However, the parties can, if they wish, state in their separation agreement that the alimony they have agreed on cannot be modified by the court. In that case, the court will follow the agreement and not modify alimony even if circumstances change. This can be risky for either party, but some people prefer certainty over uncertainty.

> **Tip** The court can always modify alimony unless you make it nonmodifiable by written agreement.

Cohabitation

As we discussed, remarriage of the person receiving alimony will terminate alimony. So, what if the person receiving alimony just decides to live with someone without marrying them? Some states provide by law that cohabitation terminates or modifies alimony. Some do not.

You can put a provision in your separation agreement that provides for termination of alimony upon marriage or cohabitation. But then you better define cohabitation. Is it living together in a marriage-type relationship with sharing of expenses or is a romantic relationship enough? And how long must the cohabitation continue? How many nights a week?

> **Tip** If you want alimony to end on cohabitation, put it in your agreement and define cohabitation.

Nonmarried Support

Although child support may be awarded to nonmarried parents, there are no such provisions for unmarried persons to receive alimonylike payments, referred to as "palimony." Palimony is actually a civil contract matter rather than a divorce matter. If you can prove there was an agreement to pay, an unmarried person may sue for breach of contract and collect damages if she wins.

Taxes and Alimony

As previously mentioned, if you are paying alimony pursuant to an agreement or court order and you are separated, you can deduct alimony on your taxes. If you are receiving alimony under these conditions, it will be taxable income to you, and you may have to file quarterly estimated tax payments.

The opposite is true for child support and payments for property interests. Child support is nondeductible for the person paying it and nontaxable to the person receiving it. And property transfers in a divorce are tax free. Clever taxpayers may be able to take advantage of this tax treatment in a divorce.

Here's an example: Mike is a lawyer who makes $165,000 a year. His wife, Jane, is a schoolteacher who makes $24,000 a year. They have three minor children. In lieu of paying child support, Mike can pay more dollars in alimony because he gets a tax deduction for it. And Jane gets to keep more dollars because she is in a lower tax bracket than Mike. In effect, the government is contributing to the family support, and so there is more money available to the family.

Conditions for Deducting Payments as Alimony

The Internal Revenue Code has certain conditions that must be met to make payments deductible as alimony for the payor:

- Payments have to be in cash or cash equivalents. Checks and money orders are treated as cash. IOUs, property, and services are not treated the same as cash. If you pay your spouse's obligations to third parties, that can qualify as deductible alimony.

- Payments have to be pursuant to a divorce decree or a written separation agreement. It is not unusual for a spouse to move out but continue to pay bills or give money to the other spouse for family expenses without having it in writing. These payments are not deductible as alimony because there is no divorce order or written agreement. And, before you ask: No, you cannot backdate your agreement to cover the last few months that you have been making payments.

- The agreement cannot say the payments are nondeductible. Remember, you can reverse the tax treatment of alimony in your agreement. If you do this, the payments will not be deductible as alimony.

- You and your ex have to be living in separate residences with separate roofs. If you live in the basement and your ex lives upstairs, it's not alimony.

- Payments stop on the death of the person receiving the payments.

- You don't file joint tax returns.

If a spouse has to pay $100,000 in a property settlement, you can see that there would be a powerful incentive on the part of the payor to try to make the payment tax deductible by calling it alimony in the agreement. The government has anticipated this. You cannot make it alimony by calling it alimony in your agreement. Even if it is called alimony, it still must meet the conditions above for it to be deductible as alimony. Since the $100,000 payment for a property settlement doesn't terminate on the death of the recipient, it doesn't pass the test for deductible alimony.

> **Tip** Alimony is tax deductible for the payor, but only if it meets certain conditions.

Alimony Recapture

The alimony recapture rule is intended to keep taxpayers from disguising tax-free property transfers as deductible alimony. Payments that are too concentrated in the first two years of alimony look like property transfers. If you don't pass the test for front-loading of alimony, then the IRS can recapture lost taxes by including excess alimony payments in the payor's income, in effect reversing some of the alimony deduction.

While you can find a calculator online if you put "alimony recapture" in a search engine, what follows is the rather-complicated formula. The first calendar year in which alimony is paid is the first year in the formula.

1. Start with the third year that alimony was paid. Add $15,000 to the amount paid and then subtract the alimony paid in the second year.
2. Next, take the amount of alimony paid in the second year and subtract the total outcome of step 1.
3. Now, take the alimony paid in the third year and add it to the result from step 2. Divide the resulting sum by two.
4. Take the result from step 3 and add $15,000. Subtract that number from the alimony paid in the first year.
5. Add the result of step 4 to the result of step 1. This is the amount of excess alimony to be added to the income of the payor and subtracted from the income of the payee in the third year.

Note that there is no recapture if the payee has remarried. Excess alimony only occurs in the first two years. It does not exist in the third year or subsequent years. If you want to avoid the calculations, there is a simple safe harbor: There is no excess alimony if payments do not go down by more than $10,000 a year in any of the first three years.

> **Tip** Watch out for alimony recapture if your payments have been front-loaded. Think through how you will pay alimony in the first three years to avoid trouble.

Child Support Disguised as Alimony

Another temptation is to disguise child support as alimony so that you can take the deduction for it. Congress is ahead of you on this one as well. It has devised three tests for what it calls alimony fixed as child support.

The first test is simple. You can't call it child support. If any payment is said to be for the support of children in your agreement or divorce decree, then it is child support, not alimony. Therefore, you can't deduct it.

The second test is that the payment can't change as a result of some event related to one of your children. For example, if you say that the payments will stop when Timmy leaves home, or the payments will reduce when Sally goes to college, the payments will be nondeductible child support. Other examples of child-related events include graduation, reaching a certain age, marriage, death, getting a job, reaching a certain earnings level, or leaving home.

The third test says you cannot change the payments based on an event that can be associated with one of the events in the second rule. IRS Regulations provide two more tests to see if you meet the third test:

1. **The Birthday Test.** If alimony is reduced or terminated within six months of the 18th or 21st birthday of a child (or the local age of majority), then it will be presumed to be child support instead.

2. **The Two or More Children Test.** If you have two or more children, you cannot deduct alimony that will change two or more times within a year before or after they reach a certain age between 18 and 24. The measuring age must be the same for both children.

In the case of Mike and Jane above, Mike passed all three tests: He didn't call his payments child support; they didn't terminate within six months of the 18th or 21st birthday of a child; and it didn't change two or more times within a year before or after a child reached a certain age between 18 and 24. Therefore, he gets to deduct the entire payment as alimony and the IRS will not recharacterize it as disguised child support.

Tip If changes in payments are tied it to an event or time associated with the children, they may not be deductible as alimony.

Health Insurance

Health insurance can be a major problem in a divorce. If you are covered by your spouse's group health insurance under a family plan with his employer, you will no longer qualify once you are divorced. The children will still be covered.

You can apply for and obtain continuing coverage under that plan for three years, but you will have to pay the premium that was formerly paid by your spouse's employer as well as the employee portion, and it will be the premium for an individual. Sometimes, this expense is included in alimony, but once again the expenses of two people living separately are more than when living together.

Life Insurance

Just as life insurance can be collateral for the obligation to pay child support, it can be used to secure alimony payments. Life insurance on the life of the payor would replace any alimony that would have been paid for spousal support if the payor had lived. You can tailor the amount and duration of the life insurance to match the obligation to pay alimony. In an acrimonious divorce, the payor may not want to buy or continue life insurance for an ex-spouse, but it can be a negotiated item in a settlement agreement.

Summary

Alimony is for the support of a spouse in addition to child support. It is not usually a calculated amount and judges have more discretion in setting the amount and duration. In the next few chapters, we will take a look at dividing up various assets acquired during the marriage.

CHAPTER 12

Property and Debt

Now we have reached the part of divorce where you and your spouse divide the things you own and the things you owe between the two of you. Property includes assets as well as liabilities, real estate, and personal property, both tangible and intangible. Property can include houses, bank accounts, stock, pensions, businesses, automobiles, and country club memberships. If you have done your homework, you have a list of everything already prepared and a notebook with tabs and supporting documents. If not, now is the time to do an inventory.

If you are not able to complete an inventory because of an uncooperative spouse, you can use the discovery rules of court to obtain information and documents from your spouse and banks, employers, pension plan administrators, and other financial institutions. Of course, this is more difficult, time consuming, and expensive than exchanging financial information and documents voluntarily.

More than nine out of ten divorce cases settle before trial. Most people are able to divide their property and debt themselves. But in order to reach a settlement, or if you are involved in that one in ten that doesn't settle, you need to know a little about the alternative, which is trial where a judge will make decisions about your property and debt.

Distributing Property and Debt

States have different ways to distribute property and debt—community property and equitable distribution.

Community Property

Arizona, California, Idaho, Louisiana, Nevada, New Mexico, Texas, Washington, Wisconsin, and Puerto Rico are community property jurisdictions. In Alaska, you can opt into a community property arrangement if you want. Even though they share a common system, the community property laws are different in each state.

In general, property acquired during the marriage is split equally. Property owned before the marriage is the separate property of the spouse who owned it. Gifts, inheritances, and property acquired after separation are also separate property. Whether the income of separate property is community or separate depends on which state you are in. A local lawyer can fill you in on the nuances of state law.

The theory behind the community property system is that because both spouses contributed to the marriage equally, each spouse has an interest in the property acquired during the marriage.

Property acquired during the marriage, except for inheritances and gifts, is community property owned by both parties jointly. It will be divided equally in the event of a divorce. There is a presumption of joint ownership unless there is specific evidence proving otherwise. Property owned by a spouse before the marriage is separate property and it stays with the spouse who owned it.

What Is Community Property?

All the earnings of both spouses during the marriage and everything acquired with those earnings is community property. Likewise, any debts incurred during the marriage are community debts.

What Is Not Community Property?

Separate property is property that the court will not divide in a divorce. After the divorce, it remains the property of the spouse who owned it. Gifts and inheritances, personal injury awards, and parts of pensions acquired before the marriage are separate property. Assets acquired with separate property are separate property. A business started prior to the marriage is separate property. However, if the business increased in value during the marriage due to the efforts of one or both spouses, a part of it may become community property.

If you or your spouse have acquired property with a combination of separate funds and community funds, the property will be part community property and part separate property.

If you mixed separate property with community property, the result may be that it becomes all community property.

Community Property Distribution

The court may divide items by splitting them or by the value of the items. In some states, the court must divide community property equally. In others, the judge has more discretion to divide community property unequally.

California requires a strict 50/50 division of community property by statute, so most disputes are over whether an item should be classified as community property or separate property. This is not an insignificant question. In the McCourt divorce in 2011, a prenuptial agreement was voided, and the dispute became whether or not the Los Angeles Dodgers baseball team was community property or not. The issue was settled before trial for around $130 million.

Equitable Distribution

All of the other states and the District of Columbia use equitable distribution of marital property. Marital property is that which is acquired during the marriage. It does not include separate gifts, inheritances, and property made marital property by subsequent agreement. It may or may not include property acquired after separation, depending upon the laws of the jurisdiction. Equitable does not mean equal in this context. It means fair. Fair to whom? Why, the judge, of course.

In some states, the judge can use separate property to make the division equitable. In others, the judge cannot transfer title to property and uses a marital award to adjust the equities in the property division, ordering one party to pay the other a dollar amount. Again, consult a local divorce attorney for the lowdown on your state.

In most equitable property jurisdictions, the legislature has given the judge a set of factors to consider in deciding whether a property distribution is equitable or not. The factors are vague enough to give the judge considerable leeway in making a decision.

Here's how it works if you take your case to trial:
- The court first identifies all the property owned by the parties, together or separately.
- The court then values the property.
- Then, the court decides which property is marital and which is not.
- Next, the court distributes the marital property. The nonmarital property stays with the person who owns it.

What Is Marital Property?

In equitable distribution jurisdictions, marital property means most property that is acquired during the marriage. Legal title doesn't matter. If one spouse buys a car, starts a business, or opens a bank account during the marriage, it is marital property. It doesn't matter whose name is on the title or account.

What Is Nonmarital Property?

Property that you owned before the marriage is nonmarital, or separate, property. Nonmarital property also includes property acquired outside the marriage, like an inheritance or gift from someone other than your spouse.

Tip You will probably be able to keep any property you brought into the marriage or acquired by inheritance or gift from a third party.

Changing Property Classification

You can change marital property into nonmarital property, and vice versa, by a written and signed agreement. You can also do it unintentionally. If you have a bank or stock account that is your separate, nonmarital property, and you have put it into joint names with your spouse, you may have converted that non-marital bank or stock account into marital property. Or you may deposit non-marital funds into a joint account, or deposit marital funds into your non-marital separate accounts. This can mingle marital and nonmarital funds to such an extent that you can no longer tell which part is marital and what part is nonmarital.

Tip Make sure you don't change separate property into marital property inadvertently.

Part Marital and Part Nonmarital Property

It is possible for something to be part marital and part nonmarital property. Pensions are a good example. If you had a pension plan when you entered the marriage and you made contributions to it during the marriage, it is part nonmarital and part marital.

Earnings and Appreciation on Nonmarital Property

The passive earnings and appreciation on nonmarital property, such as the dividends and the increase in value of IBM stock for example, are also nonmarital property. However, if you and your spouse both actively managed your stock portfolio, it may be argued that the income and appreciation are a result of marital efforts and therefore a portion of the earnings and appreciation should be marital.

Another example is a house that was owned by one spouse prior to the marriage. After the marriage, that spouse used his income to pay the mortgage, maintain the house, and make repairs. In a divorce, does the other spouse have any claim to the proceeds if the house is sold? The payments made to pay the mortgage were from marital funds. The same is true for repairs and maintenance. Therefore, it is considered that both spouses should share in that portion of appreciation resulting from these payments.

A similar situation can arise in the case of a business owned before the marriage that grew during the marriage. The difference in the value of business at the date of marriage and at the end of the marriage may be marital if the efforts of either party were responsible for that appreciation.

Date of Valuation

The date of valuation is important. It is the date the court identifies and values the property owned by the parties. The court can only value the property that is still there. In other words, if your spouse spent $10,000 on a vacation, that money is gone and not part of the assets on the valuation date.

Some states use the date of trial. Others use the date of separation. That can make a big difference in the results of your divorce. If you make pension plan contributions during your separation or deposit money in your bank account, it will be marital property or separate property according to the date of valuation in your state.

Tip Find out the date of valuation in your state. It can make a big difference in property division and planning.

Debt

Debt can be distributed by a divorce court, just like property. Some courts will only distribute debt that is used to acquire a marital asset, like a mortgage for a house or a car loan for an automobile.

No matter what the court orders, it only has jurisdiction over the debtors, not the creditors. So if you have debt in joint names, like a credit card, the creditor can still sue both of you, even if the court orders only one of you to pay it. It's better to pay off the debts at the time of divorce if you are financially able to do so.

One of the biggest joint debts is usually the mortgage on the marital residence. If you sell the house for more than the mortgage, the liability goes away. But if one spouse gets the house, the other may have to stay on the mortgage until the house is refinanced or sold some time in the future. This is called a contingent liability, and it may make it difficult for the spouse that doesn't live in the marital residence to purchase a new house.

Equitable Distribution Factors

Some courts use what's called a marital award to adjust the balance after distributing the marital property if it is not distributed equally. A marital award can be in the form of a judgment. However, the spouse who obtains a judgment must take additional legal actions to collect the award.

In determining a marital award, the court will look to certain factors, including duration of the marriage; the age, health, skills, and abilities of the parties; the separate property owned by each party; the ability of the parties to acquire future property; the financial needs and debts of the parties; taxes; and contributions (both monetary and nonmonetary) to the marriage. Fault, such as adultery or cruelty, can play a role as well, even in no-fault jurisdictions. But a lot of litigants spend 90 percent of their time on fault and 10 percent on the finances. Judges usually see it the other way around.

Note Most parties in a divorce are way more interested in establishing fault than dividing assets and debt equitably. Judges are far more interested in the latter.

Case Study

The divorce lawyer's office is quiet, dark, and wood paneled with burgundy leather chairs. There are bottles of water, sparkling glasses, and ice cubes on a tray in the side cabinet of the refrigerator. There is not a speck of dust anywhere. The lawyer asks Joe Green what his contributions were to the marriage as well as his wife's.

"I worked 70–80 hours a week to support the family," said Joe. "I was a good provider. I gave up all my time so my family could have a nice house in a good neighborhood. I did everything. My wife? My wife did nothing. She stayed at home the whole time."

As chance would have it, across town, Joe's wife, Ida Green, is meeting with her lawyer, whose office is all chrome and glass.

When they get to the same question, Ida says, "I took care of the house, the laundry, the meals, and the cleaning. I raised two kids, took care of them when they were sick, bandaged their scrapes, ferried them back and forth from sports events and after-school activities and programs, bathed them, put them to bed, and helped them with their homework. My husband? He did nothing. He just worked all the time and he was never home."

Monetary and nonmonetary contributions to the marriage are both factors in the equitable division of property, and a judge will rule accordingly.

Note Fault can be a factor in property division even in no fault states.

Who Gets Rover?

People can get very attached to their pets. There have been fights in court over pets that have run up legal fees many times the cost of the pet. When couples have children, it makes sense to let the pets stay with the parent who has primary physical custody of the children. When couples have no children or grown children, the judge might look at who purchased the pet and who cares for the pet. One judge had the parties bring the dog to court. Then he had them both call for the dog to come to them. He awarded the dog to the party that the dog approached first. But, in general, the law views pets as personal property, like a chair or a sofa. The court will decide who gets the chair and will not give the other party visitation.

Marital Dissipation

If a spouse gambled away marital funds to avoid distribution in a divorce, the court may penalize that spouse by giving more of the property to the other spouse. The same is true if a spouse spends the money on gifts, dinners, vacations, and so forth with a paramour.

Hiding Assets

Don't try hiding assets. There is usually a paper trail that will lead to them. It is bad idea, and if you are caught, you will be worse off than if you just bite the bullet and divide the assets with your spouse. The judge will not believe anything you say after that and will likely assess attorney fees against you.

When it comes to assets, don't take your spouse's word for it in a divorce. You need to see the statements. And if you suspect your spouse may be hiding assets, the following list contains the best place to look for them. You can obtain these documents by discovery in the litigation if you do not have them or your spouse will not give them to you voluntarily.

- **Interest income and stock dividends:** These earnings are reported on tax returns. You may be able to identify secret accounts in this way.

- **Business investments, partnerships, trusts, and real estate holdings:** These financial assets are all reported on an income tax return as well.

- **Bank account statements:** Review these statements to see if there are any accounts you did not know about during the marriage.

- **Savings account statements:** Check these statements for unusual deposits or withdrawals.

- **Copies of canceled checks:** Canceled checks can also show investments and amounts written to cash.

- **Loan applications:** Applications for loans contain a balance sheet where a person lists all of her assets and provides a value for each.

- **Real estate:** Check the courthouse and the county tax assessor's office for real estate owned by your spouse. Some jurisdictions allow you to access this information online.

- **Stock options, retirement funds, and salaries:** If your spouse works for a publicly traded company or an organization like the county school system, the federal government, or the World Bank, you can find a lot of information online about many of these types of benefits.

Use the rules of court discovery to find out whether your spouse has prepaid his expenses, like taxes, only to seek a refund after divorce; deferred his income, like bonuses or raises; or loaned money to a relative or a friend to hold until the divorce is over.

Tip If your spouse works for a publicly listed company, you can find a description of her benefits online.

Summary

Now you know how property and debt is divided in equitable distribution and community property states. I have explained the difference between marital property and nonmarital property and the difference between community property and noncommunity property. You have some tips on how to find hidden assets. Next, we will be looking at particular assets, starting with the marital residence.

CHAPTER 13

The House: A Play in Three Acts

The house is one of the most important assets in most divorces. It can have a large monetary value as well as a large debt. Moreover, it is shelter for the family. And people have a lot of historical and emotional attachment to their homes. I thought the various issues involving the house might best be addressed in this short play.

Act One: The Wife's Lawyer

Venerable divorce lawyer Simon Nicholas enters from stage left to start his day at his well-appointed law office, which takes up half the stage. There are freshly pointed pencils, tips upward, in a cup on his desk. He sits down at his large desk, which has only one piece of paper in the center. He picks up one of the pencils and starts to write, when the phone rings. He answers gruffly with only his last name. The other half of the stage is then lighted to show the caller, a woman named Brooke Davis, in a French-style kitchen tastefully decorated in reds, blues, yellows, and golds. Clerks continue to come in and out of Simon's office with papers, which he signs without reading while talking on the phone.

BROOKE: Mr. Nicholas, this is Brooke Davis. Remember, we talked the other day about me hiring you for my divorce.

Chapter 13 | The House: A Play in Three Acts

SIMON: Of course. How are you today, Brooke?

BROOKE: Better than when we last talked. But I woke up last night in a cold sweat: We never talked about the house. What do we do about it?

SIMON: You are right that the house is usually the first thing to be dealt with in a divorce. It is typically one of the largest assets in the marital estate. If there is other real estate, like a rental property or vacation home, you'll have to decide what to do with those as well.

BROOKE: There is no other real estate. But we worked hard and saved and sacrificed to own our own home.

SIMON: It's the American dream.

BROOKE: I love this house. Our children were born and raised here. So many memories. Some good. Some bad.

SIMON: The house is especially hard to deal with because besides being an asset, it is shelter for the family, with emotional attachments and memories.

BROOKE: Plus, I don't have the energy it would take to find a new place to live in, to pack, and to move, all in the middle of a divorce. I just can't deal with this.

SIMON: But deal with it you must. You and your husband need to decide who is going to live where, and what timesharing arrangements will be made for the children.

BROOKE: I want to keep the house, if I can, for the children's sake. But my husband says we can't afford to. We have to sell it and split the proceeds.

SIMON: Many financial experts say you should not try to hang on to the house. It's not a liquid asset. You can't feed your family on the equity in your house. But some people do keep the house in a divorce. And over time, it has paid off in appreciation. You'll have to make a budget and take a look at your finances to see if you can afford the mortgage, utilities, and upkeep for the house. We'll have to estimate some items, such as alimony and child support, and your future earnings and child care expenses. Some people are able to rent out a room in order to help with expenses.

BROOKE: Will we have to sell the house?

SIMON: That depends. These are the issues that must be negotiated and decided by the parties if possible. Otherwise, a judge will have to decide them for you. Then you will have less flexibility. For example, it is not uncommon for a judge to order the marital residence to be sold by a trustee and the proceeds to be divided equally. If you negotiate your own settlement, one spouse may be able to buy the other out and keep the house in exchange for cash or some other marital asset. If you do agree to sell it, we can ask for a right of first refusal, giving you the right to buy the house at the same price as any contract for sale you accept.

BROOKE: I want him to move out.

SIMON: Then, ask him. But if your house is in joint names, or titled as tenancy by the entireties, which is joint title by a husband and wife, you may not be able to get your spouse to move out. Ownership of property gives the owner the legal right to occupy the premises. Your spouse can move voluntarily, but he cannot be forced to leave unless he commits domestic violence. This can be a vexing situation, especially if you need separation as grounds for divorce.

BROOKE: What if he agrees to move out?

SIMON: Even when a spouse moves out, he has the right to reenter the house at will. In order to give each party privacy, and prevent claims of abandonment or desertion, the parties may enter into a move-out agreement that sets forth the mutual and voluntary nature of their separation as well as the terms for the payment of expenses and the timesharing arrangements for the children.

BROOKE: Can I change the locks?

SIMON: In the absence of an agreement, it is not a good idea to change the locks. Since he is also an owner of the house, he can call a locksmith or break a window. And this could work against you in your divorce. It could possibly cut off your spouse's responsibilities to contribute to the costs of the house. We can talk more about it when you come in. Are you looking at your calendar? How does Friday at 2:00 p.m. sound?

Act Two: The Husband's Lawyer

The scene is Marvin Scott's law office, which has a cheap desk, pictures askew, and papers strewn about in stacks. Ric Davis, Brook's husband, sits across the desk from Marvin in one of the torn leather and chrome client chairs.

RIC: I just want to make sure I'm not living in my car when this is all over.

MARVIN: You won't be living in your car. Did you purchase the house after you were married?

RIC: Yes. Why?

MARVIN: If you owned the house before the marriage and never changed it to joint ownership, it is premarital property. However, your wife might still have a claim to a marital portion of the appreciation on the house, based on mortgage payments and repairs made with marital funds during the marriage.

RIC: We bought it after we were married.

MARVIN: I'll need to see a copy of your deed. Most marital residences are held jointly. Joint ownership by a husband and wife is called a tenancy by the entireties. However, sometimes a house is bought during the marriage but put in one spouse's name only. It is still marital or community property if acquired during the marriage or put in joint names during the marriage. If you used separate property to acquire the house, you may be entitled to a credit for that contribution.

RIC: That was a long time ago. But I am pretty sure I put down $30,000 from the sale of my bachelor condo.

MARVIN: Let me tell you what proof will be required in court, and probably in settlement negotiations, if your wife's lawyer is on the ball. Proof consists of canceled checks, bank statements, and settlement forms, like HUD-1. You will need to show that the money came from your condo sale, went into your bank account, did not go through a joint account, which hopefully it didn't, and finally that it was used to purchase the marital residence. This can get even more complicated to trace if there are other sales or refinances.

RIC: Ok, let's say I can find the proof. Do I get my $30,000 back and then we split the rest?

MARVIN: There are several ways to calculate it. Some states do not permit any tracing at all. The majority do. The parties may agree on any division that they think is fair and the court will approve it. One simple way is to return each party's separate contribution plus interest at a fair investment rate. Or, if you want to get more sophisticated, you could use the percentage rate at which the house appreciated during the period you owned it.

RIC: How would the court calculate it?

MARVIN: We use what is called the Brandenburg Formula in this state. It is explained in a case by that name, and several states use it. This formula uses contributions made at the purchase of the house to determine the percentages of the sale's proceeds. So, if you bought the house for $100,000 and you each paid $30,000 from your separate assets, then your separate share is 30 percent of the proceeds. The other 70 percent is marital property and is divided equally.

RIC: She wants me to move out, but I can't afford to keep paying for the mortgage and rent a place to live. We need to sell the house, get the cash, and get out from under the mortgage payments.

MARVIN: You are not required to move out. You have all the rights of ownership. Just tell her you're not moving until you reach a settlement.

RIC: Can I list the house as for sale now?

MARVIN: You will need her agreement and signature on the listing agreement. She will also have to sign the deed when you sell the house.

RIC: What happens if we cannot agree?

MARVIN: In our state, the judge can transfer the title of the house to one or the other parties. But it is more likely that the judge will order it to be sold by a trustee. That means an extra expense, so it is better to settle if you can.

RIC: If I do move out, can I take some things, like dishes, towels, and urniture?

MARVIN: Well, they belong to both of you until the court orders otherwise. So, yes, you can take things, but I prefer you try to do it a little more smoothly. Make a list of what you want to take and let me discuss it with your wife's attorney. Maybe we can have a move-out agreement. Or maybe we can try mediation.

RIC: OK. Set it up!

Act Three: The Mediator

Stephanie Silverstein is a lawyer who now only takes cases as a mediator. Brooke and Ric are seated at a round conference table in Stephanie's office. A dish of candies sits on the table. Stephanie is standing by a blackboard with chalk in hand.

STEPHANIE (drawing a house on the blackboard): Now, what are we going to do about the house?

BROOKE: I'd like to stay in the house.

STEPHANIE: Are you prepared to buy out your husband's interest in the house?

BROOKE: I would like to. But I have no cash. How can I buy out his interest?

STEPHANIE (sitting down): Maybe we can find something you can trade for his equity in the house. One of the reasons that mediation works is because people want different things. Let me tell you a story to show you what I mean.

Mary was a scientist working for a biotech company. She owned a lot of corporate stock in her name. She was married to Tom, an engineer. They owned a townhouse together. Mary thought the prospects of her company were exciting, and real estate was a boring investment to her. Tom, on the other hand, believed that stock investments were mercurial and that real estate was a more solid investment. The equity in the house and the stock were about equal in value so it was easy for them to agree that Tom would keep the house and Mary would keep the stock. They were each taking a risk on the future of their investments, but it was a risk they both felt comfortable taking.

Chapter 13 | The House: A Play in Three Acts

BROOKE: That's a good story, but I don't have any stock to trade for the house.

STEPHANIE: No, but your husband owns a business and has a pension plan.

RIC: That's right. I'm a partner in an accounting firm and I have a 401(k) retirement plan.

STEPHANIE: If the numbers work, you may be able to trade Brooke's marital interests in the business and the pension plan for Ric's interest in the house.

RIC: How will we know if the numbers work?

STEPHANIE: We can agree on the value of the house or we can have it appraised. The same goes for the business. The value of the 401(k) plan is on your last statement.

RIC: Who pays for the appraisals?

STEPHANIE: Since they are for both of you, it would make sense to split the cost. That's better than going to court and each of you having your own appraisal done.

BROOKE: What about the mortgage?

STEPHANIE: You are going to have to take over the mortgage payments, real estate taxes, utilities, insurance, repairs, and maintenance on the house once it is transferred to you. We will have to keep that in mind when we mediate support.

RIC: How do I get my name off the mortgage?

STEPHANIE: That's important because if you try to buy another house it will be considered a contingent liability. And even though Brooke agrees to pay the mortgage, if she misses a payment, it could affect your credit and the mortgage lender can ask you to pay.

RIC: So, what's the solution?

STEPHANIE: One way to solve this problem is to give Brooke a certain amount of time to refinance the mortgage in her name alone. You agree that if she is unable to do so within that time frame, then she will sell the house.

BROOKE: How much time?

STEPHANIE: That's up to the two of you to decide. Some courts will give the party that has primary custody of the children extra time in the house so as not to upset the children's routine. Depending on the age and maturity of the children, it could be a number of years.

RIC: Will I have to pay taxes on the buyout?

STEPHANIE: No. Section 1041 of the Internal Revenue Code makes all property transfers, during a marriage or incident to a divorce, tax free.

RIC: What does "incident to a divorce" mean?

STEPHANIE: It means the transfer occurs within one year after the divorce or is related to the divorce. It is related to the divorce if it occurs within six years of the divorce and is contained in a separation agreement or decree of divorce. If the transfer occurs more than six years after your divorce or it is not mentioned in the separation agreement or divorce decree, then the IRS will presume it is not a tax-free transfer related to your divorce. However, you can still overcome this presumption if you have facts to persuade the IRS otherwise.

BROOKE: If the transfer of the house is tax free to me, will I have to pay taxes on Ric's share when I eventually sell the house?

STEPHANIE: Brooke, you will have a carryover tax basis in the house after the transfer. The tax basis is used to calculate the capital gains tax when the house is eventually sold by you, and it is the cost of the house plus improvements and sales expenses. But there is an exclusion of up to $500,000 of gains after deducting the basis for a married couple when they sell the house as long as they meet two tests: The use test requires that both of you must have lived in the house for at least two of the past five years. The ownership test requires that one of you must have owned the house for at least two years. The exclusion is $250,000 of capital gains for single taxpayers or taxpayers filing a separate return.

BROOKE: What happens if we don't sell the house for four or five years?

STEPHANIE: Ric could lose his $250,000 exclusion because he would not meet the use test for living in the house for at least two of the last five years.

RIC: I don't like that scenario.

STEPHANIE: There is a work-around. If Brooke has a court order granting the use of the house to her, Ric can add her time in the house to his. Then, Ric can meet the use test. The IRS calls this tacking.

RIC: Can you give us an example?

STEPHANIE: Sure. Let's say you both paid $200,000 for the house. If you, Ric, transfer the house to Brooke in exchange for her interest in your pension and your business, she will carry over your basis in the property. So, her basis will be the total cost of the house, or $200,000. If she sells the house for $600,000, her gain will be $400,000 (the sales price less her basis). She can exclude $250,000 of gain if she is divorced, which will leave her with $150,000 of gain. The capital gains federal tax is 15 percent, or $22,500, plus state taxes.

RIC: So, how do we avoid that?

STEPHANIE: One way to do it is this, Ric: You can both sign a separation agreement that provides that Brooke and the kids can live in the house for five years, and then they will sell it and you will both split the proceeds. If they sell it for $700,000, they will have a capital gain of $500,000 (the sales price less their basis). But now, you can tack Brooke's use onto your own. You therefore pass the ownership test as well. So, both of you can each take a $250,000 capital gains exclusion and pay no taxes. That effectively gives you $22,500 more to negotiate with, courtesy of your Uncle Sam.

RIC: That's very slick. I can see how this may work.

STEPHANIE: Yes, but Brooke, you will still have to be able to pay the mortgage. So, let's talk about support.

Summary

The house is usually one of your most important assets. You can sell it, or one spouse can buy the other out. You can use other martial assets, like pension plans or business investments, to trade for equity in the house. Transfer of the house is tax free in a divorce. With tax planning, you can avoid taxes on the sale of the house.

CHAPTER 14

Pensions, Retirement Plans, Deferred Pay, and Social Security

When dividing assets, don't forget about the retirement funds. More than half the value of assets transferred in divorces each year are retirement funds. Because retirement plans are complicated and not readily convertible to liquid assets that can be spent, they can be the last thing on your mind when you are getting divorced. But overlooking them could be a costly mistake.

Pension Plans

A pension plan may be either a defined contribution plan or a defined benefit plan.

Defined Contribution Plans

A retirement plan where the employee's annual contribution is specified is a defined contribution plan. Most companies have this type of retirement plan. A 401(k) plan is a defined contribution plan. The employee, the employer, or both may make contributions to the plan. Individual accounts are set up with the funds contributed plus the earnings on those funds. The account may be self-directed by the employee, and the investments are usually made in the stock market. Only this amount is guaranteed. Future benefits will fluctuate depending upon the investment's increase or decrease in value. The value of the plan is easily available from your last account statement.

If contributions were made to the plan before the marriage, the plan is part marital and part nonmarital property. You must calculate and subtract the nonmarital portion, including gains, losses, interest, and dividends to the date of division. The part that is left is the marital portion, which can then be divided or traded for another asset.

Defined Benefit Plans

In a defined benefit plan, the employer promises to pay certain benefits, based on a formula, to the employee upon retirement. The formula uses factors like salary history and employment duration. A determination is made each year about what amount of money the plan must have at a certain date in order to pay out those promises in the future. The investments are entirely up to the company. The plan statements will show how much money is in the plan on a given date, but that is not the value of the plan. The value has to be determined by an actuary using assumptions about retirement, life expectancy, appreciation of plan assets, and inflation rates. This is an expensive proposition and may cost you around $5,000.

If you want to trade defined benefit plan assets for another marital asset, then you will need to have the plan valued. If the plan was started before the marriage, it will be part marital and part nonmarital. The marital share is calculated as a fraction. The numerator is the number of months you have been married during your spouse's participation in the plan. The denominator is the number of months your spouse participated in the plan to the date of retirement.

In lieu of valuing the plan, the court can order it divided "if, as, and when" received." For example, the court could order the plan to pay one-half the marital share to the other spouse if, as, and when payments are made to the spouse that is the employee.

> **Note** Retirement funds can be a major part of the marital property to be divided. You may need to engage an actuary to value the plan, who will value the marital portion of the plan based on the length of your participation until retirement and the length of your marriage.

Qualified Plans

A retirement plan may either be qualified or not qualified for favorable tax treatment. If your plan meets the requirements of the Employee Retirement Income Security Act (ERISA) and Section 401(a) of the Internal Revenue Code, it is said to be tax qualified. The requirements are that the plan does not discriminate in favor of highly paid individuals and that benefits are reasonably determinable. If the plan is tax qualified, you do not have to report contributions as income and you can defer taxes until the contributions are withdrawn, usually at retirement. The contributions can grow tax free until withdrawal. In the meantime, however, your employer can deduct contributions in the year they are made.

ERISA applies to 401(k) plans, Keogh plans, money-purchase pension plans, defined benefit plans, target benefit plans, and profit-sharing plans. It does not apply to government, military, or international organization retirement plans or individual retirement accounts (IRAs). It also does not apply to some private, nonqualified plans. All of these plans fall under other rules than those of ERISA.

Alienation

Alienation is a fancy word for selling, assigning, or transferring. ERISA and the Internal Revenue Code provide that you cannot transfer your pension plan benefits to another person. These are called the antialienation provisions. They are federal law. The purpose of these provisions is to make sure your benefits are there for your support during retirement.

So, in the past when a divorce court issued an order dividing a pension and assigning a portion to the spouse of a participant in a pension plan, it raised a question: If the plan complied with the state order, did this violate the federal antialienation provisions of ERISA and cause the plan to be disqualified and lose its tax advantages for all employees?

Congress to Rescue: The QDRO

Congress made a special divorce exception to the antialienation provisions by enacting the Retirement Equity Act (REA) of 1984. That act allows qualified pension plans to be divided by state divorce courts with a special order, without losing favorable tax status. The order is directed to the plan administrator.

The order transferring retirement benefits is known as a qualified domestic relations order (QDRO). Under the QDRO exception, a state court may transfer an employee's retirement benefits to a spouse, former spouse, child, or other dependent. This transfer may be used to pay alimony, child support, or a marital property obligation. A pension plan does not have to comply with a state court ordering the division of pension benefits unless the order is a QDRO.

The Mechanics of a QDRO

As mentioned, the QDRO is a "domestic relations order." A domestic relations order is a judgment, decree, or order, including an order approving a property settlement that is made under a state's domestic relations law regarding the child support, alimony, or property rights of an alternate payee.

The judge must actually issue the order. A property settlement agreement signed by the parties cannot by itself be a QDRO unless it is approved by an order of the court.

There is no requirement that the order be signed or approved by the parties, but many judges and lawyers will have the parties sign it anyway. You do not need to present the retirement plan to the court nor make the plan administrator or the plan a party to the divorce.

The employee is referred to in the QDRO as the participant. The spouse, former spouse, child, or dependent of the participant is called the alternate payee. The plan administrator is the person or entity so identified in the plan documents. You will find the name, address, and telephone number of the plan administrator in the plan's summary plan description. The administrator is required to provide a summary plan description to each participant describing her rights and benefits under the plan.

A QDRO, which transfers retirement benefits from the participant to the alternate payee, must contain the following:

- the name and address of the participant
- the name and address of each alternate payee
- the name of the plan (note that some companies have several plans with similar names)
- the dollar amount or percentage of the benefit to be paid to the alternate payee, or a method of calculating the percentage
- the number of payments or time period to which the order applies

A QDRO must not contain the following:

- any benefit or option that is not provided by the plan
- a requirement for the plan to provide for increased benefits
- a requirement for the plan to pay benefits to an alternate payee that are required to be paid under a prior QDRO to another beneficiary
- a requirement for the plan to pay benefits to an alternate payee in the form of a qualified joint and survivor annuity for the lives of the alternate payee and his subsequent spouse

Usually, a QDRO is prepared as a separate order. That is not required, however, and it may be part of the divorce decree or part of a property settlement agreement as long as the agreement is approved by a court order.

A QDRO does not need to be issued only in a divorce. You can sue for alimony or child support without filing for divorce. Any domestic relations order that provides for support or marital property rights may be a QDRO.

A QDRO can be issued after a divorce, after the participant's retirement, or even after the participant's death. But it is a better practice to have it prepared and entered at the time of divorce. Once the QDRO is submitted to the court and signed by the judge, it is mailed to the plan administrator. The plan administrator then determines whether the order is qualified or not. For that reason, some plans provide drafting templates for QDROs and preapproval of QDROs before submitting them to the court. QDROs are also drafted with provisions that permit the court to modify them if required by the plan administrator. It is also possible to include a provision that the funds be paid from other assets if the QDRO is not approved.

Marital settlement agreements frequently provide that retirement funds will be divided but lack details on how that is to be accomplished. That leaves too much room for disputes when the QDRO is drafted later. Whose lawyer will draft the QDRO? Who will pay for it? It is better to include as much detail as possible in the agreement. The best practice is to draft it at the same time as the agreement and attach a copy.

Tip You need a QDRO to divide pension plans that are qualified for tax benefits under ERISA. Have it prepared and preapproved at the time you sign the settlement agreement or by the time of your divorce trial.

Survivor Benefit

If your QDRO provides for payments from a defined benefit plan if, as, and when received, you need to know about the survivor benefit. A survivor benefit acts like a life insurance policy. It permits the alternate payee to continue to receive benefits after the death of the participant (typically about half the benefit received during the life of the participant). There is a cost for securing the survivor benefit, and it is subtracted from the pension payments each month. The QDRO must assign this benefit to the alternate payee or all payments will stop if the participant dies.

The questions most often raised in divorces about survivor benefits are threefold: Will the alternate participant receive a survivor benefit? If so, how much of the benefit will be assigned? And who will pay for the survivor benefit?

If the plan does not provide for a survivor benefit or the participant won't agree to it, the alternate payee can buy a private life insurance policy on the participant's life.

It is possible to assign part or all of the survivor benefit. It makes sense to assign the same percentage as the percentage of benefit that the alternate party receives while the participant is living. This will leave a partial survivor benefit for a new spouse and children if the participant remarries. But it is possible to assign more than this, up to 100 percent of the survivor benefit.

The survivor benefit is paid for by deduction from the monthly pension benefit. The deduction reduces the monthly benefit paid both to the participant and the alternate payee. However, because the survivor benefit is only for the alternate payee, the parties sometimes negotiate that the entire cost will only be deducted from the alternate payee's benefit payments.

Note If you don't buy a survivor benefit, payments will stop upon the death of the employee.

Nonqualified Plans

A deferred compensation plan is the most common nonqualified plan, although it is not the only type. Companies set up nonqualified plans to reward their most highly paid executives. The employee contributes a portion of her pay to the plan and does not pay taxes on those contributions until they are withdrawn from the account at retirement.

Some nonqualified plans are fully funded currently and can be divided in a divorce. Others are not funded currently but consist of a promise to pay benefits in the future, or may have provisions that do not allow for a division in a divorce. In that case, you can have an expert value the plan and trade it for other assets or establish an agreement and court order under which the employee will pay the former spouse a percentage of the benefit if, as, and when received.

Individual Retirement Accounts

Individual retirement accounts are less complicated. They do not fall under the antialienation rules of ERISA or the QDRO exception. You do not need a court order to divide an IRA. They may be divided by an agreement of the parties. Usually, the institution holding your IRA will require only a form or a letter in order to divide the account. The court may issue an order dividing an IRA, but it is not required.

The transfer is tax free to you if it is made under a divorce decree or separation agreement incident to a divorce. The transfer must be paid into an IRA owned by your spouse in order to be tax free to him.

Sometimes a spouse needs the money at the present time and doesn't want to put it into an IRA. You would then have to pay income tax on the distribution. There is a 10 percent penalty if you withdraw funds from a qualified plan before age 59.5. This 10 percent penalty is waived for qualified plans if the distribution is pursuant to a QDRO but not for IRAs.

Note If you don't transfer part of the IRA into another IRA, and you're not yet 59.5-years-old, then you'll need to pay a 10 percent penalty for the withdrawal in addition to any income taxes due.

Federal Government Retirement Plans

All employees of the federal government have a defined benefit retirement plan (either CSRS or FERS, described below) and a defined contribution plan (TSP). The plans are divided by a qualifying court order, which is similar to but not the same as a QDRO.

Civil Service Retirement System

Federal government employees who started their civil service prior to 1984 are covered by the Civil Service Retirement System (CSRS). Since this is a defined benefit plan, it will have to be valued by an actuary or divided on an if, as, and when received basis.

Employees who are in the CSRS may also contribute up to 5 percent of their earnings to a Thrift Savings Plan, or TSP. There are no employer contributions. The administrator for the TSP is the Federal Retirement Thrift Investment Board, 805 15th Street NW, Washington, DC, 20005-2207 (telephone: 202-942-1600).

Under the CSRS, employees do not make contributions to, or qualify for, social security as a result of their government employment. When one spouse is a federal employee with CSRS and the other spouse is entitled to social security, a divorce court can divide the CSRS but is prevented from dividing social security under federal law. Some states permit the judge to make adjustments in dividing assets to take into account the fact that you cannot divide social security.

Federal Employees Retirement System

Federal employees hired after January 1, 1984, are covered by the Federal Employee Retirement System, or FERS. It is a defined benefit plan. Under FERS, employees will receive a basic benefit at retirement equal to 1 percent of their average earnings for each of their top three years of service. They are also eligible for social security. The government will contribute 1 percent of the employee's pay to her TSP and will also match the employee's contributions to the TSP dollar for dollar for the first 3 percent and half of the next 2 percent taken out of her paycheck.

International Organizations

International organizations have their own retirement plans and operate under their own rules. The World Bank and the International Monetary Fund, for example, will not accept a state court order dividing a pension benefit unless it takes the form of an order to pay alimony.

Military Pensions

Unlike in the case of civilian pensions, service members cannot borrow against or cash out early from a military pension. It is all or nothing. They cannot receive any benefit until they have served at least 20 years (or have acquired the necessary points through the Reserves or National Guard).

The Uniformed Services Former Spouse Protection Act (USFSPA) provides that state divorce courts can divide military pensions and enter an order awarding a portion of the military pension to a former spouse. You and your spouse can either agree on the division and have your attorney prepare the court order, or you can ask the judge to award you a portion of the pension if you cannot agree.

There are different ways to divide a military pension. The former spouse can receive a percentage or a specific dollar amount. You can also trade your share in a military pension for cash or other assets. In this case, you will need the pension to be valued by an expert.

Direct Pay

The government agency in charge of paying military pensions is the Defense Finance and Accounting Service (DFAS). A former spouse may receive court-ordered pension payments directly from the DFAS if he meets the following requirements:

- The decree of divorce judgment and the order dividing the military pension are both final and unappealable;
- the service member is retired or in the process of retiring; and
- the service member has served at least ten years in the military and the parties were married for ten years during the member's military service.

The DFAS cannot pay a former spouse more than 50 percent of a service member's disposable net pay nor more than 65 percent in total if there is more than one court order. If you are entitled to more than that, or you don't qualify for direct pay, you will have to collect it from another source such as a bank account or wages if the service member takes a civilian job after retirement from the military.

Disposable Retired Pay vs. Disability Pay

The benefit to the former spouse is typically a percentage of the service member's disposable retired pay. This is the monthly benefit less the following items:

- The debts owed to the United States, such as advanced pay;
- the fines assessed against the service member, such as court martial penalties;
- the amounts waived by the service member to receive an enhanced civil service retirement benefit if she goes to work for the federal government;
- the amounts waived by the service member in exchange for the receipt of disability pay; and
- the costs of a survivor benefit plan.

If a service member is eligible for disability pay, he can elect to take disability pay instead of retirement pay on a dollar-for-dollar basis. This will reduce the former spouse's share of the military pension. There is an incentive for doing this because disability pay is tax free while retirement pay is not. Disability pay is not divisible in a divorce.

Social Security

Spousal benefits and survivor benefits are a valuable feature of social security for married people. When you reach 66, the eligible retirement age, you can claim half your spouse's retirement benefit if it is higher than your own full benefit. You are also entitled to a benefit if your spouse dies.

Divorce courts won't divide social security benefits. But most of the benefits for married couples are still available to you if you get divorced; provided you are single, were married to your ex for at least ten years, are at least 62-years-old, and are not already receiving a social security benefit higher than the divorced spouse's benefit.

If your divorce has been final for at least two years, you can file for the divorced spouse's retirement benefits even if your ex is not receiving benefits.

If you remarry, you lose these benefits and you will have to be married to your new spouse for one year before you can file for benefits based on her earning record.

One strategy for divorced spouses works like this: If your own benefit is less than half your ex's benefit when you reach retirement age of 66, you can claim your divorced spouse's benefit. Then, at age 70, if your own benefit has grown in excess of your divorced spouse's benefit, you can switch to your own benefit.

Another strategy is switching back and forth between multiple ex's benefits, selecting the highest benefit, as long as you have been married to each of them for at least ten years.

■ **Note** Social Security benefits are not divisible by the divorce court, but some states allow the judge discretion to take them into account in dividing other marital property.

Summary

When dividing marital property, retirement funds can be a valuable asset. Sometimes, retirement funds are part marital and part premarital property. Defined contribution plans can be readily valued by looking at the current account statement. Defined benefit plans require valuation by an actuary or division if, as, and when received. It takes a QDRO to divide plans covered under ERISA. Other plans are divided by different methods. The survivor benefit is a valuable part of a pension plan but must be paid for on an ongoing basis. Social security benefits are not divisible in a divorce court, but divorced spouses are entitled to certain benefits.

The next chapter will discuss how to divide a business in a divorce.

CHAPTER 15

Business Investments

Businesses present their own challenges when dividing property and establishing income in a divorce. A business can be anything from a retail store to a home-based operation. It can be a medical practice, a construction business, a day care center, a dental practice, a law firm, or some other business. Businesses can be owned in several different ways. They can operate as sole proprietorships, partnerships, corporations, or various other business entities.

You Have a Silent Partner in Your Business: Your Spouse

It was 3:00 on a hot afternoon when Vince Reed, MD, rolled into his divorce lawyer's parking lot in his new Jaguar. The sign on the door read, "Lauren West, Attorney and Counselor at Law."

Vince and Carla Reed had been married for eighteen years when they decided to get divorced. Vince is a successful orthopedic surgeon.

During the marriage, he joined a group of other physicians providing medical services in a surgery center owned by Emery Surgery Center, LLC, a limited liability company. Vince owned one share in the center equaling 1 percent. He had paid $30,000 for it. The center was so profitable that Vince recovered his entire investment in the first two months.

"OK, so I went to medical school," Vince explained to his lawyer as he sat down at her desk. "I earned the money to invest in the surgery center. I found the investment. I worked each day to make it successful. And you're telling me she gets half? I don't get it."

"It's marital property," Lauren responded.

■ **Tip** A business started or acquired during the marriage is marital or community property no matter whose name it is in.

How Businesses Are Valued in a Divorce

The conversation between Vince and Lauren continued. They discuss the division of property in a separation agreement and what to offer Carla for Vince's share of the surgery center.

"Then offer her $15,000," Vince said. "That's half of what I paid for the surgery center. It's also half of what I would get if I left the practice."

"Your wife's attorney wants to have a business appraiser value your interest in the surgery center," Lauren said.

"OK. A business appraiser will tell her it's worth $30,000," Vince suggested.

"No. He won't. It doesn't work like that," Lauren informed him. "He'll want a lot of information. Then, he'll put it all in his computer and come up with a much higher number."

"What information?"

"Articles of incorporation, operating agreement, amendments, a list of members, ledgers, accounts receivable, a profit and loss statement, and a balance sheet, to name a few," said Lauren.

"That's a big list."

Documents

Six months later, Vince was still sending documents to his attorney to forward to his wife's business appraiser.

It was a rainy afternoon when Vince called his lawyer to say, "It seems like every time I give them what they ask for, they want something more. Is this ever going to end?"

"I'll call them," Lauren assured Vince. "Maybe I will be able to expedite matters."

Lauren called Carla's attorney, Mitch Handelman. "Hi, Mitch. Lauren West here. What can we do to speed up the Reed case?"

"Get me all the documents my expert needs," answered Mitch.

"Isn't there some way around that?" asked Lauren. "What if we make a generous settlement offer?"

"I can't advise my client whether an offer is generous or not until I know the value of the business," said Mitch. "And I can't know the value of the business until my business valuation expert gets all the documents he needs."

"Once you get all the documents, how long will it take your expert to give us his opinion of value?" Lauren proceeded to ask.

"Two weeks," said Mitch.

"I'll hold you to that."

The Wife's Expert

A month later, Mitch set up a meeting with Lauren to present the opinion he received from the expert. When he got to her office, he handed Lauren the written summary.

"You'll see that our expert used the projected cash flow of the business to value your client's shares," said Mitch. "He used very conservative assumptions."

"And what does he say it's worth?" asked Lauren.

"Between $1 and 1.5 million."

There was silence in the room. Finally, Lauren stated, "Well, we'll see what *our* expert says and get back to you."

The Husband's Expert

Vince and Lauren got her expert, Albert Cassini, on a conference call. "Vince bought his interest in the surgery center for $30,000. The expert told them two other doctors have been brought into the practice and they each paid $30,000 for their shares. The best determination of the fair market value of something is what it sells for. There have been three sales in the recent past. So, the correct value is $30,000."

"What about the opinion claimed by the expert for Carla's lawyer suggesting that it's worth between one and one-and-a-half-million dollars?" Lauren asked.

"He just put numbers in his computer spreadsheet and took the result it gave him without thinking it through," replied Albert. "That's a common mistake in our occupation. You have to look at the numbers, but you have to apply common sense as well."

"Why would the sellers sell such an attractive income stream for so little?" asked Lauren.

"Because they want to acquire more patients and grow. So they are looking for doctors with a good client following. That limits the number of qualified buyers. A small number of qualified buyers means the buyers can negotiate a lower price. The doctors know they can buy the income stream at another clinic for $30,000 if they can't get it at this one," explained Albert.

Discounts

Lauren's expert proceeded to educate Lauren and Vince. "There are also certain discounts that may be applied to value a business properly."

"Like what?" asked Vince.

"There are four things," explained the expert and then went on to describe them. They can be categorized as follows:

- **Lack of Control:** As stated by the expert, "We can discount the share value for lack of control. Since your shares aren't the controlling ones for the business, they are worth less than shares that are."

- **Lack of Marketability:** The next point the expert made was, "When a business interest would be hard to sell, its lack of marketability creates a discount. IBM stock is easy to sell because there is a market for it. An interest in a medical practice is not as marketable."

- **Personal Goodwill:** The next discount he described to them was goodwill. "You are also entitled to a discount for personal goodwill. Goodwill is the portion of the business that is attributed to the owner rather than the business. For example, if people come to the business because of the reputation and skill of the owner, that's personal goodwill. If a business has several different stores and employees, then there may be less personal goodwill and more business goodwill. Many states treat personal goodwill as separate property in a divorce, subtracting it from the value of the business."

- **Uncle Sam:** "If you sell your business at a profit, you would have to pay a capital gains tax," said the business valuator. "Future taxes will therefore also be considered as a discount to value. However, some judges will not take taxes into account because there is no actual sale of the business in a divorce."

"These, among other reasons, are why your portion of the business, Vince, is worth just $30,000 in my view," the expert concluded.

Lauren thanks the expert, and the call is ended. She and Vince continue talking.

"Vince, there are a couple of other things you need to know," Lauren says.

Tip Have your business valued by an expert. If your spouse has an expert, be prepared to argue for your value compared with the value she comes up with.

Double-Dipping

"There is also an argument that your spouse is double-dipping," said Lauren.

"What do you mean?" asked Vincent.

"The double-dipping argument goes like this," started Lauren. "First, the judge determines alimony and child support based on your income. The income he considers is all from the earnings of the business. Next, the judge will determine a division of marital property. The judge may choose to use the value presented by your wife's expert, in which case you will have to pay half the present value of your future earnings to your wife for a buyout. Your wife's expert will use the future earnings of the business to come up with the value. That's in addition to support. So, she has effectively used the same earnings twice, once for alimony and once for the business buyout. That's double-dipping."

"So what do we do?" asked Vince.

"We try to settle," replied Lauren. "We agree on a price and terms for you to buy her interest with payments over time.

"And what if we can't settle?"

"Then the judge will listen to both experts and decide for you."

Valuing Business Assets

The family business is usually a main source of income. Therefore, it is probably a valuable asset worth fighting over in a divorce.

You fail to value the family business at your own peril in a divorce. Take Ron, who bought a tree-chipping company. He had several contracts with local governments and was very successful. In his divorce, he told his wife, Louise, that his accountant had valued the business at about $250,000. He offered to pay her half of that. Louise ran that by her attorney, who recommended she get the business valued on her own. She did and the appraiser said it was worth $600,000. She finally settled on a $250,000 payment. Although she had to pay $5,000 for the appraisal, it was worth it for her to receive $125,000 more than the original offer.

A business owner may benefit from an evaluation also. Steve owned a company that sold paper rolls for cash registers and credit card machines. His wife, Sandy, was a salesperson for the company and responsible for most of its success. Her accountant valued the business at $2 million based on its discounted future earnings. Steve's expert valued the business at $600,000 and then discounted that by 50 percent for lack of marketability. The judge found Steve's expert to be more believable and gave Sandy an award of $300,000.

There is a temptation to hire the accountant for the business to value it. After all, the accountant already has the financial information. This may work for settlement purposes. But for trial, your accountant must have expertise in valuing businesses in order to qualify to testify as an expert and give an opinion of value. Otherwise, consider hiring a certified business appraiser (CBA).

But be aware that even experts can make mistakes. In one case, Sarah bought a company that published an advertising magazine for realtors. She and her husband, Mark, also owned a home and a rental property. She offered to trade his interest in her business for her interest in the couple's real estate. In order to do this, they agreed to jointly hire an expert to value the business. The expert discovered the lingerie she purchased at Victoria's Secret on the company credit card but somehow failed to notice the $300,000 she paid to herself and her husband last year as dividends. He valued the company at $150,000. The equity in the two real properties also totaled about $150,000, so the deal was made.

So ask your expert to identify any errors or weaknesses in the report of your spouse's expert. Appraisers use assumptions when valuing a business. So different appraisers can have widely differing values.

Sometimes, people confuse business assets and individual assets. For example, if your spouse has an automobile, you will want to examine the title to see if it is owned by your spouse or your spouse's business. If it is owned by the business, it will be taken into account when the business is valued. In other words, the value of the automobile will be included in the price of the stock owned your spouse (if the business is a corporation). The same goes for office equipment, computers, and inventory.

What to Do with the Business

If you both own the business, one option is to do nothing. You can continue to operate the business as partners after the divorce. Some people are able to do this successfully. But most couples prefer not to continue in business with an ex-spouse.

Stan and Stella owned a jewelry business together with four stores. Stella was in charge of buying and selling jewelry. Stan took care of hiring and firing people, negotiating the leases, and supervising the build-out of the stores. They tried running the business together after their divorce, but they had constant disputes, causing Stella to hide some of the inventory and Stan to sue to appoint a receiver. They finally reached an agreement for Stella to buy out Stan's interest in the business over time.

If you are lucky enough to have a business that can be divided into two approximately equal businesses, then each spouse can take one part of the business.

You can also sell the business outright and split the proceeds. Doing this will allow the parties to take the proceeds and start new businesses on their own if they wish or retire. You will need to agree on how decisions will be made until a buyer is found. And it may take a while to find the right buyer. Also, there will be a capital gains tax to be paid if the business is sold for a profit.

The approach that most people take is for one spouse to buy the other's interest in the business. You can pay in cash or trade other assets, like a pension plan or equity in the house. If there is not enough cash or other assets, you can agree to payments over time. The parties can agree on a buyout price or have their business appraised. When one spouse transfers appreciated assets in a divorce, there is no capital gains tax. That tax will be collected from the spouse who keeps the business if it is sold for a profit in a subsequent transaction.

Note Unless you can work together after the divorce, or the business is easily divided, you will have to sell it or one of you will have to buy out the other.

Professional Degrees and Licenses

Rachel sacrificed her own education to work to put Tim through medical school. Once Tim graduated and started his internship, they separated and Tim filed for divorce. Is this fair to Rachel? Should she be compensated somehow? How much?

Most states say a degree or license is not property and cannot be equitably divided in a divorce.

A few states, like New York and Massachusetts, disagree. They permit an expert to place a value on a degree. This is usually accomplished by estimating the difference in lifetime earnings of the person with a professional degree and the one without a degree.

Louisiana allows a spouse in this situation to claim reimbursement for the cost of obtaining the degree.

Intellectual Property: Patents, Trademarks, Copyrights, Royalties

Max was a famous painter. His artwork sold in galleries around the world. While he was a gifted artist, it was his wife Nora who inspired him to paint for a living and who managed the business aspects of his career and artwork. It was she, for example, who obtained the contracts for reprints. In their divorce, they were able to agree on support and dividing his inventory of paintings, but they were stuck on how to divide future royalties that he would receive for reprints of paintings created during the marriage. They ultimately agreed to set up a trust for their children and deposit a portion of the royalties into that trust.

In dividing a marital estate, don't overlook intellectual property like inventions, patents, trademarks, copyrights, royalties, and trade secrets that were acquired during the marriage.

■ **Note** Professional degrees and licenses are not marital property in most states, but intellectual property is.

Income

The income of a business owner is used to determine child support, and it is one of the factors considered in determining spousal support. But a business owner who has control is able to manipulate income and even hide money.

In the year of the divorce, a business owner can delay collection of receivables or even lose payments by customers in a desk drawer and forget to deposit them.

A business owner can speed up the payment of bills and pay in advance. Most business owners pay estimated taxes quarterly. One trick is to pay more taxes than you owe and then file for a refund after the divorce.

A business owner can also stock up on inventory. There will usually be a line of credit from a bank. A business owner can borrow to meet cash flow needs and claim these are borrowed funds rather than income. Then the owner can pay the loan off after the divorce.

An accountant or the expert you use to value the business can determine the true income of a business owner by looking at the books and records of the business. The expert will look at the records for several years of business operations and not just for the year of the divorce.

Tip A business owner with control can manipulate income for the year of the divorce. An accountant or other financial expert can tell if there has been manipulation in the figures and give an opinion of true income. So, have your expert take a good look if you suspect there is more income to be uncovered in a business.

Summary

A family business can add complexity to dividing marital assets and determining income in a divorce. You will need your own expert to value the business and determine the income it produces. If your and your spouse's experts have opinions that are far apart, the judge may have to decide. In most states, a professional degree or license is not marital property. Neither is the personal goodwill of a business. In the next chapter, we'll examine the division of bank accounts, stocks, and other assets.

CHAPTER 16

Bank Accounts, Stock, and Other Assets

Deciding how to divide liquid assets like bank accounts and stocks is not quite as complicated as dividing houses, retirement funds, and businesses. But it can still have some twists and turns of its own.

Dividing Bank Accounts

Remember, we are dividing marital property only. If you have a bank account in your individual name that is from before the marriage or an inheritance or gift, then it stays your separate property after divorce. But if the bank account was opened during the marriage, and is not inherited or gifted funds, then it is marital property whether it is in joint names or individual names.

The easiest way to divide joint bank accounts is to close them and split the amount equally. That is, unless you have an argument about why the amount should not be divided equally. For example, maybe the money you put in that account is from premarital property.

If you can withdraw funds from your joint account with just one signature, you may want to go ahead and split up the account before you reach an agreement. This is a protective step to prevent your spouse from taking more than half of the funds without your knowledge.

You can divide marital bank accounts that are in individual names equally, or each person can keep the funds from their own account if they have approximately equal balances. If not, then an equalizing adjustment can be made when dividing other assets.

Date of Division

If you have an agreement about how to divide the joint bank accounts, pay particular attention to the balances and the dates. You can make the date of division the same as that of the agreement, the day you go to the bank, or some other date. But balances change as bills are paid, and it can make a difference whether you divide the bank account balance on the day before or the day after your spouse pays the rent or mortgage.

The following story demonstrates some of the complexities that can arise in the seemingly simple task of dividing bank accounts.

Anne calls her divorce attorney, Lee Francis, and says, "Hi, Lee. Jason is harassing me about wanting his half of the money that was in the bank the date we signed the papers. I was always under the impression that the money that would be divided when we actually divorce would be based on what was in the accounts at the time we signed the separation agreement."

"Hold on while I get the agreement," Lee says and goes to find the document.

"Let's see, it says here, 'The parties have a joint checking account with Bank of America that has a balance of $2,500 as of May 29, 2013. The parties agree to close this account and equally divide the balance on the day this agreement is signed.'"

"Do I wait until we are divorced to pay him? Or should I pay him now?" asks Anne.

"You can pay him now," Lee tells her.

"And how do I prove that I paid him if I give him any part of the money now?"

"As for proof of payment, you can have him sign a receipt if you give him cash, or just use a copy of your canceled check if you give him a check."

"Here's another problem. On the day we signed the separation agreement, I withdrew $600 in cash. I have an ATM receipt that shows the date. I gave Jason $300 of the money for his half of the tax refund. He signed a receipt saying that I gave him that cash. There was no witness or notary. So the problem is that he will get that money twice because the $600 was not subtracted from the account by the bank until the next morning," Anne adds.

"Did he know the tax refund was in the account?" Lee asks her.

"Yes, he knew the tax money was in there. He never asked to see the balances. I tried to show them to him on my phone, but he wouldn't look at them. So how do I prove that I paid him the correct amount?" Anne wants to know.

"The $300 was an advance payment to him of half the account. You did pay him the correct amount. And you can prove it with your receipts, bank statements, and canceled checks," Lee tells her.

"Thanks," Anne replies. "Jason is going out of control right now. He says he's going to take me to court. That's because he's going off the numbers that were on the agreement from a month ago. He's ignoring the part that says he gets half of the balance on the day we signed the agreement. He's wrong on that, isn't he?"

"Yes. Just go by the agreement."

"And he is saying that the tax money shouldn't come out of his half. The check I gave him was for half of the balance minus the $300 I paid him for the taxes. I'm worried now. Can he go to court over this?" asks Anne.

"Anybody can go to court over anything, but I don't think he will win" is Lee's response.

Note The date of division can be an important detail in dividing bank accounts.

Don't Try to Hide Bank Accounts from Your Attorney

Amy was halfway through her initial conference with Carrie, her divorce lawyer, when they started talking about bank accounts.

"Do you and your husband have any joint bank accounts?" asks Carrie.

"No, we have separated everything already."

"Do you have a checking account?" Carrie goes on.

"Yes," replies Amy.

"How much is in it?"

"About $200."

"And in your savings account?"

"I don't have a savings account."

"I see on your tax return that you have some interest from an account at M&T Bank," Carrie remarks.

Amy leans forward in her chair. "I can't touch that money!" she says.

"Why not?"

"That's the only money I have left to live on."

Carrie was left to explain to Amy that despite what she thinks, the court has the power to distribute assets acquired during the marriage. It does not matter whose name is on the account. The court can leave the money in the account and give the other spouse a marital award to adjust the equities. The spouse granted the award can then use the powers of the court to have the money paid directly from that account or other asset. Carrie told her client that you can't make a bank account disappear by ignoring it or hiding it although many have tried.

Don't Try to Hide Bank Accounts from the Court

Andre fidgeted in the witness chair as Judge Martin questioned him about the financial statement he submitted to the court. He was clearly uncomfortable.

"Let me show you Plaintiff's Exhibit 1," says the judge. "Do you recognize that?"

"Yes," answers Andre.

"What is it?"

"A statement from my bank."

"And it says you have $100,000 in that account. Am I reading that correctly?"

"Yes."

"Now show me where you disclosed that bank account on your financial statement," proceeds Judge Martin.

"I didn't. That money was left to me by my mother. My wife has no claim to that money!"

Andre ended up accomplishing two things by not reporting his bank account. He destroyed his credibility with the judge and he made him unsympathetic to his situation. The judge ordered Andre to pay $10,000 of his wife's attorney fees.

Note You can't make a bank account disappear by pretending it doesn't exist.

Finding Hidden Bank Accounts

If you suspect that your spouse is hiding money somewhere, you need to take action, or have your attorney take action, to find any hidden assets so that they are properly divided in your divorce. Hiding assets in a divorce is illegal, but people still try to do it.

Some people let their spouse handle all of the family finances. This can include all of the bank accounts as well as investments, such as the home, vacation property, rental property, stock, stock options, retirement plans, life insurance, and the family business. That's a lot of things to keep track of, especially if you have no experience or are not mathematically or financially inclined.

Once you file for divorce, the rules of the divorce court concerning discovery, which we will discuss later, will give you tools to help find your spouse's assets. You can also hire a private investigator to do an asset search even before you file. Or you can hire an accountant (sometimes called a forensic accountant) or a financial planner (some are certified for divorce) to analyze the family's finances. They can determine if expenses match income, assets, and loans. If the expenses are larger than the known resources, there may be some hidden income or bank accounts.

Tip If you suspect a spouse of dishonesty in reporting assets, consider hiring a forensic accountant. He will analyze your family finances and may be able to sniff out unreported accounts.

Tricks Used to Hide Money in a Divorce

You have a better chance of finding hidden bank accounts or other assets if you know some of the schemes that are used to hide money in divorces. Become financially aware and keep your eyes open for tricks like these that are used to hide money:

1. *Reducing or delaying income.* A business owner might hold customer checks in a desk drawer and not record them until the divorce is over. An employee might tell an employer to defer income or delay raises, bonuses, and commissions. A spouse might put the sale of a business or new employment contract on hold.

2. *Speeding up payment of expenses.* Tricks for speeding up expenses and thus reducing income include paying a mortgage early, buying extra inventory if you own a business, paying estimated income taxes for the whole year in advance, and paying off credit cards that are in one spouse's name only.

3. *Purchasing assets.* Be on the lookout for the spouse who buys a new car or adds to a collection of antiques, artwork, coins, gold, or miniature railroad cars.

4. *Hiding money.* Some spouses put cash under the mattress, in the attic, or inside a safe or safe deposit box.

5. *Cheating.* A spouse might report lesson a financial statement or tax return than was actually earned.

6. *Transferring funds.* Watch out for a spouse asking a friend, relative, or other trusted party to hold money until the divorce is over.

7. *Putting funds in another's name.* Be on the lookout for a spouse who transfers money to the children by putting it in custodial accounts.

Having knowledge of your family finances is the best way to detect hidden money and protect yourself in a divorce. You should know about family finances anyway in case your spouse becomes incapacitated or dies. Know where your bank accounts are held. Actually read your tax returns and ask questions. Don't just sign them without looking.

Tip If your spouse handles the family finances, start learning more about her and where all the accounts are held.

Stock

Stock is divided by the delivery of stock certificates, but usually you never see the certificates because they are held by a stockbroker. If you reach an agreement on how to divide your stock, you can simply give instructions to your broker to transfer the shares to another brokerage account in the name of your spouse.

Stock is different than cash for the reason that it may carry with it a hidden tax burden. If you sell stock for more than you paid for it, you have to pay taxes on the gain.

Gain on stock is not taxed when it is transferred in a divorce. Instead, the cost or tax basis of the stock is transferred with the stock. The spouse who receives the stock will have to pay the taxes on any gain when the stock is sold. So $10,000 worth of stock may be worth somewhat less than that amount in cash once you account for the taxes that may have to be paid in the future.

Stock is not favored on your taxes with an exemption, as is real estate, nor in a deduction and deferral of taxes, as in the case of retirement funds. So take care when you trade different asset classes for one another in a divorce that you are taking tax aspects into account and not just trading dollar for dollar.

Just like in the case of bank accounts, the value of stock fluctuates daily. So if you are dividing a stock account equally, the value of the stock is a moving target and the date of division becomes important. If you are willing to take the risk that the value of the stock might go up or down, you can agree to distribute a percentage to each party on the day the stock is divided instead of a set dollar amount.

Note   Stock may have a hidden tax burden when transferred in a divorce that makes it not as valuable as cash or other assets.

Stock Options

A stock option enables a person with the right to buy stock at a set price. Stock options are sometimes offered to employees as additional compensation.

A stock option may have value even if the current price of the stock is below the set value. This is because stock prices go up and down and experts are able to value the probability that you will be able to exercise the option at a gain sometime in the future.

Vested stock options are marital property because they have been earned during the marriage. Unvested stock options are also usually considered to be marital property as long as they are awarded for work performed during the marriage.

Stock options follow the law of marital property. If they are acquired during the marriage or are awarded for work performed during the marriage, then they are marital property. If they were granted before the marriage, they are part marital and part premarital and an expert will have to value them for you unless you can agree on a value or a percentage to be transferred.

Automobiles and Other Vehicles

To divide the automobiles in a divorce, you could sell them, pay off any car loans, and divide any proceeds that are left over. But those options are not practical in most cases, and people usually want to keep the automobiles they have been driving.

If you do these things, you can adjust for the difference in values with cash or other assets. The value of your automobile is available on the Web at www.kbb.com. Subtract any car loans to get the net equity value.

Ownership of an automobile is transferred by title. Its transfer in a divorce is usually exempt from automobile transfer taxes if you submit certain forms at the Department of Motor Vehicles when you register your title. After the transfer, you may have to change your automobile insurance if you have family coverage or your spouse is listed as another driver.

All of this applies to other vehicles as well, including trucks, motorcycles, and boats.

It is always a good idea to have assets valued when splitting them up in a divorce. Take the following case of one husband and wife who were getting divorced and dividing up their marital assets. The husband had purchased a couple of cars a few years earlier. One was a beautifully restored 1966 Plymouth Valiant convertible that the wife drove. The other was a 1970 Plymouth convertible that he drove from time to time.

The husband suggested that his wife keep the 1966 Plymouth Valiant and he keep the 1970 Plymouth. She didn't see any problem with this and readily agreed. Her lawyer, however, recommended that she have both cars appraised just to be sure they were approximately the same value.

The appraiser valued the wife's 1966 Plymouth at $15,000. The husband's car, on the other hand, was a rare and valuable Hemi Cuda convertible and was appraised at over $1 million.

It is too late to appraise assets after the settlement agreement or after the divorce. Be sure you have your assets identified and values determined before you sign an agreement or you may regret it later.

Tip   Have your assets appraised. They may be worth more than you think.

Furniture and Furnishings

Furniture, furnishings, clothes, jewelry, towels, dishes, silverware, and other miscellaneous household items are usually not worth much compared to the house and retirement plan. They can be replaced rather easily. But they sometimes carry emotional value or symbolize the end of the marriage and can become the tail that wags the dog.

Most judges hate disputes over these small items and will simply order the things to be sold by a trustee if necessary and the proceeds divided equally.

If you can agree on a division of household items, you will save time and legal fees. If you cannot, here's a method for dividing them: First, make a list of every item room by room. Then flip a coin to decide who goes first. The winner picks an item on the list that he wants. The other spouse picks next. Go back and forth until everything is settled.

Frequent Flyer Miles and Award Points

Airline frequent flyer miles and credit card award points can add up during a marriage, especially if one or both spouses travel a lot for business purposes. If the company will allow it, the straightforward way of splitting up these things is to divide the points equally into separate individual accounts for each spouse. There may be fees for this, which should be equally divided as well.

Some companies do not permit the transfer of award points in a divorce. In that case, you can value the points and negotiate for something of equivalent value. If there is not a point-to-dollar conversion, you can do an estimate based on the value of services or products you can trade the points for.

Other Assets

Other assets to be divided in a divorce include time-shares, country club memberships, oil wells, wine collections, paintings, sculptures, coin collections, annuities, and cash values of life insurance policies.

You should know that life insurance policies can be term or whole life. Term policies have a face value, which is the amount that will be paid on death, but no cash value. So they have zero value as an asset. Whole-life policies have both a face value and a cash value. The cash value is what they are worth, and you can collect that amount by surrendering the policy to the company that issued it.

One adventure-loving couple had had hand-crafted his-and-her kayaks custom built for themselves during their marriage. When they got divorced, the wife proposed that each take one. The husband's argument was that they were a uniquely matched pair that were more valuable together than alone. He wanted both of them. The wife finally decided that it was a matter of money, not emotion. So she let him keep them, but he had to pay a high price for getting his way.

Summary

We have talked about how to divide the house, the retirement funds, the businesses, the bank accounts, the stock, and other assets. During these discussions, we've touched upon some of the tax consequences of a divorce. Now we're going to review all those aspects together in the next chapter, on taxes.

CHAPTER 17

Taxes

There's a lot going on in a divorce. You might be paying or receiving alimony and child support. The marital home, retirement funds, and businesses may be sold or transferred. It will be determined who gets what tax benefits for the children. Your tax filing status will change. Taxes affect every divorce. This chapter will view various divorce transactions from the tax point of view. You may use it as a checklist for tax issues in negotiations, settlement, and litigation.

Tax Filing Status

Your marital status on the last day of the year, December 31, determines your filing status for federal income tax. And your filing status determines which tax rates apply to your income.

Married Filing Jointly

If you are married on the last day of the year, you can file a joint tax return with your spouse and your status will be "Married filing jointly." This filing status has the lowest tax rates. Even if you are separated, you can still file joint tax returns to take advantage of the lower tax rates.

Married Filing Separately

If you file separate tax returns, your status will be "Married filing separately." This filing status has the highest tax rates. Let's listen in on a conversation that will show you the types of disputes that may arise over tax-filing status in a divorce. The conversation takes place at the offices of the wife's lawyer during the deposition of the husband with both spouses and their lawyers present.

Randy asks his wife, Susie, "Are you going to sign the joint tax return?"

Susie's lawyer, Gloria, responds for her: "Since you are working and Susie is not, we calculate that you will save $10,000 in taxes by filing a joint return."

"So?" says Randy.

"Susie won't owe any taxes whether she files jointly or separately," says Gloria. "So, we propose that Susie will file jointly with you if you agree to pay her $5,000 of your tax refund."

"Why, that's blackmail!" shouts Randy. He stands up and walks out.

Randy's lawyer looks at Gloria and says, "Let's talk. Maybe we can work something out."

When one spouse has a higher income than the other, that spouse may gain a significant tax savings by filing jointly. However, when spouses are divorcing, sometimes anger gets in the way of their commonsense (and common cents). The high-income earner may have to share some of the tax savings with the low-income spouse to get an agreement to file joint tax returns.

Tip If you and your spouse file jointly, you cannot file amended separate tax returns later. But if you file separately, you can file an amended joint return if you reach a settlement after filing your taxes.

Single

If you are not married on the last day of the year, you may file your tax returns as "Single," which has the third-lowest tax rates.

You can still file your tax returns as single even if you are married on the last day of the year if you meet all of the following conditions:

- You and your spouse file separate returns;
- A child lives for more than half a year at your home and you are eligible to claim him as a dependent;
- You provide more than half the cost of maintaining your home during the year; and
- Your spouse did not live in the same house during the last six months of the previous year.

Head of Household

If you are not married on the last day of the year, you can file as "Head of household," which has the second-lowest tax rates, if you meet all of the following requirements:

- you maintain the home of a qualified dependent for more than half the year;
- you pay more than half of the cost of the home for the qualified dependent;
- your spouse or former spouse is not a member of your household; and
- you do not file a joint return.

If you have one child, only one parent can qualify for the head-of-household status because of the requirement of furnishing more than one-half of the support of the household for a qualified dependent. If you have more than one child, both parents can meet the terms for the status.

Tip Your marital status on the last day of the year determines your filing status. There are different tax rates for each status. "Married filing jointly" is the lowest status, and "Married filing separately" is the highest.

Alimony

Alimony is tax deductible if you are paying it and taxable income if you are receiving it. There is no withholding tax on alimony income so you may have to make estimated tax payments quarterly if you receive alimony. If you forget to do this, and many people do, you will have a big tax bill on April 15th.

Child support, by contrast, is not deductible for the person paying it, and it is not taxable income for the person receiving it. So a high earner will be better off paying more alimony and less child support due to the tax deduction for alimony. And the person receiving payments will be better off with more nontaxable child support and less taxable alimony.

The Internal Revenue Code requires that payments meet all of the following conditions to be deductible as alimony:

- they must be made to or on behalf of a spouse or former spouse;
- they must be made in cash or a cash equivalent;
- they must be pursuant to a written divorce agreement or order;

- the agreement or order does not say the payment is not alimony;
- the parties do not live in same household;
- the payments terminate upon the death of the person receiving alimony;
- they are not made in a year for which the parties file a joint return;
- they are not for child support; and
- they are not disqualified under the IRS alimony recapture rules.

Here's an example: When David and Sue agreed to separate in January, David agreed that he would continue to be the breadwinner and support the family by paying Sue $5,000 a month. He paid her $60,000 during the year.

David asked his accountant if he could file a separate tax return for the year and deduct the $60,000 he had paid as alimony.

The accountant told him no, because the payments were not made under a written divorce agreement. David could have saved thousands of dollars if he had only put the agreement in writing.

Fortunately for him, Sue agreed to file joint returns for that year. Had she not, David would have had to pay the higher tax rates for filing as "Married filing separately," and he would not be able to take the alimony deductions that he would have had if he had a written agreement.

There are tax complications for the spouse who receives alimony as well. An example is the Earned Income Credit, which phases out as your income rises. Alimony may increase your income to the point that you lose the Earned Income Credit.

Tip Even if you call it alimony, it may not be deductible unless you meet the IRS requirements for alimony.

Alimony vs. Child Support

The IRS has rules designed to prevent you from turning nondeductible child support payments into deductible alimony payments, discussed in the earlier chapter on alimony. Basically, since child support ends when a child becomes an adult, these rules disallow deductions for alimony payments that are tied to an event in the child's life.

Alimony vs. Property Transfer

The IRS also has rules to prevent you from turning a nontaxable property transfer into deductible alimony. These rules were discussed in detail in the chapter on alimony. They allow the IRS to recapture deductions for alimony payments that are front end loaded into the first two years of alimony payments.

The Family Home

There are favorable tax benefits associated with owning a family home, including tax deductions and exclusion of some capital gains on a sale. You need to consider these tax benefits in a divorce.

Deductions for a Home

A taxpayer may deduct interest she paid on mortgages and real estate taxes for her primary residence. She may also take those deductions after she moves out of the family home if she still has a dependent living in the home.

If you have a divorce agreement or divorce order that gives the use and possession of a jointly owned home to your spouse and requires you to pay all of the mortgage and taxes, you are entitled to deduct half of these payments as alimony plus half of the interest and taxes.

If the home is in your name alone, however, you can deduct all the interest and taxes, but there is no deduction for alimony because you are paying your expenses and not those of your spouse.

Sale of a Home

Upon the sale of a home, you may exclude up to $250,000 in gain from your income and your spouse can also exclude up to $250,000. Gain is the sales price less your tax basis. Tax basis is costs plus selling expenses and improvements minus any depreciation you have taken for tax purposes.

The home must be your principal residence. A principal residence is defined by the IRS as a home you've owned and lived in for at least two of the five years before the sale. There are exceptions to this rule for military members, vacation homes, homes bought less than two years prior, and certain hardships and other circumstances.

If you reach an agreement to sell the house at the time of divorce, then you will be able to exclude up to $500,000 of gain from your taxes if you meet the personal residence requirements.

But if you buy out your spouse in a divorce, that transfer will be tax free for both of you. Your spouse won't pay any capital gains tax. If you stay in the house and sell it later, you can exclude $250,000 of the gain as long as the house qualifies as your personal residence.

Here's an example: George and Jill lived in their house for twenty months before they divorced. In the divorce, the court granted Jill the right to live in the house for three more years or until it was sold, whichever came first. They would continue to own the house together and split the proceeds when it was sold. Jill sold the house a year later. Since she had lived in the house for more than two years, she was entitled to the $250,000 tax exclusion.

What about George? He had only lived in the house for twenty months at the time of the divorce, less than the two years required for the exclusion. Fortunately, the IRS permitted him to tack on to his time the period that Jill was living in the house exclusively under the divorce decree. So George would also get the $250,000 exclusion. Note that he could have lost his exclusion entirely if he had not obtained a written agreement or divorce decree within three years of moving out of the house. That is because he would not have lived in the house for two of the prior five years and could not tack on Jill's time because it was not pursuant to a divorce decree or instrument.

Tip   You can deduct up to $250,000 of gain from the sale of your home if you meet the IRS tests for ownership and use.

All Property Transfers in Divorce Are Tax Free

Property transfers from one spouse to another in a divorce are nontaxable events. You do not report any gains or losses on the transaction in your tax returns.

Your tax basis is transferred to your spouse with the property. The tax basis is the cost of the asset with certain adjustments provided by the tax code like selling costs and depreciation. When you sell the asset, that is a taxable event. The sales price less the tax basis is your capital gain or loss for tax purposes.

Cash vs. Stock

Jeff and Lisa were in the process of getting divorced. As part of their property settlement, Jeff agreed to pay Lisa $50,000. During their marriage, they had purchased some Apple stock together for $10,000. The stock was now worth $100,000. If Lisa were to transfer her half of the Apple stock to Jeff, would she be paying him $50,000? Maybe not. If Jeff were to try to turn the stock into cash by selling it, he would have to pay taxes on the capital gains. The capital gains are the sales price of $50,000 less the original cost of $5,000, which equals $45,000. If the taxes are 20 percent of his $45,000 in capital gains, he will owe $9,000 in taxes on the stock sale. Due to the tax consequences, Jeff would be better off insisting that Lisa pay him $50,000 in cash instead of stock.

Tip Property transfers in a divorce are tax free, but not all assets are equal due to the tax consequences when they are sold later.

Retirement Funds

Retirement funds in qualified pension plans and traditional individual retirement accounts are not taxed when they are earned; they are taxed when the funds are withdrawn. There is no tax on the transfer of retirement funds pursuant to a divorce order. But retirement funds carry an income tax burden with them like the previous stock example. And this income will be taxed at ordinary income rates, which may be higher than the capital gains rate.

401(k) Plans

The division of 401(k) plans is done tax free with a Qualified Domestic Relations Order issued by the divorce court. The plans continue to earn interest and dividends tax free until they are withdrawn. When withdrawn, they are taxed as earned income. If a person withdraws funds from a 401(k) before they reach age fifty-nine-and-a-half, they are subject to a 10 percent penalty tax. There is one important exception to the 10 percent penalty rule. Here's an example to illustrate the exception.

Carlos, Helen's divorce attorney, was young, tall, and thin. He was dressed impeccably in a dark-navy suit, white starched button-down shirt, and red tie for his meeting with Steve, the divorce attorney of Helen's husband, Nelson. Steve was a short, slightly pudgy man, with wisps of grey hair framing his bald head. Carlos went to the other lawyer's office for the meeting.

"The problem Helen has with your client's settlement," Carlos tells Steve, "is that there is no money for her to make a down payment on a new place to live."

"What about the $100,000 she's getting from the 401(k)?" asks Steve.

"Well, she can't use that because she will have to pay the 10 percent early withdrawal penalty," Carlos remarks.

"Ah ha!" exclaims Steve as he jumps up from his desk. "Follow me."

Carlos followed as Steve strode spryly out of his office and down a long hallway into another office where a young associate labored over a desk piled high with books.

"Hi Alex," says Steve. "Can you find that little obscure provision in the Internal Revenue Code that provides that 401(k) plans can be distributed in a divorce without a 10 percent early withdrawal penalty?"

Alex grabbed his dog-eared copy of the Internal Revenue Code and thumbed through it quickly. He laid it open on the desk and pointed to a provision with the tip of his pencil.

"Here it is," Alex tells them. "In section 72, if go all the way down to subparagraph (t), and then look below that at subparagraph (2)(C), it says that the 10 percent early withdrawal penalty does not apply to: 'Any distribution to an alternate payee pursuant to a qualified domestic relations order.'"

"Wow!" Carlos remarks. "That's something they never taught me in law school."

Individual Retirement Account

Parties can transfer funds from one spouse's individual retirement account, or IRA, to the other spouse's IRA tax free in a divorce. You do not need a Qualified Domestic Relations Order to divide an IRA because IRAs do not fall within the ERISA requirements of the Internal Revenue Code, which govern 401(k) and other so-called qualified plans.

The institution where you have your IRA will probably want to see a copy of the divorce decree and separation agreement upon the transfer. They may have a form for you to sign requesting the transfer or they may ask you to send a letter requesting it. After the transfer is completed, the new IRA will be treated in the same as any other IRA: the taxes will be deferred until the funds are withdrawn. Note that we're talking about transferring money in a divorce. If you actually cash out to pay off a spouse, that's different, and it would be a taxable event. If you take an early distribution from the new IRA, you will have to pay taxes and the 10 percent early withdrawal penalty. The divorce exception to the early withdrawal penalty that we saw in the previous story does not apply to IRAs. So you will have to pay the taxes and the penalty if you withdraw the money before the age of fifty-nine-and-a-half.

■ **Caution**   Distributions in a divorce from a qualified pension plan are exempt from the early withdrawal penalty but not IRAs.

Children

You can negotiate or ask the court to decide the allocation of tax benefits associated with children in your divorce, namely the dependent exemption, the child tax credit, the child care credit, and the head-of-household filing status.

Dependency Exemption

You are entitled to take a personal exemption for your own income and for each dependent you support. An exemption works just like a deduction, by reducing your tax. The amount of the exemption for 2013 is $3,900. The exemption is phased out as your income increases for each filing status.

Beginning in 2013, the phaseout for each filing status is as follows:

- "Married filing jointly" (phase-out begins at $300,000 and ends at $422,500 of adjusted gross income)
- "Head of household" (phase-out begins at $275,000 and ends at $397,500 of adjusted gross income)
- "Single" (phase-out begins at $250,000 and ends at $372,500 of adjusted gross income)
- "Married filing separately" (phase-out begins at $150,000 and ends at $211,250 of adjusted gross income)

A custodial parent is entitled to the dependency exemption if the following requirements are met. You are a custodial parent if the child lives with you for more than half the year.

- Children and stepchildren qualify for the exemption as well as certain other dependents.
- The parents together provided more than one-half of the child's support.
- The child was in the custody of one or both parents for a total of more than half of the year.
- The parents were divorced or legally separated by court decree, separated under a separation agreement, or lived apart for the entire last six months of the year.
- The child was either under age nineteen or the child was a full-time student for at least five months and under the age of twenty-four at the end of the year.

A custodial parent may release the dependency exemption to a noncustodial parent. This might occur as a result of negotiations in a settlement or in a case where a high-income custodial parent is phased out of the exemption and cannot use it anyway.

The release requires IRS form 8332 to be completed and signed by the custodial parent and attached to the noncustodial parent's tax return. The release either applies to all future years or in cases where it is conditioned on child support being paid, the custodial parent may sign it for one year at a time.

Tax Planning with Dependency Exemptions

In order to qualify for head-of-household filing status and a lower tax rate, you need to have a qualified dependent. If there are two or more children, each parent should claim at least one of them as a dependent, so that both parents can qualify. Otherwise, the parent with the highest income will get the most benefit from the exemptions, unless that income is high enough to trigger the phaseout provisions.

Tip   You can allocate dependency exemptions between parents in a divorce to achieve the best tax results.

Child Tax Credit

You can take a $1,000 child tax credit in 2013 for each child under age seventeen whom you claim as a dependent. This is a dollar-for-dollar reduction in your taxes (not a deduction from your income).

The child tax credit is gradually reduced as your income goes up. The phaseout begins at these income levels:

- $55,000 for married couples filing separately
- $75,000 for a person who is single and the head of a household
- $110,000 for married couples filing jointly

The child tax credit is reduced by $50 for each $1,000 of income above these amounts.

The child tax credit accompanies the dependency exemption. So if you are the custodial parent, you are entitled to this credit unless you have released it to the noncustodial parent.

Child Care Expenses

You may be entitled to the dependent care credit for child care expenses that enable you to work or look for work, such as day care or summer camp. This is available to custodial parents, and it may be released to noncustodial parents with the dependency exemption using IRS form 8832. The child must be under thirteen years of age on the last day of the year for you to qualify.

In 2013, the credit is 20 percent of your child care expenses if your adjusted gross income is over $43,000 and gradually goes up according to your income, with a maximum of 35 percent if your adjusted gross income is less than $15,000. The credit is capped at $3,000 per child.

Some employers offer benefit plans that allow employees to take part of their income as tax-free reimbursement of day care expenses. This could be more advantageous to you than claiming the dependent care credit, depending on your circumstances.

Summary

Every divorce transaction should be viewed through the lens of its tax consequences. There is no getting around the fact that the tax code is complex and complicated. That's why we have accountants and tax lawyers. But being knowledgeable about the general principles of taxes and divorce that we have discussed in this chapter will help you as you proceed through the divorce process. Next we will talk about how to settle your divorce case.

CHAPTER 18

Prenuptial Agreements

Prenuptial agreements, also called premarital agreements or antenuptial agreements, are commonly referred to as prenups. They are contracts executed before the wedding by the two people getting married. After the wedding, the couple may draw up a postnuptial agreement if they wish. The contract has provisions for dividing property and support upon divorce, separation, or death.

If you have a prenuptial agreement and you are getting divorced, this chapter will help you whether you are trying to defend it or set it aside. If you don't have a prenuptial agreement, read this chapter so you will know how to protect yourself with a prenuptial agreement the next time you get married.

Background

Before 1968, American divorce courts viewed prenuptial agreements unfavorably, as being destructive to marriage, and refused to enforce many of them. Then, an appellate case out of Florida held that prenuptial agreements were in contemplation of marriage rather than in contemplation of divorce.

That was enough for the court to declare that they were not against public policy and therefore valid and enforceable. The popularity of prenuptial agreements bloomed as people became more realistic about marriage and divorce.

The Uniform Premarital Agreement Act (UPAA), providing for the enforcement of prenuptial agreements, has been adopted by twenty-six states and the District of Columbia in one form or another. Premarital agreements are permitted in the other states by statute or case law.

Why Don't More People Have Prenuptial Agreements?

Most people don't think they need, or could benefit from, a prenuptial agreement. A poll of Americans by Harris Interactive shows that:

- Twenty-eight percent believe prenuptial agreements make smart financial sense.
- Twenty-five percent think they are only for the rich and famous, not regular people.
- Nineteen percent think they are not needed when two people really love one another.
- Fifteen percent say a prenup dooms a marriage from the start.

On the other hand, forty-nine percent of divorced people believe prenuptial agreements make good financial sense.

Other studies have shown that while most people are aware of the fact that half of marriages end in divorce, only about ten percent believe it will happen to them.

You Already Have a Prenuptial Agreement

Your prenuptial agreement is already in writing. It is thousands of pages long. You probably won't know the terms of it unless and until you get divorced. You agreed to it by getting married.

Where is it? It is in the family laws of your state and the cases interpreting those laws.

So while you may think your choice is between having or not having a prenuptial agreement, it is really between using the prenuptial agreement set forth in the laws of your state or using a prenuptial agreement that you negotiate and write.

Most people contemplating marriage don't think about divorce. Yet one in two marriages will end in divorce. Love sometimes makes people lose their commonsense. They think a prenuptial agreement will ruin the romance. After all, there is nothing very romantic about a prenuptial agreement. To some, it shows a lack of commitment to the marriage, which is supposed to be "Until death do us part." To others, it may indicate a lack of trust that their partner will be fair and reasonable in the event of divorce.

But is it a bad thing to have an open and honest conversation with your partner about financial planning for your marriage? It may actually be beneficial to the relationship to explore your views on marriage, money, family, support, and property with one another. It may even make a divorce less likely. And if there is a divorce, the parties do not have to fight over the property and alimony because the terms are already agreed upon.

Tip The family law of your state will be your default prenuptial agreement if you don't make one for yourself.

The Elements of a Prenuptial Agreement

Prenuptial agreements are valid and enforceable in all fifty states and the District of Columbia provided that all these conditions are met:

- there is full financial disclosure;
- there is no duress;
- the agreement is fair and there is no overreaching; and
- the agreement is in writing, signed by both parties and acknowledged before a notary public.

Full Disclosure

Both parties to a prenuptial agreement must make a full and complete financial disclosure. This requires a frank, complete, and truthful disclosure or actual knowledge of what rights are being given up by the agreement. The most practical way to do this is to attach documents showing each party's assets, liabilities, and incomes. You can back this up with tax returns and statements if you wish.

The reason for this is that both parties must have full knowledge of the facts so they know what they are giving up and what they are getting.

Example: Jo and William met when she was forty and he was fifty. They had both been married before, so they decided to enter into a prenuptial agreement. Jo waived her right to alimony. But William had failed to disclose to Jo that he was worth $3 million because he wanted to leave it all to his daughter from a prior marriage. During the divorce proceedings, the truth came out about William's net worth. Jo was able to contest the prenuptial agreement because she said she never would have waived alimony if there had been full disclosure.

The agreement should provide that the parties have made a full disclosure of their finances to one another, and it should be executed with full knowledge of this and should not have the potential to be invalidated for lack of financial disclosure.

No Duress

You need sufficient time to negotiate and consider all the legal consequences of a prenuptial agreement. Consider this situation:

"What's this?" says Fiona as she looks at the papers that Todd, her fiancé, has just handed her.

"Oh, that's a prenup that my lawyer prepared," says Todd matter-of-factly. "Just sign it on the last page."

"Are you kidding?" cries Fiona. "It's two weeks before the wedding. The invitations have gone out. I've bought my wedding dress. We've paid deposits for the caterer and reception. People have made travel plans and bought wedding gifts."

"Well, my lawyer says I can't get married without it," says Todd.

"All right, I'm signing, but I'm not even reading it," retorts Fiona.

This agreement can be contested on the basis that it was signed under duress being that Fiona signed it just so the wedding could go forward as planned. To have a valid prenuptial agreement, you have to begin negotiations far in advance of the wedding and include in the agreement that you have negotiated over an ample period of time so that neither of you feels pressured to sign. You must be able to show that both of you entered into it freely and voluntarily without duress.

Here's another example from a recent case in New York. Elizabeth claimed that her husband, Peter, who controlled $20 million in real estate, fraudulently induced her to sign a prenuptial agreement four days before the wedding.

Elizabeth said that Peter threatened to call off the wedding if she didn't sign. She said she felt coerced into signing against her will. Her father had already paid $40,000 for the reception when the prenup was presented to her.

She also told the court that Peter had promised he would tear up the prenup once they had children. They had three. Peter denied that he made any such promise. The Brooklyn Appellate Court threw out the prenup. The divorce proceeded without it.

> **Note** You need to sign your prenup long before the wedding if you want it to hold up in court.

No Overreaching

The court can set aside a prenuptial agreement that it considers to be too unfair. An agreement can be one-sided, but if one party gives up all rights and the other gives up none, the agreement will be subject to attack on grounds of fairness and inequity.

To test this, the court will look at what the agreement provides and compare this to what the law would provide in the absence of an agreement.

Some lopsided agreements can be saved by a sunset provision, whereby certain terms or the entire agreement end after a period of time during the marriage.

There are people who want to keep everything separate during the marriage, including their incomes and assets they will acquire. They may have a need for control or they may have been burned in a prior divorce. Marriage is a sharing of life, however, and people who share income and assets in creating a marital estate together seem to have a greater sense of purpose and satisfaction. Marriage is not only a physical and emotional union but a financial one as well.

Put It in Proper Form

The prenuptial agreement must be in writing. Oral prenups will not be enforced. It must be signed by the two parties to the marriage. Their lawyers cannot sign for them. And their signatures must be properly acknowledged by a notary public.

One attorney should not try to represent both sides to a prenuptial agreement. Each party needs to have his own independent lawyer.

If one party has an attorney draw the document and the other party does not have an attorney, like Jo above, the unrepresented party can attack the agreement in the future by saying, "I didn't understand it. It was all legal talk. I just signed it without knowing what it said."

You want to be able to prove that you both signed the agreement with full knowledge of its meaning and effect.

The Bulletproof Prenup

First, the bad news. There is no such thing as a bulletproof premarital agreement. This is a fantasy that clients have based on the movies and television shows. No one can guarantee your prenup will hold up in court or that some judge somewhere will not set it aside.

You can however, make it defensible by incorporating the elements of time, disclosure, voluntariness, and proper execution.

> **Tip** No prenuptial agreement is bulletproof, but you can make it more likely to be upheld by the court with full financial disclosure, freedom from duress, fairness, and proper execution.

Why You Need a Prenup Before You Get Married Again

A prenuptial agreement can help you answer questions like these:

- How will any premarital real estate be paid for during the marriage, and what will happen to the proceeds on sale?
- What will happen to a business opened before the marriage or after the marriage?
- What alimony will be paid in the event of a divorce?
- How will premarital and postmarital retirement assets be divided in the event of a divorce?
- Will one party support the other in obtaining a professional degree?
- Are there children from prior marriages or parents who need to be taken care of?
- Which property will be identified as separate property and which will be identified as marital or community property?
- Which debt will be identified as separate debt and which will be identified as marital or community debt?
- How will we leave family property to one another and other family members?
- Who gets what in the case of a divorce?
- Who will handle the finances?
- How will we pay the family bills?
- Will we have joint accounts?
- Will we have a budget?
- How will we buy a house together?
- How will we pay for savings, college, insurance, and credit cards?

A prenup can bring clarity and security to your relationship. If you have more assets or income than your spouse-to-be, it will allow you to be assured they will be protected. On the other hand, it will let the other spouse-to-be to have some sense of financial security if things do not work out.

How to Bring Up the Subject

Bring up the subject of a prenuptial agreement as early as possible, preferably even before the engagement. Be honest and candid. Let your intended know that you would like to discuss a prenuptial agreement. Be considerate of the other person's concerns and questions.

Be prepared for some give and take. You and your fiancé will not agree on everything. Allow plenty of time for discussion.

Although this is a touchy subject, and may even lead to an argument, it is a good test of the communication and conflict-resolution skills that you will need in a marriage.

Ideally, each of you will have a separate lawyer review the terms of your prenup and explain to you how they differ from the family law of your state so that you know what you are getting and what you are giving up.

It's Your Marriage, Not the Lawyer's

The legal system is adversarial. So, if you ask a lawyer to draft a prenuptial agreement, it is going to be one-sided in your favor. An alternative method is to sit down with your sweetheart and work out the basic provisions between the two of you. Prepare an outline or a memorandum and present that to the lawyer to put in a more formal agreement. The result will be a balanced and fair agreement.

What to Put in Your Prenup

The beginning of the prenup should refer to the UPAA or other laws of your state governing prenuptial agreements. There should be some recitation of the circumstances of the parties, such as age, health, prior marriages, children, occupations, income, and other personal information. There should be a clause providing for financial disclosure. The agreement should include an acknowledgment that both parties think it is fair and they are signing it voluntarily.

Next, the agreement will carefully define what property is to be considered the separate possession of each party. Then, it will set forth rules for how income and property acquired during the marriage are to be treated.

There are usually special provisions for waiving rights and benefits in qualified retirement plans as well as what happens to contributions made during the marriage. You may also wish to have specific provisions for a business, especially when both of you will be working in it.

You will probably both be contributing money to any real estate you own, so you will want to clarify how that would be handled in the event of separation, divorce, or death. The agreement will also address alimony, whether it is waived or provided for in the event of separation or divorce.

You can contract for life insurance and will provisions in a prenuptial agreement. You may also wish to have a sunset provision stating that the agreement, or parts of the agreement, will expire after a certain period of marriage. In Maine and a few other states, the agreement lapses by law upon the birth of a child unless it is renewed by the parties. Some states provide a sunset provision after a certain number of years by operation of law.

The law of the state where the parties get divorced is the law that will control the interpretation of the prenup. But you can change this by choosing to include in your agreement a provision as to which state law will apply.

Lifestyle Clauses

Prenuptial agreements mostly deal with what will happen in the event of death or divorce. But they can also be used to set up how a couple will handle their finances during the marriage.

It is also possible to put nonfinancial provisions in a prenuptial agreement. These are called lifestyle clauses. A couple can agree on who does which household chores. They can provide for how much television watching is permitted. They can even say how many times a week they will have sex. You can set a weight limit. You can agree to a penalty for cheating.

Some couples find these provisions to be valuable. They view them as a mission statement for their marriage or an extension of their vows. Others find them negative, saying that a marriage with lifestyle clauses is doomed from the beginning.

How they would be enforced is another question. For example, would a court order an overweight spouse to lose ten pounds?

■ **Tip**   You can include lifestyle clauses in your prenup, but it may be difficult to enforce them.

What a Prenup Cannot Do

A prenuptial agreement covers many issues, but as you will recall from the chapters on custody and child support, the court always retains jurisdiction on these issues. Thus, even if a couple agrees to certain provisions regarding children in a prenuptial agreement, those provisions would be void and unenforceable in court.

Keeping the Prenup Current

You may want to review your prenup from time to time to see if it is still current. There may be new events in your life and your marriage, like starting a business, or buying a house, for example.

You may have changed banks and accounts and added your spouse's name to accounts that were formerly in your name.

It is possible for the parties to defeat the purpose of a prenup unintentionally by commingling separate and marital property if they do not keep those distinctions in mind.

Summary

We discussed different types of support and property division under the family laws of your state. These laws provide a template for how support will be determined and property will be divided if you get a divorce. You can change this template by a written prenuptial agreement. To be valid, the agreement must provide full financial disclosure, be fair and have no overreaching, and be signed without duress. Next, we'll take a look at separation agreements.

PART IV

Settlement

A well-crafted settlement agreement can keep you out of the courtroom, a place best avoided. Legal battles, especially, are not for the fainthearted.

CHAPTER 19

Separation Agreements

Let's say you got married without a prenuptial agreement (as most people do). It's not too late. You can still agree on all the matters we discussed in the previous chapter and define what will happen in the event of death or divorce in a written contract signed after the wedding. Postnuptial agreements are just as valid as prenuptial agreements.

Of course, the bargaining positions are different after you are married. If your spouse refuses to sign a postnuptial agreement, the family laws of your state will apply. But some couples find that a postnuptial agreement gives them peace of mind, security, and more certainty about the future. It can sometimes help resolve marital difficulties.

But when the difficulties become so significant that separation or divorce is the next step, then the postnuptial agreement takes the form of a separation agreement.

Why a Separation Agreement Is Better than a Divorce

Kathy had decided she wanted a divorce from her husband, John, so she calls Larry, a divorce lawyer recommended to her by a friend.

"I want a divorce" is the first thing Kathy says to Larry.

"Let's talk about that," replies Larry. "Only the court can grant a divorce. And the court requires that you have reasons for a divorce. These reasons are called grounds for divorce. They are set out by statute and they differ in every state. But in our state, we have the traditional fault grounds of adultery, cruelty, and desertion."

"None of those apply," responds Kathy.

"Then, we have the no-fault grounds of separation for one year."

"But we're still living together!" cries Kathy. "And I need a divorce now! You're saying I can't get one?"

Note You cannot file a complaint for a divorce until you have grounds for the divorce. No matter where you live in the United States, the law requires that you have certain specific reasons for wanting a divorce.

"There may be another way to solve the problem," says Larry.

"What is it?"

"A separation agreement."

"How does that work?" asks Kathy.

"A separation agreement is a written contract between two married people," Larry tells her. "It includes all the terms that a decree of divorce would contain. It is like a private divorce." The separation agreement is 98 percent of your divorce. It contains all the details. Once you have a separation agreement signed, you may still have to wait for the separation period to run out before you can file for divorce, but then you will have a ten minute, uncontested divorce trial. Your complaint says to the judge that all disputes have been settled and resolved and there is nothing left for the judge to decide."

"Do I need grounds for a separation agreement?" asks Kathy.

"No."

"Do we have to be separated to have a separation agreement?"

"No."

"That sounds great!" remarks Kathy.

"Yes, it is," Larry replies. "A separation agreement can give you almost everything a divorce can, except the right to remarry."

Tip You can still get almost everything a divorce can give you with a separation agreement even if you don't meet the requirements for divorce.

When to Get a Divorce

"Only problem is I want to get divorced as soon as possible," Kathy continues.

"Most people do," responds the lawyer. "But ironically, once you have a separation agreement, you no longer need a divorce. As a matter of fact, you can take as long as you like to file for a divorce. That is, unless you want to get married again right away. I even had one client who went from his divorce proceedings on the fourth floor of the courthouse to the marriage license bureau on the first floor that same afternoon."

"I don't have anyone beating down my door to get remarried, but will I be able to date legally with a separation agreement?" inquires Kathy.

"Technically, you are married until you are divorced," he tells her. "So it is possible to commit adultery even when you have a separation agreement. Adultery is grounds for divorce in our state. But the areas where adultery matters are alimony and property distribution. Once you have agreed to the terms of these in a separation agreement, the court will not change them even in the case of adultery."

"So, can I get a divorce a year after we sign the separation agreement?" Kathy proceeds.

"You can file for divorce a year after you physically separate, which means live in different homes in this state. Or if there has been adultery, you can file for divorce immediately without separating and without waiting a year. Once you file for divorce, it takes a little time to actually get your divorce."

Filing the Separation Agreement

Next, they get on to topic of what to do with the actual agreement. "Do I file the separation agreement with the court?" Kathy asks the lawyer.

"Not immediately upon signing it." Larry replies. "Should we go through with this, you'll keep it somewhere safe until your divorce and I'll keep an original in my office files as well. When you file for divorce, we'll attach a copy of the separation agreement to the complaint or submit it at the uncontested divorce hearing. It will be incorporated into your decree of divorce and then become an order of the court."

Advantages

"So, Larry, do you think a settlement agreement is the way to go?" asks Kathy.

"Definitely," he answers. "You can negotiate the outcome rather than let a judge, who is a stranger to your marriage, decide. Judges are trained as lawyers, not family social workers. And the legislature has limited the judge's power by statute. For instance, the judge cannot transfer ownership of assets in our state except in limited circumstances. But the parties can transfer assets by agreement and the court will follow that agreement. You may go into greater detail in a separation agreement than with what a court typically orders in a divorce decree."

Disadvantages

"What's the downside?" asks Kathy.

"There is only one," Larry tells her. "We have to get your husband to agree. If he doesn't, then you have a contested divorce trial, which means more time, stress, legal fees, and uncertainty of outcome."

What to Include

"I'm sold," declares Kathy. "What do we include in a separation agreement?"

"The separation agreement includes all the issues regarding divorce, including division of property, alimony, child custody, child support, taxes, and legal fees, among other things," the lawyer tells and hands her a checklist.

I reproduce a typical checklist in the sidebar. (You will notice a certain symmetry between this list and the things we have talked about so far.)

CHECKLIST FOR SEPARATION AGREEMENT

The following is a list of items that typically need to be included or addressed in the separation agreement. Sit down with your spouse and go over this list, and agree on how you will handle each particular item and provide the information requested. Be sure to have an answer for each of the items; it will save you time and attorney's fees.

<u>Facts (sometimes called "recitals")</u>

- ❏ The names of the husband and wife.
- ❏ The date of the marriage.
- ❏ The names and birthdates of the child(ren).
- ❏ The date of separation (the actual date or the intended future date if you are still living together)

Consideration

In order to make a contract valid, the law requires that the parties exchange something of value. In a separation agreement, the mutual promises the husband and wife make to one another are what is considered to be the thing of value. Sometimes lawyers state in the agreement that one dollar has been exchanged. This is a legal formality and the statement itself is good enough to make the agreement valid. You don't really have to pay the dollar.

The Separation

- ❑ The date of the actual or intended separation.
- ❑ A mutually signed confirmation that you will live separate and apart after that date.
- ❑ A mutual confirmation that you can both live as though you were single people.
- ❑ A mutual confirmation that you will not interfere with one another's lives.
- ❑ A mutual confirmation that you have no further marital interest in one another's property.
- ❑ A mutual confirmation that you have no further marital interest in one another's property.
- ❑ A mutual confirmation that spouses have no further interest in one another's income.

Legal Custody of Children (Long-Term Parenting Decisions)

Education

- ❑ School (public or private): which will the children attend?
- ❑ Tutors: Permissible? Who pays?
- ❑ Extracurricular activities: Anything off limits? By mutual agreement? Who pays?

Medical Care

- ❑ Name of the child(ren)'s pediatrician and other doctors.
- ❑ Name of the children's dentist.
- ❑ Name of permissible medications.
- ❑ Braces: OK? Who pays?

- ❏ Cosmetic treatment: OK? Who pays?
- ❏ Therapy: OK? Who pays?

Other

- ❏ Child(ren)'s religion: which one?
- ❏ Last name: which parent's name will be used?
- ❏ Must both parents consent for child(ren) to join the military before they reach the age of adulthood?
- ❏ Who has the right to select the lawyer if the child(ren) have a lawsuit?

Access to Children (Time-Sharing, Visitation)

- ❏ Where will the child(ren) live most of the time (residential custody)?
- ❏ What are the daily routines at each of the homes (homework, television, bedtimes)?
- ❏ What is the schedule for each parent's access (weekly, holidays, summer vacations)?
- ❏ Pickup and drop-off: where, who, when?
- ❏ Relocation: permitted, prohibited, new schedule?
- ❏ Introduction of the child(ren) to new people in parent's lives: will it be allowed?

Child Support

- ❏ A determination of the child(ren)'s financial needs.
- ❏ A calculation of child support: which party will pay child support to the other?
- ❏ Payment of child support: by check or through wage-withholding order?
- ❏ Payment terms: Monthly, semimonthly, or biweekly? Is there an adjustment for inflation?
- ❏ Review of child support calculation and exchange of financial information: how often?
- ❏ Termination of child support: when does it end and for what reasons?

- ❏ Health insurance: who covers the child(ren)?
- ❏ Child(ren)'s uncovered medical expenses: who pays?
- ❏ Life insurance to replace child support if parent dies: Necessary? Who pays?
- ❏ Day care: who pays?
- ❏ Summer camps: Permitted? Who pays?
- ❏ Extracurricular activities: permitted?
- ❏ Religious celebrations, weddings, automobiles: who pays?
- ❏ College expenses: who pays?

Alimony

- ❏ What is the amount of alimony that will be paid?
- ❏ How long will it be paid for?
- ❏ Modifiable or nonmodifiable?
- ❏ Cost-of-living adjustments that will be included.
- ❏ Its terms for termination.
- ❏ Its terms for cohabitation.
- ❏ Health insurance benefits included.
- ❏ Life insurance benefits it specifies.
- ❏ Does it include legal fees for a divorce?

Real Property

- ❏ The marital home: Sell it? When? Price?
- ❏ Other real estate owned: who gets what?
- ❏ Division of proceeds.
- ❏ Spousal buyout of the other: price and terms?
- ❏ Mortgage in joint names: Can spouse buying the home take the other spouse's name off the mortgage by refinancing? How long will it take?
- ❏ Cost of deed preparation and transfer fees: who pays?

Personal Property

- Bank accounts, cash, certificates of deposit, money market accounts: who gets what?
- Contents of safe deposit box: how are they divided?
- Stock, brokerage accounts, stock options: who gets what?
- Family business: Sold? Divided? Continue to own jointly?
- Automobiles: who gets which ones?
- Household furnishings and furniture: who gets what?
- Jewelry: who gets what?
- Collections: who gets what?
- Clothing and other personal items: who gets what?
- Time-shares: how are they divided?
- Life insurance: who gets it?
- Frequent-flyer miles and credit-card reward points: who gets them?

Retirement Funds

- Defined-contribution or defined-benefit plans?
- Value of each account.
- Division between spouses and in what amounts?
- Qualified orders: required?
- Lawyer who will draft orders: which one?
- Which party pays for survivor benefit?

Taxes

- Tax-filing status: "Joint" or "Married filing separately"?
- Child exemptions and related tax benefits: who can claim them?
- Apportioning taxes due: how should this be done?
- Dividing refunds: how should this be done?
- Costs of preparing returns: who pays?

Summary

The divorce issues we have discussed in previous chapters can be resolved with a separation agreement. A separation agreement has many advantages over a divorce trial and can give you almost as much as a divorce can give you except for the right to remarry. Use the checklist in this chapter to learn about the items to include in your separation agreement.

There are several different ways to get a separation agreement, which we will discuss in the next chapter.

CHAPTER 20

Different Ways to Get a Separation Agreement

When you go to a doctor, he usually starts with the least invasive and least expensive medical intervention, like "Take two aspirins and call me in the morning." Then maybe he will order some tests. The most invasive and most expensive intervention is surgery.

Likewise, there are different ways to reach a settlement and obtain the goal of a fair-and-balanced separation agreement. They vary in complexity and cost. We will discuss each of the following, from the least invasive and expensive to the most invasive and expensive:

1. Negotiation of your own agreement
2. Mediation
3. Collaborative law
4. Negotiation by attorneys
5. Arbitration
6. Trial

Negotiate Your Own Separation Agreement

The most straightforward way to reach an agreement is to sit down at the kitchen table with your spouse and talk about it. Use the checklist for a separation agreement in the last chapter. Go through the items one by one. Take notes.

Then, flip a coin to see who goes first. Have each person state a position on the first item. You and your spouse should not interrupt one another.

If you can find a compromise between the two positions that you both agree on, mark that on the checklist with an "A" for "agreed" and move on to the next item. If you get stuck on an item, mark it with "NA" for "not agreed" and come back to it after you get through the whole list.

It may help to make a rule that agreement on each item is conditioned on full agreement on all items. That way, no one feels locked in until they get a chance to look at the whole checklist.

Gather Information

Listen carefully and ask questions. The first stage of negotiations is to obtain information. If you reach an impasse on a certain item, a key question is "Why?"

Here's an example: "I want 50 percent of the time with the children," says Theodore.

"I want every weekday with the children," says Charlotte.

Theodore's first thought is "No way!" But then he has a second thought. "Why do you want every weekday with the children?" he asks her.

"Because you don't help them with their homework for school," she tells him.

"What if we put in the separation agreement that I will help them with their homework each night that they are with me, and that I will initial their worksheet and put it in their school notebook so you can see that I did it?"

"Well, that might work. I'll have to think about it," Charlotte replies.

Tip When negotiating at the kitchen table, ask questions, gather information, and create options.

Interest-Based Bargaining vs. Position-Based Bargaining

Interest-based bargaining works in negotiations because people want different things. The metaphor, often used by mediators and popularized by the classic book *Getting to Yes*,[1] is an orange on the kitchen table. Both parties want the orange. That's their position and the negotiations can go no further. They have reached an impasse.

But then you ask them why they want the orange. It turns out that one likes the pulp. The other wants orange juice. Both can get what they want. By asking why, you have pierced through their position and can get to their interest. Position-based bargaining creates an impasse. Interest-based bargaining opens up other options for resolution. I'll give you some more tips for negotiating your own separation agreement in the next chapter.

Tip Try to find the interest behind the position. It's one of the best ways to break through logjams to negotiation.

Good Communication Skills

Success in kitchen table negotiations requires good communication skills. We all think that if we talk and talk and talk, the other person will finally see that we are right. That won't work in this case. You will have to ask questions and listen to the answers in order to find a compromise that meets the interests of both of you and your children.

It is very hard to have good communication skills in the middle of the stress and upheaval of a divorce in which you are worried about your future, where you are going to live, and how you will pay for basic expenses. After all, if the two of you were able to communicate and reach agreements during your marriage, you might not be getting divorced.

Once you reach an agreement, write up your checklist and notes as a "memorandum of agreement," or what the business lawyers call a "deal memo." Both of you should initial it. Then, give it to a lawyer to turn it into a more formal legal document.

Note Someone once said that a good settlement is one in which each side gives up 60 percent.

---

[1] Roger Fisher, William L. Ury, and Bruce Patton, *Getting to Yes: Negotiating Agreement Without Giving In* (New York: Penguin, 2011).

Mediation

When the parties are unable to reach an agreement by themselves, they can seek the help of a neutral third party, called a mediator, to guide them through the process of reaching an agreement. The mediator can be a lawyer, a psychologist, or anyone else with the proper training.

Neutral means the mediator does not represent either party. The mediator is there to guide the discussions and explore various options to resolve the issues that need to be addressed in a separation agreement.

Mediation proceeds through a series of meetings with the parties and the mediator. Lawyers can be present as well if the parties desire, but many meetings take place without them. They usually last about two hours. It may take several of them to cover all of the issues. The cost is divided between the parties.

The first meeting is usually an orientation. The mediator will introduce himself and go over the process. The mediator may also give you financial forms to fill out and bring to the next meeting.

Mediation also works on the principles of interest-based bargaining. The mediator attempts to facilitate a problem-solving approach and minimize conflict. The mediator's training and experience in family law allows him to propose different options for solving the issues in a divorce.

Another useful technique used by mediators is reframing the problem. That means viewing and stating the issue in a different way. For example, "Why should she get a penny from me when she is to blame?" would be reframed as "How can we arrange our finances and resources so that both of us can be self-supporting in the shortest possible time?"

The mediator can help translate for parties that have stopped listening to one another. Sometimes a mediator has to say, "She heard what you proposed. Did you hear her say no?"

The mediator will usually take the issues one by one and more or less track the separation agreement checklist I provided for you in the previous chapter.

To go this route, both parties have to agree to private mediation. A court may order the parties in a divorce to attend mandatory mediation. In both cases, mediation is nonbinding. That means you do not have to reach an agreement in mediation if you are not satisfied with the terms.

If there is an imbalance of power between the parties, it is the job of the mediator to level the playing field. Most mediation is done with both parties present. But you may request to meet with the mediator alone if there is something you want to say privately. Or the mediator may split the parties up if that will help resolve more sensitive conflicts.

The end result may be a memorandum of understanding that you would then take to a lawyer to put in the form of a "separation agreement." Or the mediator might prepare the final separation agreement for you to review with a lawyer before signing.

Tip If you are unsuccessful in negotiating with your spouse on your own, try a mediator who can guide both of you through the process of settling your divorce.

Collaborative Law

The legal system is adversarial. It is a form of civilized combat. The theory is that the divorce case is presented by advocates for each side and the judge will be able to discern the truth from this conflict.

In fact, a large majority of divorce cases settle before trial. Yet the lawyer must start thinking about trial the moment you walk in the door. Collaborative law divides the process into the two parts, namely settlement and trial.

The collaborative lawyers are the settlement lawyers. They are specially trained for this function. You engage them only for the purposes of settling your case. If they do not succeed, then they must withdraw from the case and you will have to hire different lawyers to try your case.

The approach collaborative lawyers take is to engage in problem solving to minimize conflict, just as in mediation. They cooperate with each other to solve disputes rather than fighting with each other to get the most out of the divorce for their respective clients. The parties agree to disclose all financial matters early and voluntarily.

An important principle of collaborative law is that the lawyers and the parties should be able to explore long-term nonfinancial goals, such as having a beneficial parenting relationship with each other after the divorce, rather than burning all their bridges.

Collaborative law proceeds through a series of four-way meetings, meaning that both parties and their lawyers are present. This is an advantage in that there is no delay or misunderstanding in communications, and everyone can ask questions to clarify. You don't have to talk to your lawyer, who talks to your spouse's lawyer, who talks to your spouse.

After the four-way meeting, the lawyers talk between themselves to summarize the progress and plan the agenda for the next meeting.

If an impasse is reached, say about child time-sharing, another professional, like a custody expert, may be called in to give recommendations.

Like mediation, collaborative law is nonbinding, meaning you don't have to reach an agreement during the process if you don't want to. But in collaborative law, if you fail to reach an agreement, you have to find new counsel to litigate your case. That can sometimes work to encourage a settlement.

> **Note** In collaborative law, the goals can include long-term nonfinancial objectives.

Negotiation by Attorneys

Using an attorney is the traditional approach to reaching a settlement agreement. The advantage is that the attorneys are one step removed from the emotional whirlwinds of the divorce. This allows them to concentrate on the issues that need to be decided with respect to the children and the finances with a minimum amount of drama.

Usually, the first thing that happens after your initial consultation is that the attorney will send a letter to your spouse. The letter informs your spouse that the attorney has been retained and wishes to discuss a separation agreement.

If your spouse hires an attorney, that attorney will contact your attorney. The next step is information gathering, which they do by arranging for an exchange of financial information. This is sometimes called voluntary discovery since it is not conducted under the more formal and onerous rules of discovery that apply once litigation is commenced.

It will help your attorney to have a written summary of your objectives. The days are past when the client gave a problem to an attorney and the attorney simply came back with a solution. Nowadays, the attorney keeps you advised of the negotiations and sends you copies of all letters, faxes, and e-mails that go back and forth between the two attorneys. The attorney cannot make agreements without your consent, but once you give your consent, your attorney speaks for you.

One of the attorneys usually prepares a written settlement proposal and the other answers with a counterproposal. Negotiations go back and forth between them and hopefully get closer together to the settlement with each iteration, each side making concessions and compromises, until all issues are resolved.

In principled negotiations, one side makes a proposal and the other responds with specific objections or a counterproposal. This reduces the number of disputes. The lawyers then negotiate each area of dispute, making compromises until there are no disputes left.

Negotiations can proceed even after the litigation has started. They can take place in person, by telephone, or by correspondence.

> **Tip** Lawyers are one step removed from the divorce, so they can negotiate a settlement without emotional turmoil.

Arbitration

Unlike a mediator, who offers only options and suggestions, an arbitrator will listen to both you and your spouse as well as both of your lawyers and then issue a written decision in your case.

You can define by agreement how you want to set up your arbitration. It can be binding or nonbinding. You can suggest whether or not you want the arbitrator to be limited, as is the judge, by the family law of your state.

You can also select nonbinding arbitration, in which case the decision is advisory only. It may help you settle your case to see how an arbitrator views it. If you don't choose to go this route, you will have to try your case before a judge.

If you select binding arbitration, you can file the decision of the arbitrator with the court and it will become a court order. You can appeal this decision in court unless you have agreed to waive your appeal rights.

The advantage of arbitration is that usually it costs less and you can get a decision sooner than in a trial.

Trial

If you are unable to reach an agreement, then you will have to have a trial, which I will discuss in Part 6. This, like surgery, is the most invasive and expensive approach. The trial may last a day, a week, or longer. Both sides will offer evidence and witnesses. The judge will then make an agreement for you, which is called the "decree of divorce."

Summary

With what you have learned about child custody, alimony, and property division in a divorce, and the advantages of a separation agreement, you are probably ready to use your checklist to try to reach a settlement. There is more than one way to obtain a separation agreement. Select the one that feels most comfortable to your personality and style. See if your spouse agrees.

Next, we'll take a look at some tips and techniques for negotiating a separation agreement.

CHAPTER 21

Tactics and Strategies for Negotiating Your Own Separation Agreement

People spend thousands of dollars negotiating and litigating their divorces. But the truth is you can settle most divorces in a few hours if both people are willing to negotiate a settlement. If you decide to try to negotiate your own separation agreement, this chapter will provide you with some tips on how to do it.

You Need to Know Your BATNA

We have discussed how the judge determines such things as custody, visitation, alimony, child support, and alimony in previous chapters. When you have agreed to settle, knowing your BATNA will help you to know what a fair and reasonable settlement of these issues is. BATNA stands for "best alternative to a negotiated agreement." It refers to what would happen if you end up walking away from the negotiations. In the case of divorce, it is what the judge will do if you try your case. Knowing this will keep you at the settlement table if you are making progress toward your objectives and it will tell you when to walk away if you are not.

You need to know what you want in a business negotiation. In such situations, the negotiator always goes in with a written list of goals and objectives. Further, these objectives are given a best-case, worst-case, and middle-case scenario. Then, they are numbered in order of priorities from the highest to the lowest. You would do well to follow this strategy.

It has been shown that people who enter negotiations with high expectations tend to end up with a better result than those who have lower expectations. So don't be afraid to ask for the sun and the moon in your best-case scenarios. It can be your starting position.

At the same time, you also have to be flexible to reach a settlement. Being unyielding or acting like a bully rarely works in negotiations. First of all, we tend to be more giving in negotiations when we are treated nicely by the other person. When people are rude or controlling, we dig in our heels and become defensive.

It is possible to be an aggressive negotiator and polite at the same time. You just need to be clear and firm in stating your positions. Studies have shown that polite-but-firm negotiators are more successful in their settlements than negotiators who try to intimidate the other party.

Avoid ultimatums and take-it-or-leave-it declarations. These can shut down negotiations.

You can reframe threats in a constructive way. For example, rather than saying, "If we can't settle, we'll have to go to court and pay tons of money to lawyers," you might instead say, "If we are able to settle, we'll save tons of money on lawyers."

Tip Know what you want to achieve in a settlement and what your best alternative is.

Time and Place

When negotiating a separation agreement, the sooner you start the better. Schedule a regular time with your spouse when there will be no distractions. Turn off your cell phones and television. Plan for a couple of hours for each negotiation session. It takes a lot of concentration and energy. Set a time limit and stick to it. Don't let the negotiations keep going without any real progress.

Pick a time when the children are asleep or at school or on a playdate. Keep the children out of any disputes between you and your spouse. This is a time they will need all the love and attention you can give them. They need to know that you will always be their parent no matter what happens.

Pick a neutral place like the kitchen table where both of you can feel comfortable. Plan an agenda using the settlement negotiation checklist provided earlier. Agree on what you will cover ahead of time. For instance, you might state, "This week we will discuss custody, and next week time-sharing schedules."

Don't be afraid to reschedule as necessary. If one of you gets angry or you both get bogged down, or even if you are losing an argument, you can end the negotiation early and try again in the next session. However, try to avoid leaving the negotiation open, even if the only agreement you can reach is when the next meeting will be.

You must take the timing of negotiations into consideration. If one spouse wants to stay married, he may not be capable of negotiating a separation agreement with you until sufficient time has passed for him to accept the idea of a divorce and heal emotionally. Unfortunately, this is often accompanied by the other spouse's impatience to negotiate a settlement agreement.

Information Gathering

You have filled out your financial forms and prepared your settlement notebook in the previous chapters. You have thought about what you want and your priorities. These preparations will keep you calm and focused in your negotiations. With all these powerful weapons at your disposal, you will probably control the negotiations.

But you may not have access to the complete financial picture of your marriage. If this is the case, you will need to obtain information from your spouse, like her income, retirement funds, investments, and so forth.

You also need to know what your spouse wants. In fact, to make sure you are not shooting too low in what you are asking for, you can request that your spouse makes the first offer. Of course, if your spouse does not know what she wants, and many do not, then you will need to ask questions to get her to decide or you will need to state what you want first.

In order to reach a settlement, you will have to make some compromises. Be flexible. You usually can't get everything you want. But you can get your high-priority items. The best way to find out what your spouse wants is to ask questions.

The Value of Questions

Many people think they know what their spouses want in a settlement. But this makes them skip a step. They are trying to practice mind reading. But all you have to do is ask. Sometimes the answers are not what you think at all.

Demands, confrontations, and arguments do not settle cases. Questions are a nonthreatening way of obtaining information.

We have already discussed interest-based bargaining involving using the question "Why?" to pierce through a person's position and get to the interest behind it.

Other powerful questions include:

- "What would that look like to you?"
- "If you got your wish on this item, what would it be?"
- "How would you feel if we solve this problem like this?
- "Is that the best you can do?"
- "Do you have any room to negotiate?"
- "Do you see any other options?"

Tip Find out what your spouse wants by asking questions, not mind reading.

How to Answer Questions

There is no harm in answering questions truthfully. This is a part of any successful negotiation. Try not to be evasive in your answers. A lot of people feel uncomfortable saying what they want or talking about money. But you are going to have to take your thoughts out of your head and put them into your mouth.

Start with the Easy Items

Discuss the easy items first. Find as many things as you can that you agree on. Then build on those agreements. If you can find nothing else, agree that your marriage is in trouble or that you have cute children.

Don't Push Buttons

Even couples that have only been married a short time know what buttons to push to make their spouse crazy. This is not the time to push those buttons. Negotiation is best done in a cool and calm state of mind.

And don't let your buttons get pushed. Try to control your emotions. Stick to your agenda and keep your focus on the checklist. Do not get sidetracked by arguments. Your objective is not to get revenge or prove that you are the better spouse. Your objective is to get a fair and reasonable separation agreement.

In negotiation strategy, it is fair to use histrionics, emotions, and drama as tactics, just as long as you're acting and don't really lose control. For example, if your spouse has engaged in marital misconduct and feels guilty about it, you are free to use that guilt to obtain an advantage in negotiations.

If you are the one faced with histrionics, try not to get caught up in the emotional reactions. Stick to the finances or issue at hand. Imagine you are negotiating a business deal.

Process Is Just as Important as Substance

Let's consider this situation: Ned had seen a crystal decanter with green glass inlays at an antique shop that he liked. He looked at the price tag. It was $180.

Ned decided he would come back next week and buy the decanter.

Ned took off work Monday morning and stopped by the bank to withdraw $200 in cash.

He went to the antique store but was disappointed to find that the decanter was not on the shelf where it had been. He asked the man sitting behind the counter in the center of the store if the decanter with the green inlay had been sold.

"No," said the salesperson. "I moved it to a cabinet in the back of the store." He directed Ned to it with a glance.

Ned was delighted to find the decanter sitting there. He lifted it in his hands. It felt heavy and cool to his touch. He brought it to the counter and asked the man if the price was negotiable for cash, expecting him to say no.

"Hold on," said the employee. "I'll call the owner."

He dialed the phone on his desk. "Someone wants to buy the green inlay decanter for all cash. He wants to know if you will sell it for less. Uh huh. Uh huh. Got it."

Chapter 21 | Tactics and Strategies for Negotiating Your Own Separation Agreement

The man hung up. "She says $150 is the lowest she can go."

"I'll take it!" Ned exclaimed.

He left the shop humming to himself. Not only had he found the perfect decanter but he had been given a great deal and still had $50 in cash in his wallet.

Now imagine that the price was originally marked $150 and no negotiation took place. The result would be the same with Ned, but he would have been far less satisfied with his purchase. People need process—the sense they are successful in getting their spouses to give up something they want—in negotiations as much, or sometimes more, than they need results. So, be aware of the need for process and give it proper respect in your negotiations. Don't be in such a hurry to get to results.

In fact, if everything is going your way in the negotiations and you are winning on every point, you might want to slow down. It is a sign that your spouse is just caving in to your demands. This is a spouse that will have buyer's remorse and not sign the final agreement once negotiations are completed. You need to take your time and make sure the agreement is something that both sides can agree to.

■ **Note** The negotiation process can be as important as the result. If only you get everything you want in the negotiation, your spouse might later exhibit signs of buyer's remorse and refuse to the sign the separation agreement.

Watch for Verbal Clues

Listen carefully to the answers your spouse gives to your questions during the negotiation process. This will allow you to gather the information you need to complete the blanks in your financial information. You will find out what your spouse really wants in a settlement. And sometimes additional information is leaked in the answers. Verbal clues may be telegraphed unconsciously.

For example, "$3,000 a month in support is about the most I can afford" does not mean it is the most she can afford. It means she can afford more.

A professional negotiator will tell you when he has reached his worst-case scenario and is prepared to walk away by saying that this is his "best and final offer." Until then, you can keep bargaining.

Make your offers in small and decreasing increments. Your objective is to pay your husband $150,000 or less for his share of the house. Your current offer is $100,000. If your next offer is $125,000, you show you have lots of room to move. But if your next offer is $105,000 and the one after that is $107,000, it sends a message that you are getting close to your limit.

Successful negotiation is a patient and gradual process.

Tip Listen for verbal clues that can give you important insights while negotiating.

Different Negotiating Techniques

Knowing different negotiating techniques will allow you to try them out for effectiveness or recognize them when they are tried on you.

Here's an example: Terry was getting frustrated in negotiating the renewal of his lease. He had been to his landlord's office several times in the past month and had made no progress in the negotiations. So, he was trying again.

"You are using brick wall negotiation tactics," Terry accused his landlord.

"What are those?" the landlord came back.

"Every time I ask you for a concession, you say no. It's like hitting my head against a brick wall. Bang, bang, bang."

"And you are using water torture negotiation," said the landlord.

"What is that?" asked Terry.

"You keep asking for more concessions. It's like water torture. Drip, drip, drip."

What's happening here? Both sides are using the technique of repetition. Repetition of a request will sometimes work as a negotiating technique. The best example of this is when your children ask for something over and over again no matter how many times you say no. Finally you just give in. This can work for you, too, in negotiating your separation agreement.

Segmentation

Another negotiating tactic is called segmenting. If the elephant is too big to tackle all at once, try cutting it into thinner and thinner slices. If you can't solve a problem, try breaking it into separate parts and tackling one part at a time. For example, if time-sharing seems too overwhelming, try starting with what the first week will look like.

Nibbling

On television, Detective Columbo would always turn away from the suspect and start to leave. Then, he would turn back and say, "Oh, I forgot. Just one more thing."

The nibbler uses the same technique. Near the end of negotiations, the parties are tired and relieved that the end is in sight, and there may be a certain amount of goodwill built up by the agreements made so far. There is pressure to keep the deal you have made so far. You are about to conclude the negotiations. And then the nibbler says, "Oh, just one more thing."

This is a dangerous point. Most concessions are made in the last 10 percent of negotiations. You need to be on guard.

Note Most concessions are made in the last 10 percent of negotiations. Don't be on the receiving end of "nibbling" if you can avoid it.

Quid Pro Quo

Quid pro quo is Latin for "This for that." In the context of negotiations, it means, "If I agree to what you want, what will you give me?"

This is how you deal with the nibbler. Typically, the nibbler will not want to make any concessions and will go back to the original deal.

On the other hand, you may want to try the nibbling technique yourself to see if it works for you.

Avoid Vague Statements in Your Agreement

Some people don't want to be pinned down in negotiations. If your spouse refuses to be pinned down, it may make it impossible to negotiate an agreement. But you should try to be as precise and detailed as you can in the agreement. The whole idea is to avoid disputes later.

For example, you can agree that time-sharing will be "reasonable," or "liberal," or "to be agreed between the parties," but this may lead to disputes over who gets which weekend or holiday. Now is the time to pin it down with a detailed schedule.

For the spouse who does not like to be pinned down, you can add a clause that says the parties will be flexible with one another when work requires a change in the schedule.

Best to Have Your Lawyer to Draft the Formal Agreement

If you have taken good notes in the negotiations, you should be able to turn them into a "memorandum of understanding" or a "deal memo" fairly easily. You just need to list each item and the agreement reached with respect to it. Then have both parties initial it. Don't sign it, because that might turn it into a final agreement prematurely. A good rule to follow is not to sign anything before your lawyer reviews it.

Suggest to your spouse that your lawyer will prepare the first draft of a more formal "separation agreement" from the memorandum of understanding. Having your lawyer draft the agreement will allow you to find subtle ways to spin the words in your favor.

It is a false economy to think you will save money by having your spouse's attorney prepare the first draft. Your attorney will probably charge you just as much to review the draft, but this is OK because she may save you money by catching any provisions that have been spun in your spouse's favor by his attorney.

Reframe the Conversation

Suppose your spouse comes at you with, "I'm paying you alimony and child support and you want me to pay for college?" There is no good way to answer this question. Responding that it is because you are the economically independent parent is not very persuasive.

But most parents do want their children to go to college. So you need to reframe the question. Take the emphasis off the parties and put the focus on the children.

The reframed question could be, "How do we pay for college?" You can then consider various options such as the resources and incomes of both spouses and the grandparents and discuss loans, financial aid, and the costs of college. This allows it to become a financial-planning issue and not a question of one spouse versus the other.

Reframing is a useful negotiation technique for you to have in your toolbox. It can sometimes allow you to easily remove what seem to be intractable problems.

Summary

Armed with knowledge and preparation, and the strategy and tactics outlined in this chapter, you can negotiate your own separation agreement with your spouse. You have nothing to lose by trying. If it doesn't work, then you'll need the chapters in the next part of this book, which are all about trying your case before a judge.

CHAPTER 22

Pleadings

In order to get in front of a judge who can make a decision in your case for divorce, you have to file pleadings. The judge starts off as passive in regard to your case. It is up to you and your lawyer to ask her to sign an order. You also have to convince her to do so, usually in the face of opposition by your spouse's attorney. This is requested in a formal written document that you file with the court clerk. The clerk then puts the document in a case file and it is presented to the judge. *Pleadings* refers to all of the documents filed in a case.

Note Pleadings are documents filed with the court in a lawsuit that ask the judge to order something you want. The first pleading in a divorce is a complaint for divorce.

Rules for Pleadings

Almost every court has detailed rules about the way pleadings must be filed. The court might tell you, for example, that pleadings must be printed on a 8.5-by-11-inch white sheet of paper and be double-spaced and in black, twelve-point Times New Roman type.

The rules will also tell you the titles of pleadings, what information they must contain, and who must sign what. They may say whether faxed signatures are acceptable or original signatures are required. Some pleadings may require an affidavit (a sworn statement signed by you before a notary) in a certain form or using certain words.

There are also timing rules for when pleadings must be responded to and instructions on what to do if the date falls on a weekend or a holiday when the court is closed.

There are rules for lawyers entering or leaving a case and substitutions of counsel.

Complaint for Divorce

You start a divorce with a complaint for divorce. Also referred to as a petition or a bill in certain jurisdictions, a "complaint for divorce" is the first pleading that opens your case and starts the litigation process. Your lawyer files the complaint with the clerk's office in the courthouse in the county where you live. He hands it across the desk to the clerk in a similar way as making a bank deposit. There is a filing fee, typically around $100. The clerk then stamps a copy of the complaint with a date for you to keep for your files and records.

What's in the Complaint

The heading of the complaint, called the *caption*, contains the name of the court, the names and addresses of you and your spouse, a place for the clerk to put a case number, and the title of the pleading, which in this case is "complaint for divorce." The person filing the complaint is the *plaintiff*, and the other person is the *defendant*. Within the complaint is a series of numbered paragraphs that provide brief statements of each of the facts necessary for your case. The following sections contain a few examples.

The Parties

1. The plaintiff is an adult resident of (name of state) and has been such for (number of) years before the filing of this complaint.

2. The defendant is an adult resident of (state) and has been such for (number of) years before the filing of this complaint.

The Marriage

3. The parties were married on (date) in (town, state) in accordance with the laws of (state).

Children

4. There were (number of) children born or adopted of the marriage of the parties, namely (child's name), who was born on (date), and (child's name), who was born on (date).

5. The children are in the case and custody of the plaintiff.

6. The children have resided with the plaintiff and defendant during the past (number of) years until the parties separated.

7. The plaintiff is a fit and proper person to have custody of the children.

8. The plaintiff is unaware of any other proceeding or case involving the custody of the children.

Grounds for Divorce

9. The parties separated on (date), and they have lived separate and apart without marital relations for more than a year prior to the filing of this complaint.

Note You may file alternative grounds for divorce if you have more than one. You only have to prove one to obtain a divorce.

Support

10. The defendant is employed as a (job title) and makes approximately (number of) dollars per year and is well able to pay child support and alimony.

11. The plaintiff is employed as a (job title) and makes approximately (number of) dollars per year, which is not sufficient for him to be both self-supporting and support the children of the parties.

Property

12. During their marriage, the parties have acquired a marital residence, bank accounts, automobiles, retirement funds, and other assets in their joint names or individual names, which are marital property.

Debt

13. The parties obtained a mortgage in their joint names to purchase the marital residence, and the mortgage is marital debt.

Prayer for Relief (What You Are Asking For)

For the foregoing reasons, the plaintiff prays that the court:

1. grant him a divorce from the defendant;
2. award him custody of the children;
3. determine an access schedule for the defendant;

4. determine the amount of child support and order the defendant to pay that amount through an earnings withholding order;

5. award an amount of alimony to the plaintiff and order the defendant to pay that amount through an earnings withholding order;

6. identify and value the marital property of the parties;

7. determine an equitable distribution of marital property and enter appropriate orders for division, transfer, and sale of marital property;

8. order the defendant to pay him a monetary award to adjust the equities of the parties and reduce the monetary award to a judgment;

9. order the defendant to pay or contribute to his attorney's fees;

10. grant him any other appropriate relief

Signature and Verification

Your attorney will sign the complaint and add her address and telephone number. You will probably also have to sign the complaint, under penalties of perjury, to verify that it is true and accurate.

Attachments

The rules will require attachments to the complaint, such as an information cover sheet and your financial statement.

Caution The complaint outlined here is only an example. If you are going to try to prepare your own complaint, you will have to revise it to state the facts in your case and to comply with the laws and rules of your state. Check the Internet or the court clerk's office to see if there are complaint forms available, or check out a divorce file at the clerk's office to see how other lawyers prepare complaints.

Summons

When you file your complaint, the clerk will assign the next-available case number to it and write it on the complaint. Bring an extra copy of the complaint to the clerk's office when you file. The clerk will attach a summons to the copy and give it back to you. This is called the *service copy*.

Serving the summons and complaint on your spouse will give him notice that a complaint has been filed and the opportunity to be heard in court. The summons tells the defendant that he must respond to the complaint within a certain number of days or the court may find him in default (which is like forfeiting a basketball game by not showing up) and rule against him.

The legal term for notifying your spouse by serving him a copy of the summons and complaint is called *service of process*. It is the process by which the court obtains personal jurisdiction over the defendant so he is bound by the court's decision.

Each state has different rules for how service of process is to be accomplished.

Personal Service

Personal service involves someone handing the summons and complaint to your spouse. It can be served at home or work or anywhere else. You can ask the sheriff to do it or hire a professional process server or ask someone you know to do it. Most courts won't let you serve it yourself. The person who serves it then files an affidavit of service with the court stating who, when, and what pleadings were served. Most states require you to serve the defendant, but some states will permit service on any person of suitable age and discretion who regularly resides in the same dwelling as the defendant.

Certified Mail

Your state may authorize service by certified mail, restricted delivery, or signed return requested. If your spouse won't sign for the mail, then this won't work. If it does go through, you can file a copy of the original signed return with the court with an "affidavit of service by mail."

Alternative Service

If you cannot find your spouse, or your spouse is actively evading service, you can file a motion for alternative service. A *motion* is another type of pleading that asks the court to do something that is filed after the initial complaint.

You have to attach an affidavit that you have made diligent efforts to locate or serve your spouse and have been unsuccessful. Describe those efforts one by one, such as service attempts at different times during the day; searches of the phone book and Internet; and inquiries to her last-known employer, friends, relatives, and neighbors.

Alternative service may consist of posting notice on the courthouse bulletin board, posting or mailing to your spouse's last-known address, or publishing notice in your local newspaper.

After service of the initial complaint, all other pleadings are served by regular mail or hand delivery. Each pleading will include a certificate of service that states you mailed or hand delivered a copy to your spouse at her address of record and the date of mailing or hand delivery. E-mails and faxes are not proper methods of service under most court rules.

Note You must serve a copy of the complaint and summons on your spouse in order for the court to have jurisdiction over her.

Preliminary Motions

The defendant may respond to the complaint with preliminary motions to dismiss the complaint for various reasons, including lack of jurisdiction, defective service of process, or failure to state a cause of action.

She may file a motion for a more definite statement, which means the complaint is not clear enough to put her on notice of your claims.

If you have both unknowingly filed complaints and opened two separate divorce cases, a motion to consolidate is in order.

A motion for summary judgment may be filed when there are no facts in dispute and the court can decide the case on the law. In a contested divorce, however, the facts are always in dispute.

Motions may be accompanied by a memorandum, points and authorities, an affidavit, and a proposed order. You must include a certificate of service and mail a copy to your spouse.

Other motions may be filed as the need arises during the proceedings when you want the court to act.

You may file an opposition to your spouse's motion within the number of days provided by the rules for opposing the motion. The opposition will include a memorandum, citations to laws and appellate opinions in previous cases, a proposed order, and a certificate of service.

The defendant may file a reply to your opposition.

After the time provided in the rules for opposition and reply have passed, the court may rule on a motion or set a hearing for the parties to argue the motion prior to ruling. The court will either grant or deny the motion.

Motion for Default Judgment

If no answer is filed within the required time limit, you may file a motion for a default judgment. The clerk's office will then enter the default on the court's record and send notice to the defendant giving her one last chance to respond.

If the defendant still does not answer, the court will hold a hearing with only the plaintiff and his attorney and most likely give the defendant everything he is asking for, including custody, child support, alimony, and attorney's fees.

To avoid this result, the defendant must file a motion to set aside the default showing good reasons why she did not file an answer in time. If successful, the defendant will be allowed to file an answer to your complaint for divorce.

Answer

Once the preliminary motions, if any, are decided, the defendant must file an answer to the complaint. The answer tracks the complaint. It has a caption with the name of the court, the parties, the case number, and title of the pleading and is known as an "answer to complaint for absolute divorce."

The answer will have numbered paragraphs that correspond to those in the complaint. In each paragraph, the defendant will write one of the following statements:

- An admission of the allegations in paragraph (#) of the complaint
- A denial of the allegations in paragraph (#) of the complaint
- A claim to be lacking sufficient information to admit or deny the allegations in paragraph (#) of the complaint

The defendant can also admit part of an allegation and deny another part. For example, it would be proper to answer, "The defendant admits the allegation in paragraph 10 of the complaint that he makes approximately $100,000 a year and denies that he can well afford to pay alimony and child support."

She can also add a brief statement to an answer when it is appropriate. For example: "The defendant admits the allegation of paragraph 7 of the complaint that the plaintiff is a fit and proper person to have custody of the children and states that the defendant is also a fit and proper person to have custody of the children."

The answer concludes with a prayer for relief asking the court to:
1. dismiss the plaintiff's complaint for divorce; and
2. grant the defendant such other relief as may be proper.

The answer will be signed by the lawyer and verified by the defendant. Add a certificate of service, an information cover sheet, and a financial statement.

Note You may want the case dismissed if you don't want a divorce or just don't want to deal with it right now. Or you may want the plaintiff's case dismissed so you can proceed on your countercomplaint.

Countercomplaint

The defendant is permitted to file a countercomplaint (which may be called a counterclaim, or cross-bill, or some other name in your jurisdiction).

The countercomplaint is in the same format as the plaintiff's complaint. It is the pleading in which the defendant tells the judge her side of the story and asks the court for the relief she wants.

A countercomplaint is not required, but if you do submit one and your spouse withdraws his complaint, you do have the option of proceeding with your countercomplaint. Otherwise, you have to start all over.

Response to Countercomplaint

You will have a certain amount of time to respond to the countercomplaint or you will be in default. You may respond with a motion if you wish, but after any motions have been ruled upon, you will be required to also file an answer to the countercomplaint. The answer to the countercomplaint follows the same rules as does the defendant's answer to the previous complaint.

Summary

You begin the legal process of obtaining a divorce by filing a complaint with the clerk of the court. The complaint and other documents filed in your case are called pleadings and are governed by the rules of the court. In the next chapters, we will discuss the rules of evidence, the legal process, and what happens in your divorce trial after the initial pleadings are filed.

PART V

Trial

Sometimes, you just can't settle, and the only way to resolve your divorce case is to let the judge decide. This part will help you prepare for trial and tell you what you need to know if you have to go to trial.

CHAPTER 23

Evidence: Proving Your Case

During your first interview with a lawyer, the lawyer is already thinking about the trial. As you are telling her the facts of your marital difficulties, she is organizing in her head how she will present your story to the judge. The lawyer starts from what she needs to prove at the trial and works backward from there. The testimony and documents presented to the judge are used to prove the allegations made in your complaint for divorce. This proof is what we call evidence.

You Tell Your Story to the Judge by Answering Questions

You don't just tell your story to the judge. A trial is not a conversation. Your story is presented to the judge through your answers to questions asked by your lawyer. This may seem like a crazy way to do it, but these are the rules of court. You will be better prepared for it if I walk you through some typical testimonies. You can also go to the courthouse and view some actual divorce trials. They are open to the public.

> **Tip** Visit the courthouse and watch a divorce trial. You'll get an idea of what you can expect at your own trial. (It might even motivate you to pursue an alternative to trial.)

Evidence for a Divorce Case

The judge may call the attorneys into her chambers (the judge's office) before the start of trial for any last-minute discussions about witnesses or organization of the trial. Then, the judge will enter the courtroom and sit behind an elevated desk called the bench. Everyone will stand when the judge enters the room.

Next, the bailiff, a court officer, who keeps order in the court, will announce the case. You and your spouse along with your lawyers will be seated at tables in front of the bench. The judge will ask if everyone is ready to proceed. Then the lawyers will introduce themselves and their clients. The trial is recorded so that a transcript may be prepared if there is an appeal.

Preliminary Matters: The Rule on Witnesses

You may hear one of the lawyers say, "Your honor, as a preliminary matter, we invoke the rule on witnesses." The *rule on witnesses* says that anyone who will testify in the case, other than the husband and wife, must leave the courtroom until they are called to testify. This is so that their testimony will not be influenced by what they hear prior to it. If not invoked, the rule is waived, and it usually is waived in uncontested divorces.

Taking the Witness Stand: Your Testimony

The lawyers then make their opening statements, which usually begin with "The evidence will show ...," after which they summarize what they hope to prove. Then, the judge says to the lawyer who filed the complaint, "Call your first witness."

If your lawyer is the one who filed the complaint, that will be you. You will take the witness stand, which is a desk next to the judge's bench. The bailiff will ask you to raise your right hand and swear to tell the truth under penalties of perjury. That means you could go to jail if you lie.

> **Note** It usually doesn't matter who files first, whether it is the spouse who is out for blood or the one who decides that negotiations aren't going anywhere. The other spouse will have a chance to file a countercomplaint that will be treated the same as the original complaint.

Your lawyer will ask you questions designed to produce answers that can be used as evidence for the judge to prove the allegations in your complaint. This is called direct examination. In direct examination, your lawyer cannot suggest the answer to a question. So the lawyer cannot say, "Did your spouse desert you on September 15, 2012?" The lawyer must ask, "What happened on September 15, 2012?"

Your spouse's lawyer will then have an opportunity to examine you. This is called cross-examination. It is all about asking leading questions. It is more or less a chance for your spouse's lawyer to argue his case to the judge. An example might be, "You refused to pay for little Johnny's braces, is that right?" If your case is uncontested, however, your spouse's lawyer will probably not ask you any questions.

Direct Examination

Let's assume the wife, whose lawyer filed the complaint, is on the witness stand and being questioned by her own lawyer. What follows are the questions the lawyer will likely ask her client in an uncontested divorce.

Background Facts

The lawyer will ask a series of questions relating to the facts of the case.

Wife's lawyer: In a loud and clear voice, please state your name, age, and address.

Wife: April Jones, twenty-eight, 555 Oakwood Drive, Corolla, North Carolina.

Lawyer: Do you know the defendant in this case?

Wife: Yes.

Lawyer: How do you know him?

Wife: He's my husband.

Lawyer: When and where were you married?

Wife: May 6, 2008, in Duck, North Carolina.

HANDLING DOCUMENTARY EVIDENCE

There are special rules of evidence for documents. They must have a proper foundation. Their relation to the case must be clear. The witness has to authenticate them. This means they must be able to recognize them and be able to identify them by telling the judge what each document is.

Documents are handled in a special, formal way in court. First, your attorney has your marriage certificate marked by the clerk of the court, and the clerk affixes a sticker that says "plaintiff's exhibit no. 1." Then, your lawyer gives it to your spouse's lawyer to examine.

Exhibit No. 1: The Marriage Certificate

Now, the attorney introduces the marriage certificate by handing it to her client and asking more questions.

Wife's lawyer: I show you what's been marked as 'plaintiff's exhibit no. 1.' Can you identify this document?

Wife: Yes, it's my marriage certificate.

Lawyer: Your honor, I move plaintiff's exhibit no. 1 into evidence.

Judge: Any objections?

Husband's lawyer: None, your honor.

Judge: It will be admitted.

Caution If the lawyer forgets to move the admission of an exhibit into evidence, it will not be looked at as part of the evidence the judge considers in making a decision.

Children

If you have children, expect questions to be asked about them.

Wife's lawyer: Were any children born or adopted as a result of your marriage?

Wife: Yes.

Lawyer: What are their names and dates of birth?

Wife: Rose, January 22, 2000, and Leon, March 3, 2003.

Grounds for Divorce

Next, the lawyer will delve into the details of why her client is getting divorced from her husband.

Wife's lawyer: Are you and your husband living together now?

Wife: No.

Lawyer: When did you separate?

Wife: August 13, 2012.

Lawyer: Was it your intention that the separation be permanent?

Wife: Yes.

Lawyer: Have you remained separated without marital relations since the date of separation?

Wife: Yes.

Lawyer: Is there is any reasonable or likely prospect of a reconciliation?

Wife: No.

Exhibit No. 2: The Separation Agreement

Next up are questions the lawyer will ask her client about the separation agreement.

Wife's lawyer: I show you what's been marked as "plaintiff's exhibit no. 2." Can you tell the judge what this is?

Wife: Our separation agreement.

Lawyer: What is the date of the agreement?

Wife: August 1, 2012.

Lawyer: Is that your signature on the last page of the agreement?

Wife: Yes.

Lawyer: Would you recognize your husband's signature?

Wife: Yes.

Lawyer: Is that your husband's signature on the last page of the agreement?

Wife: Yes.

Lawyer: You honor, I move the admission of plaintiff's exhibit 2.

Husband's lawyer: No objections, your honor.

Judge: It will be admitted.

Custody

The lawyer will proceed to ask her client about custody arrangements.

Wife's lawyer: What does the agreement provide for custody?

Wife: We will have joint legal and shared physical custody.

Lawyer: Are both you and your husband fit and proper people to have joint legal and shared physical custody?

Wife: Yes.

Child Support

And, of course, the questioning will get into child support.

Wife's lawyer: What does the agreement say about child support?

Wife: My husband will pay me $200 a month.

The lawyer then authenticates "plaintiff's exhibit no. 3," the child-support guidelines worksheet, and moves its admission into evidence to show the judge that the agreed-upon child support is consistent with the guidelines.

Retirement Funds

The judge will want to see that you have agreed on a division of retirement funds.

Wife's lawyer: Does the agreement provide for the division of any retirement funds?

Wife: Yes.

Lawyer: Your honor, we submit the proposed qualified domestic relations orders, which have been signed by the parties and counsel.

Judge: They will be received.

Incorporation but Not Merger

The lawyer will ask this next question to make sure her client has all the legal remedies available to enforce her agreement.

Lawyer: Are you asking the court to incorporate, but not merge, the separation agreement into the final decree of divorce?

Wife: Yes.

> **Note** In addition to the contract remedies available for breach of your separation agreement, incorporation into a court order will make any noncompliance subject to sanctions for contempt of court. If you merged the agreement with the order, you would lose the contract remedies.

Name Change

Last, the wife's lawyer will declare to the court that she is taking back her original name.

Lawyer: Are you asking the court to restore you to your maiden name?

Wife: Yes.

Lawyer: Are you asking this for any illegal, immoral, or fraudulent purpose?

Wife: No.

Lawyer: And what is your maiden name?

You: Fletcher.

Lawyer: Your honor, that is the plaintiff's case.

> **Note** Some states require that all the testimony in your case be corroborated by an independent witness other than your spouse.

The Judge Rules

The judge will then ask the husband's lawyer if he has any evidence to present. In an uncontested case, the response is usually, "No, Your Honor."

The judge will then state the facts that she finds to be true (which are the ones alleged in the complaint) and most likely say, "Plaintiff's divorce from defendant will be granted." The judge will then order alimony and child support as agreed and sign any orders required to divide pensions.

If There Is No Separation Agreement

If you do not have a separation agreement, your case is contested, and it will take much longer to present all of your testimony, documents, and witnesses. What follows is a rundown of the issues you'll need to address and for which you'll need convincing evidence if the judge is to rule in your favor.

Custody

Whether you're seeking sole or joint custody with an access schedule, you'll have to present evidence to show the judge why that is in the children's best interest. If the children are living with you now, and you want to keep it that way, you will try to prove the children are doing well in school and are emotionally stable, and therefore the judge should not change anything. If you're on the other side, you will want to show that the children are not doing well or could be doing better if things were changed. In either case, you should keep the emphasis on what's best for the children, not what's best for you.

Your evidence will include temporary custody agreements or orders in place, report cards, doctor's visits, or calendars that show the current arrangements. You can also submit pictures of you and the children having a good time at soccer or karate practice.

You can call witnesses to testify that you are a good parent and have a good relationship with the children. Anyone who has seen you interact with the children can testify, including relatives, neighbors, coaches, religious leaders, and teachers.

The court may order a custody evaluator to conduct a study and make recommendations to the court regarding custody and visitation. If the report is unfavorable, you are permitted to attack it by showing any weaknesses in the report.

Possible defenses against an unfavorable custody report include the following claims:

- The evaluator was biased.
- The evaluator was inexperienced.
- The evaluator had little experience with families like yours.
- The evaluator talked to the wrong people.
- The evaluator's report is internally inconsistent (the recommendation doesn't match the facts).
- The evaluator failed to consider a crucial fact.

Although the judge can consider the preferences of the children in a custody case, calling the children as witnesses is usually a very bad idea. It puts them in the uncomfortable position of having to choose between mom and dad. No matter what happens, they will think they are responsible for the outcome.

The court can appoint an attorney to represent the children. He is called a best interest attorney, or a BIA. The BIA can present the children's preference to the court. If the judge does decide to hear from the children, she will probably interview them privately in her chambers rather than in open court.

Tip Never put your children on the witness stand in a divorce trial. If you do, they may have to choose between mom or dad, and they may feel the outcome depends on their testimony. This is an unfair burden to place on children in most cases.

Support

Your attorney will introduce your financial statement, tax returns, and pay statements through your testimony and those of your spouse through his testimony.

If you believe your spouse is unemployed or underemployed intentionally to avoid paying support, you will need to call a vocational rehabilitation expert to prove it. Expert witnesses differ from other witness in that they are allowed to state their expert opinions in court. Other witnesses can only testify about facts.

First, the court has to qualify your witness as an expert in the area on which you are offering her opinion. This is accomplished by your attorney asking her questions about her education and experience.

The expert witness will give her opinion about the income your spouse could be earning given his background, employment history, training, and jobs available in your area.

Your husband can defend against any charges of willful un(der)employment by showing that he has made numerous attempts to find employment and that his reduction in income is involuntary.

Tip Expert witnesses are different from fact witnesses in that they can give opinions in their area of expertise. Possible expert witnesses in your case might include experts on custody; vocational rehabilitation; and appraisers of real estate, businesses, pensions, and other assets.

Property

The wife's lawyer will then ask her more questions about her financial statement, or joint property statement if required by the court, taking her item by item through her assets and liabilities. He will also introduce supporting documents like bank statements, deeds, automobile titles, and mortgage statements.

She will testify about the value of property and which portion is marital and which is nonmarital. She will also testify about monetary and nonmonetary contributions she made to the acquisition of marital property, fault in the termination of the marriage, and any other factor used to determine how property is distributed in her state.

She may need to call upon additional witnesses, including experts for valuing real estate, pensions, and other assets.

Tips for Testifying

Here are some important tips to remember when you are on the witness stand:

- Answer the questions that are asked, directly and concisely. Don't ramble on or answer a question that has not been asked.
- Direct your answers to the judge.
- Do not get upset or angry. The calm, rational party is the one that usually does best in court.
- Do not guess at the answer. It is OK to say you don't understand the question, or that you don't know the answer, or you can't remember.

Rules of Evidence

As we said at the beginning of this chapter, you won't simply tell the judge your story. The court follows rather arcane rules of evidence to guarantee a fair trial. These rules will sometimes interrupt the free flow of information from you to the judge.

For example, say you are telling the judge about the children's preference of where to live.

You: What the children told me they would like is ....

Husband's Lawyer: Objection. Hearsay.

Judge: Sustained. Don't tell me what the children said. Next question, Counsel.

Lawyers make objections when they believe some testimony violates one of the rules of evidence.

The hearsay objection prohibits testimony about bringing in statements made outside the courtroom. This is enforced because counsel cannot examine the person who made the statement in regard to her perception, credibility, memory, and so forth.

There are many exceptions to the hearsay rule. One important exception is that the rule does not apply to the parties to the lawsuit because they are present in court and thus can be examined about their out-of-court statements. When a lawyer objects, stop talking. The judge will decide whether the question will be allowed ("Objection overruled") or not allowed ("Objection sustained").

Summary

You now see how everything discussed in previous chapters—understanding divorce laws, gathering information, negotiating a separation agreement, and the pleadings—forms the foundation of your trial. This chapter has given you some familiarity with the evidence you will need to present at trial and the rules of evidence that the court uses. In the next chapter, we will discuss legal procedures the court follows in a divorce trial.

CHAPTER 24

Trial Procedure

One of the things you will learn about divorce is that it is a process, not an event. Trial procedure involves various hearings and meetings along the way to a trial. The following describes the procedure of a typical divorce trial. The rules of procedure in your jurisdiction may differ in some details but will generally follow those that will be described.

The Scheduling Hearing

Once the complaint has been filed and served, the court will notify the parties of a scheduling hearing. Many courts use scheduling hearings for calendar control. At this hearing, you can ask for certain court services and the judge sets several dates for your trial.

Services

Many courts provide some or all of the following services in divorce cases:

- Parenting classes can be scheduled for couples who dispute physical custody.
- A custody evaluation or an attorney can be requested to represent the children.
- An interpreter may be provided if you require one during the proceedings.
- A drug test or mental health examination can be performed upon your spouse.
- Mediators may be appointed by the court for temporary support, custody, and other financial issues.

> **Note** The attorney representing the children may be called a "children's attorney" or a "guardian ad litem" in your jurisdiction. The difference lies in the scope of representation. The American Bar Association recommends calling them "best interest attorneys" and defining their duties in the court order appointing a best interest attorney.

Dates

The court will set the following dates at the scheduling hearing:

- A date by which discovery must be completed (the discovery process will be explained in the following sections)
- Upon request, a date for a *pendente lite* hearing (this will also be discussed)
- A date by which financial statements are due
- A date by which the parties will be ordered to file joint-property statements
- A date by which the parties must file a pretrial statement
- A date for a pretrial settlement conference, at which the trial date will usually be set

If your case involves a custody dispute, many courts will bifurcate the case. This means they will split your case into two trials, one to resolve custody and the other to resolve everything else. If that happens, you will have two sets of dates for mediation, discovery, and other pretrial matters. The court will issue a scheduling order with all the dates that were set at the scheduling hearing. The judge will not make any decisions in your case at the scheduling hearing except for the setting of dates.

> **Note** Some courts do not have scheduling hearings but instead leave it up to the attorneys to call the clerk and schedule dates.

Pendente Lite Hearing

Pendente lite is Latin for "pending the litigation." A *pendente lite* hearing is held to determine temporary issues. You may hear the judge and attorneys refer to it in shorthand as a "p.l. hearing" or ask if there are any p.l. issues. Temporary issues refer to those that need to be addressed between now and the trial. This can be a long time, especially if you are the one who is paying support and the trial is several months away. You may want to ask the court for temporary orders for child custody, access, child support, alimony, or attorney and expert-witness fees. At the trial, these issues are considered anew and a permanent order is entered by the trial judge.

The purpose of the p.l. hearing is to maintain the status quo so that both parties are able to continue with the litigation until trial. If the wife controls all the assets of the marriage, for example, the court might order her to pay for the husband's attorney fees and expert-witness costs to level the playing field so that she doesn't have an unfair financial advantage over the husband in the litigation process.

Discovery

If pleadings are the first phase of divorce litigation and the trial is the last phase, then discovery is the middle phase. Discovery means finding out information about the other party that you don't know. The discovery rules of the court set forth the methods by which each party is able to find out about the other's case. The reason for discovery is that it prevents surprises at trial and it encourages settlement. Discovery mainly takes place between the parties and the results are not filed with the court. You have a continuing duty to update the other party on the responses you give through discovery. In fact, the opposing counsel may send you a trial subpoena, which is an order to bring updated account statements and other documents to court on the day of the trial.

What May Be Discovered

The scope of discovery is very broad. You are entitled to discover any evidence relevant to your case and also anything that might lead to relevant evidence. In a divorce, this means anything related to the marriage, children, property, debt, income, or expenses.

Interrogatories

A party may serve the other party with written questions. An example is "Where are you employed and what is your salary?" The other party has a certain number of days to respond with the answers in writing, sworn and signed under penalties of perjury. The answers may be used in trial in the same way as testimony.

If the party that has been served does not respond in the time provided by the rules of discovery, the counsel for the party processing the interrogatories will try to contact the other counsel by telephone and written correspondence to make a good-faith effort to resolve a discovery dispute outside of court. If those attempts are unsuccessful, the attorney requesting the interrogatories may file a motion for sanctions with the court. The sanctions range from attorney fees to prohibiting the nonanswering party from presenting or defending claims.

The answering party may set forth any objections he has to the questions in an answer to the interrogatories. But if the responses are incomplete or insufficient, then the requesting party's counsel will usually send a deficiency letter stating what is still needed. If that is unsuccessful, the requesting party can file a motion to compel discovery and the court will issue an order. If the nonanswering party does not comply with the order compelling discovery, the requesting party can ask for sanctions.

A motion for a protective order can also be filed against burdensome or oppressive discovery requests.

Note It may not seem fair, but answering your discovery is not dependent on your spouse answering her discovery.

Document Requests

You can ask the other party to produce certain documents or other items or to permit you to enter his residence and inspect his property. This rule is usually used in divorces to obtain copies of tax returns, pay statements, bank statements, and credit card statements. You can also ask your spouse to produce deeds, car titles, loan applications, resumes, telephone bills, calendars, diaries, report cards, legal bills, investigator reports, and other documents.

Like with interrogatories, you can object to replying to document requests, but failure to respond or to respond adequately can lead to a motion to compel production of documents and sanctions.

Request for Admissions

You can also send your spouse a request that she admit certain statements of fact. For example, you might write, "You broke into our house and removed all the furniture."

Your wife has a certain number of days to admit or deny these statements.

If your spouse does not respond, the requests are considered admitted by the court.

> **Caution** If you fail to answer a request for admissions promptly, the statements will be considered as being admitted by you, which can have dire consequences for your case.

Depositions

Depositions are events where a lawyer asks verbal questions of a witness and the witness gives verbal answers after being sworn to tell the truth under penalties of perjury. You may depose your spouse and other witnesses. You may request the witness to bring documents to the deposition. The deposition is before a court reporter. The court reporter can make a transcript of the deposition that can be used later at trial if the witness changes his testimony.

An examination at trial using your deposition transcript might go like this:

Wife's lawyer: And you think your wife should get nothing, right?

Husband: I think she should get a fair amount.

Lawyer: Do you remember giving your deposition in my office on July 12, 2013?

Husband: Yes.

Lawyer: And you swore to tell the truth in that deposition, right?

Husband: Yes.

Lawyer: Directing your attention to page 25, line 5, of the transcript, you see the question "How much do you think your wife should get?" Your answer is: "She deserves to get nothing." Did I read that correctly?

Husband: Yes.

The lawyer has impeached the witness's credibility by using his deposition. In closing, the lawyer can argue that we don't know if the husband is telling the truth today or at his deposition, but we do know one thing: He speaks out of both sides of his mouth and should not be trusted on anything.

Third-Party Subpoena

You can send subpoenas to your spouse's employer, bank, pension plan administrator, and other third parties to obtain statements directly from them instead of relying on your spouse to produce them.

Court-Ordered Mediation

The court can order the parties to go to mediation. The fact is that the majority of divorce cases settle before trial. If the parties are not speaking and their lawyers are focused on litigation, court-ordered mediation may be the first time that everyone is in the same room at the same time talking about a settlement.

Pretrial Hearing

Typically, the parties will be required to submit a pretrial statement to the court at the pretrial hearing. The pretrial statement tells the judge the status of mediation, discovery, and motions and about the disputes at issue, any agreements, trial exhibits, and witnesses. The judge will usually ask the lawyers whether there is a chance for settlement.

Stipulations

Uncontested facts may be stipulated. For example, there should be little dispute over the age and health of the parties, the date of the marriage, or the names and birthdays of the children. Make as many agreements as you can, like what property is marital and what property is not.

Getting Ready for Trial

Before the trial, read the pleadings, the discovery responses, the trial exhibits, and the deposition transcripts. Your lawyer will probably go over your testimony and exhibits with you and your witnesses as well.

The Trial

The trial is the big show. It is the climax of all that we have discussed so far. The bailiff will say something formal like, "Oyez, Oyez, Oyez. The court of the Honorable Judge Arnold Andrew is now in session. All draw near and give your attention."

Opening Statements

The court will allow the lawyers to summarize their cases in opening statements. The plaintiff's lawyer goes first and then the defendant's lawyer. After opening statements, the plaintiff's lawyer will call the first witness, which will likely be you if you are the plaintiff.

Direct Examination

Your lawyer will conduct your direct examination and present all the facts in your case. She will ask you questions about the courtship, your marriage, the children, the troubles in your marriage, and the separation.

Then, she will ask questions about your income, property, and legal fees. She will ask about getting a name change if you want one.

Your spouse's lawyer has the right to object to testimony that violates the rules of evidence, and the judge will rule on the objection. Then, you may continue to testify.

Cross-Examination

During the subsequent cross-examination, your spouse's attorney can ask you questions about anything you said on direct examination.

Redirect Examination

Your attorney will have a chance during the redirect examination to question you again about anything you said on cross-examination that wasn't clear or needs to be explained.

Other Witnesses

Your lawyer will call your other witnesses and they will be examined one by one by your lawyer and your spouse's lawyer with direct, cross-, and redirect examination. Expert witnesses will be qualified and testify as to their opinions. (To qualify an expert, your lawyer will call the expert to the stand and ask him questions about his education and experience and then ask the court to approve his qualification as an expert.) If alimony or child support are issues in your case, then you will need to present evidence of your spouse's income. Sometimes the only way to do this is by calling your spouse as the last witness in your case only for this purpose. Then the plaintiff rests.

Defendant's Case

Now, it is your spouse's turn to present his case. His lawyer will ask him questions on direct examination and your lawyer will have a chance to cross-examine him. The case will proceed as yours did until the defendant rests.

Rebuttal

The plaintiff may call additional witnesses to rebut any evidence that came up in the defendant's case and which was not addressed in the plaintiff's case. Likewise, the defendant may call witnesses to rebut what the plaintiff's witnesses say.

Closing Arguments

At the conclusion of the trial, the lawyers are permitted to make closing arguments to the judge. They will direct the judge's attention to that evidence and law that favors what their client is asking for. The plaintiff's lawyer goes first and then the defendant's lawyer, and the plaintiff's lawyer is allowed to respond to what the defendant's lawyer says.

Decision

The judge may announce a decision immediately or take the case under advisement and issue a decision on a later date. The court's decision is your decree of divorce. If you are dissatisfied with the result, you have a short amount of time to file a motion for reconsideration or a notice of appeal. A motion for reconsideration will be ruled on by the same judge who tried your case. An appeal will be decided by a panel of different judges.

Summary

Divorce-trial procedure consists of several hearings and meetings. The discovery procedures are used to avoid surprises at trial and encourage settlement. Everything you have learned in this book comes together at the trial. In the next chapter, I will discuss the latest developments in family law involving same-sex couples, and the last chapter will deal with postdivorce issues.

CHAPTER 25

Same-Sex Marriage and Divorce

When same-sex marriage was approved in the District of Columbia, the DC Marriage Bureau had to change its preprinted forms from asking for the name of the "bride and groom" to the name of each "spouse." And officers performing marriage ceremonies changed "I now pronounce you husband and wife" to "I now pronounce you legally married."

As of August 2013, there are fourteen jurisdictions that allow same-sex couples to marry in the United States. They are California, Connecticut, Delaware, District of Columbia, Iowa, Maine, Maryland, Massachusetts, Minnesota, New Hampshire, New York, Rhode Island, Vermont, and Washington. There are twenty-nine states that have constitutional provisions prohibiting same-sex marriages and six states that prohibit it by statute.

Colorado, Hawaii, Illinois, New Jersey, Nevada, Oregon, and Wisconsin have created legal unions for same-sex couples. They are similar but not equal to the marriage laws of those jurisdictions.

Opposition

Opponents of same-sex marriage have attempted to pass an amendment to the Constitution of the United States to define marriage as a union between one man and one woman. The Federal Marriage Amendment, prohibiting states from recognizing same-sex marriages, was approved by the Senate Judiciary Committee in 2006. It was debated in the US Senate, but ultimately defeated in both houses of Congress.

Opponents of same-sex marriage base their arguments on concerns that same-sex marriage partners are not fit parents. They also cite religious convictions that are opposed to same-sex marriages. Finally, they are concerned that broadening the traditional definition of marriage would eventually lead to the inclusion of incest or polygamy.

The Defense of Marriage Act

The Defense of Marriage Act (DOMA) was enacted by Congress in 1996. It declared that marriage is between a man and a woman only. This prevented the federal government from recognizing same-sex marriages or providing the same federal benefits to same-sex couples that were available in heterosexual marriages. It also allowed each state to refuse to recognize same-sex marriages performed in other states.

Edith and Thea

Edith Windsor and Thea Spyer had lived together in a romantic relationship for forty years and they wanted to get married in 2007. The only problem was that they were both women and they lived in New York. New York did not permit same-sex marriages in 2007.

So they got married in Canada, where same-sex marriages were legal.

In 2009, Spyer died, leaving her estate to Windsor. The federal estate taxes were $363,053, but there is an exemption for surviving spouses.

The IRS said that the exemption was not available in same-sex marriages. It found that Windsor did not meet the definition of a spouse under DOMA and denied her claim.

Windsor paid the tax and filed suit against the United States for a refund on November 9, 2010, in New York. The lawsuit claimed that DOMA treated legally married same-sex couples differently than other similarly situated couples without justification.

The US District Court in New York ruled on June 6, 2012, that section 3 of DOMA was unconstitutional and that it violated the due-process clause of the Fifth Amendment. The judge ordered the tax refund to be paid to Windsor plus interest. The US Second Circuit Court of Appeals affirmed.

The Justice Department and a group called Bipartisan Legal Advisory Group appealed the case to the US Supreme Court. On June 26, 2013, in a 5–4 decision, the US Supreme Court held that section 3 of DOMA was unconstitutional in *United States v. Windsor*. The majority opinion said:

> DOMA's principal effect is to identify a subset of state-sanctioned marriages and make them unequal. The principal purpose is to impose inequality, not for other reasons like governmental efficiency.... By this dynamic DOMA undermines both the public and private significance of state-sanctioned same-sex marriages; for it tells those couples, and all the world, that their otherwise valid marriages are unworthy of federal recognition. This places same-sex couples in an unstable position of being in a second-tier marriage. The differentiation demeans the couple, whose moral and sexual choices the Constitution protects ... and whose relationship the State has sought to dignify. And it humiliates tens of thousands of children now being raised by same-sex couples. The law in question makes it even more difficult for the children to understand the integrity and closeness of their own family and its concord with other families in their community and in their daily lives.

Besides this section, the rest of DOMA remains intact, including section 2, which provides that states do not have to recognize valid marriages between same-sex couples from other states. However, the Windsor decision provides ammunition for legal challenges in those states. Cases have already been filed in New Mexico, Michigan, New Jersey, Arkansas, and Oklahoma.

Note The *Windsor* decision by the US Supreme Court extends federal rights and benefits for married couples to same-sex marriages.

Kristin and Sandra

In May 2008, the California Supreme Court held that state laws limiting marriage to opposite-sex couples were unconstitutional. However, in November 2008, the California electorate voted in adopt Proposition 8, a constitutional amendment prohibiting same sex-marriages. On May 26, 2009, the California Supreme Court upheld Proposition 8.

In May 2009, Kristin Perry and Sandra Stier applied for a marriage license in Alameda County, California. It was denied by the clerk-registrar because they are a same-sex couple. Paul Katami and Jeffrey Zarillo were denied a marriage license for the same reason in Los Angeles County. Both couples sued the county clerk and other government officials they were involved with.

Attorney General Jerry Brown and Governor Arnold Schwarzenegger refused to defend the suit. The official proponents of Proposition 8, www.ProtectMarriage.com, led by then-Senator Dennis Hollingsworth, proceeded with the case, taking it all the way to the US Supreme Court.

In 2013, on the same day as the Windsor decision, the US Supreme Court, in *Hollingsworth v. Perry*, issued a 5–4 opinion ruling that Hollingsworth was not the proper party to bring the appeal on behalf of the state of California. This decision allowed same-sex marriages to resume in California. Kristin and Sandra are now legally married.

Divorce for Same-Sex Couples

In states that permit same-sex marriages, divorce for same-sex couples is the same as divorce for heterosexual couples. The same laws, rules, and procedures that have been discussed in previous chapters apply to divorce for same-sex marriages. The courts will have to work out some of the details. For example, in states where adultery is grounds for divorce, what is the definition of adultery for a same-sex couple?

In states that do not recognize same-sex marriages, it is difficult if not impossible to obtain a same-sex divorce. Arizona, New Mexico, and Wyoming are exceptions. They do not have same-sex marriage but do permit same-sex couples to divorce.

If a same-sex couple has no way to divorce, they can still split up their assets with an agreement, but if they cannot agree on how to do so, they will have to ask the court to divide them in a civil lawsuit.

Delaware, Minnesota, and DC gave their courts the right to grant same-sex divorces to same-sex couples who were married in those jurisdictions but who now live in jurisdictions that don't recognize same-sex marriages.

Rights of Same Sex-Couples

Besides the estate-tax exemption for spouses, there are 1,137 federal rights, benefits, and privileges granted to married couples by the federal government. You can see a list of them at www.hrc.org/resources/entry/an-overview-of-federal-rights-and-protections-granted-to-married-couples. Even though states that recognized same-sex marriages gave same-sex spouses equal benefits, none were previously available from the federal government, including those related to taxes, benefits, and property.

Now, as a result of the Windsor decision, same-sex couples will have these rights.

Some examples of rights for married couple that may now be available to same-sex couples include:

- If you work for the federal government, you can have your spouse covered under your health insurance.
- If you work for a state government or a private employer and you live in a state that recognizes same-sex marriages, you can have your spouse added to your benefits.
- Married couples may file joint federal tax returns, pay lower tax rates, and amend past returns accordingly for up to three years prior.
- Married couples may claim a deceased spouse's social security benefits.
- Members of same-sex couples may be eligible to receive a refund of the capital gains taxes or estate taxes provided by these revisions retroactively.

It is not clear yet whether the federal government will retroactively apply Windsor to the date of marriage, or only prospectively.

The Social Security Administration has issued a statement that it will begin processing applications for death and retirement benefits for same-sex spouses. These benefits include: (a) the right to receive half your spouse's benefit if it is higher than yours upon your retirement, (b) the right to receive a benefit equal to your spouse's benefit if it is higher than yours and your spouse dies, and (c) the $250 death benefit.

The Social Security Administration is limiting applications to marriages that were performed in the state in which the higher earning spouse is living at the time of application. But this may be expanded later to spouses who were legally married whether or not they now live in a state that recognizes same sex marriages.

The IRS has issued a Guidance that says a validly married same-sex couple will be considered married for IRS purposes no matter where they live. This means that the IRS has adopted the "place of celebration" rule.

Why *Windsor* Is Important in Future Cases

In striking down part of DOMA, the US Supreme Court based its decision, at least in part, on the right to equal protection. That right protects certain classes from discrimination. The same argument could be applied to any state law that bars same-sex marriages.

Even Justice Scalia says in his dissent in the Windsor case:

> In my opinion, however, the view that this Court will take of state prohibition of same-sex marriage is indicated beyond mistaking by today's opinion. As I have said, the real rationale of today's opinion, whatever disappearing trail of its legalistic argle-bargle one chooses to follow, is that DOMA is motivated by 'bare ... desire to harm' couples in same-sex marriages .... How easy it is, indeed how inevitable, to reach the same conclusion with regard to state laws denying same-sex couples marital status. Windsor, 570 U.S. ___ (2013), (Docket No. 12-307) (Scalia, J., dissenting slip op.).

Note The *Windsor* decision opens the door to legal challenges of state laws prohibiting same-sex marriages.

Effect on the Federal Budget

Although the *Windsor* decision means that more people will be entitled to receive the federal benefits for married couples, there are some disadvantages to being married. These include the so-called "marriage penalty" in taxes, which means that married couples in some brackets pay more taxes than they would if each member could file as single. Also, a married couple's assets are included in means tests for welfare and disability assistance.

The Congressional Budget Office did a study in 2004, which estimated that legalizing same-sex marriage throughout the United States would actually improve the federal budget's bottom line to a small extent. Government expenses for Social Security and Federal Employee Health Benefits would increase. But that would be made up for by a decrease in expenses for Medicaid, Medicare, and Supplemental Security Income.

Public Opinion

Public Policy Polling surveyed more than 1,500 Massachusetts voters in May 2013. Twenty-five percent of voters said same-sex marriage had a positive impact on their lives. Sixty percent said it had no impact. And fifteen percent said it had a negative impact.

A similar survey by Public Policy Polling in Iowa in July 2013 found that of 668 Iowa voters polled, 11 percent said same-sex marriage had a positive impact on their lives and 63 percent said it had no impact. And 26 percent said it had a negative impact.

Expansion of Same-Sex Marriage in the United States

Here is a state-by-state history showing how same-sex marriage laws have been expanding nationally.

Massachusetts. Same-sex marriage was first recognized in the United States by the Massachusetts Supreme Judicial Court in *Goodridge v. Dept of Public Health* on November 18, 2003. The court said:

> No one disputes that the plaintiff couples are families, that many are parents, and that the children they are raising, like all children, need and should have the fullest opportunity to grow up in a secure, protected family unit. Similarly, no one disputes that, under the rubric of marriage, the State provides a cornucopia of substantial benefits to married parents and their children. The preferential treatment of civil marriage reflects the Legislature's conclusion that marriage "is the foremost setting for the education and socialization of children" precisely because it "encourages parents to remain committed to each other and to their children as they grow." In this case, we are confronted with an entire, sizeable class of parents raising children who have absolutely no access to civil marriage and its protections because they are forbidden from procuring a marriage license. It cannot be rational under our laws, and indeed it is not permitted, to penalize children by depriving them of State benefits because the State disapproves of their parents' sexual orientation.

California. The Supreme Court of California issued a decision on May 15, 2008, holding that California's statutory definition of marriage limiting it to a union between one man and one woman violated the state constitution. Voters restored the definition by approving a constitutional amendment known as Proposition 8. The US Supreme Court dismissed an appeal by supporters of Proposition 8 for lack of standing on June 26, 2013, in *Hollingsworth v. Perry*. This decision restored same-sex marriages in California.

Connecticut. The Connecticut Supreme Court legalized same-sex marriages when it overturned the state's civil-unions statute on October 20, 2008. It ruled the statute was unconstitutional because it discriminated against same-sex couples.

Iowa. The Iowa Supreme Court legalized same-sex marriage in a unanimous decision in *Varnum v. Brien* on April 3, 2009.

Vermont. On April 7, 2009, Vermont became the first state to legalize same-sex marriage through legislation. The governor first vetoed the law, but he was overridden by the legislature.

New Hampshire. On June 3, 2009, New Hampshire became the sixth state to legalize same-sex marriage.

District of Columbia. The DC City Council passed a same-sex marriage bill and it was signed into law by the DC mayor on December 18, 2009.

New York. On July 24, 2011, New York legalized same-sex marriages by legislation.

■ **Note** In the November elections of 2012, voters approved same-sex marriage by popular vote for the first time in three states—Washington, Maine, and Maryland.

Washington. The first same-sex marriage licenses in Washington were issued on December 9, 2012.

Maine. Maine's same-sex marriage law took effect December 19, 2012.

Maryland. Maryland's same-sex marriage law took effect on January 1, 2013.

Rhode Island. Lawmakers in Rhode Island passed a bill legalizing same-sex marriage on May 2, 2013, which became effective August 1, 2013.

Delaware. Delaware's legislature legalized same-sex marriages May 7, 2013, and the law took effect on July 1, 2013.

Minnesota. Minnesota's legislature passed a same-sex marriage bill signed by the governor on May 14, 2013, which became effective August 1, 2013.

Summary

Divorce basically operates in the same way for same-sex couples as it does for opposite-sex couples. With the expansion of valid same-sex marriages in the United States as well as two recent US Supreme Court decisions, we will be seeing more same-sex marriage challenges to state laws and, of course, more same-sex divorces.

CHAPTER 26

Postdivorce

Congratulations. You made it through your divorce. It's all over now Right? It's not?

Postdivorce Checklist

Teresa thought she had made a good deal in her divorce settlement with Clark. Clark had agreed to pay her $55,000 as a property settlement and she would get to keep her pension plan worth $70,000.

She was happy when she got a check from Clark for the $55,000. But a year later, a letter arrived from the IRS. It said Teresa owed $15,000 for taxes and an early-withdrawal penalty from her pension plan even though she had not made any withdrawals.

When she called the plan administrator, she discovered that Clark had withdrawn the funds to pay her property settlement. He was able to do so because she had given him power of attorney during the marriage, which she forgot to revoke after her divorce. Now, Teresa is back in court suing Clark to get the money back, plus what she owes in taxes and penalties.

Use this chapter to make your postdivorce checklist so things like what happened to Teresa won't happen to you.

The First Things to Do

The first order of business after your divorce is to revoke any powers of attorney in writing. Send copies of the revocation of your power of attorney to your ex, your bank, your broker, and your pension plan administrator. Update your will and the beneficiaries on your life insurance and pension plans.

Then, set up an IRA if you need to roll over any pension funds transferred by your spouse. After you get your pension orders, you will need to send them to the appropriate pension plan administrators and follow up to make sure you receive the money.

Next, close joint bank accounts and credit cards. Transfer bank accounts, stock, real estate, and automobile titles into the name of the spouse that gets them under your agreement or divorce decree. Notify the IRS and state that you have a new address if you have moved.

The House

You may still have to cooperate with your ex to sell the house. It may need repairs in order to get the best price. If your spouse doesn't want to move, he can make showing the house to prospective buyers difficult for the real estate agent. There may be deeds to prepare and record if you are refinancing, transferring the house to your spouse, or selling it to a third party. Household items may need to be transferred from one ex to the other. The court may have ordered a period of use and possession before sale or sale by a trustee is permitted.

Child Custody and Access

The court always maintains jurisdiction over issues affecting the children. If circumstances change, a parent may petition the court to change custody and access. Relocation is one such change. One parent may not be able to handle a difficult child and the other parent may be more capable of dealing with the child. Or the child may be having difficulty in school or be experiencing emotional problems.

If you file a petition to modify custody or access, you will have to serve the other parent with a copy of the petition and give her an opportunity to respond.

The court will hold a hearing, which is much like the custody trial you have already been through.

Child Support

A parent may petition the court to modify child support if there is a change in circumstances. A change in circumstances might include a change in custody, emancipation of a child, or fluctuation in the income of the parents.

You are not likely to get the court to modify child support for changes that you knew were coming, like the children having become more expensive now that they are older. The court is more likely to consider unexpected changes like, "I was fired when my company was sold and I haven't been able to find a new job."

If you are paying child support or alimony, you should pay by check so you will have a record. If you must pay in cash, get a receipt, or you will have problems proving you paid it. If you overpay, you probably won't recover any of the excess. The court considers overpayments to be voluntary and in the best interests of the child. If you are receiving child support or alimony, keep good records so you can prove what you did not receive if you have to go back to court.

> **Note** Federal law prohibits retroactive changes to child support.

Alimony

If you are awarded alimony by the court or it is agreed to by the parties, you may not realize in the first year of payment that taxes will be due on the alimony for that year. There is no withholding on alimony. So you must make quarterly estimated tax payments.

If the court has ordered alimony in a trial, it is modifiable in the event of a change in circumstances. Changes in income of either party qualify as changes in circumstances. The court may impute income to a party who voluntarily impoverishes himself.

> **Caution** Make estimated tax payments quarterly if you receive alimony.

Amendments

You and your spouse can change the terms of a separation agreement by a mutual agreement. The amendment must be in writing and signed by both parties. It should be executed with the same formality as the separation agreement, signed by witnesses and notaries.

A sample amendment looks like this:

AMENDMENT NO. 1 TO SEPARATION AGREEMENT

THIS AMENDMENT NO. 1 to the Settlement Agreement dated November 30, 2012 (hereinafter referred to as the "Agreement"), by and between John Keeling (hereinafter referred to as "John") and Patricia Keeling (hereinafter referred to as "Patricia"), is made this 19th day of August, 2013.

WITNESSETH:

WHEREAS, on November 30, 2012, the parties hereto entered into the Agreement which provided, among other things, for child support for their three minor children, namely Dashiell Keeling, Joseph Keeling, and Lillian Keeling (hereinafter referred to separately as "child" and together as "children"); and

WHEREAS, the Agreement was incorporated, but not merged, with the Judgment of Absolute Divorce entered by the Court on January 26, 2013; and

WHEREAS, John has had a substantial increase in salary; and the parties believe that it is in the best interest of the children to modify child support accordingly, as more fully set forth below;

NOW THEREFORE, in consideration of the mutual promises made herein, it is mutually agreed by and between the parties that effective upon the date of this Amendment No. 1 as set forth above:

1. John shall pay ONE THOUSAND TWO HUNDRED FIFTY DOLLARS ($1,250.00) a month, directly to Patricia by mail and not through payroll withholding, commencing September 1, 2013. Said child support payments shall continue on the first day of each month thereafter until the first to occur of the following: the death of a child, the death of John, a child's marriage, a child's entrance into the armed forces, a child no longer having principal residence with Patricia, a child obtaining full-time employment (other than employment during school recesses), or a child attaining the age of eighteen (18); provided, if a child has not graduated high school by his eighteenth birthday, child support shall continue until graduation or the nineteenth (19th) birthday of that child, whichever occurs first.

2. The parties agree that no child support arrearage exists on the part of either at the signing of this Agreement.

3. The parties will notify each other promptly upon any change in income or employment. The parties will exchange tax returns by May 1 of each year, or within fifteen (15) days of filing, if extended.

In all other respects, the Agreement shall remain unchanged, and bind the parties.

IN WITNESS WHEREOF, the parties hereto have set their hands and seals to this Amendment No. 1 in one or more counterparts, each of which shall constitute an original thereof, having done so as of the date and year first written above, but each actually having signed and sealed on the date set forth below his or her own name.

_____   _____

John Keeling   Patricia Keeling

Date _____   Date _____

State of _____

) ss:

County of _____

On this _____ day of _____, 2013, before me a Notary Public in and for the aforesaid jurisdiction, personally came Patricia Keeling, personally known to or made known to me to be "Patricia," who executed the foregoing instrument, and made oath under the penalties of perjury that the facts and statements contained in this document are true and that she acknowledged to me that she freely and voluntarily executed the same for the purposes named herein.

               Notary Public _____

               My Commission Expires _____

State of _____

) ss:

County of _____

On this _____ day of _____, 2013, before me a Notary Public in and for the aforesaid jurisdiction, personally came John Keeling, personally known to or made known to me to be "John," who executed the foregoing instrument, and made oath under the penalties of perjury that the facts and statements contained in this document are true and that he acknowledged to me that he freely and voluntarily executed the same for purposes named herein.

               Notary Public _____

               My Commission Expires _____

Consent Orders

If there is a court order, the only way to change it is by another court order. But you may agree to change it without filing a petition to modify, by means of a consent order.

If your ex tells you don't have to pay child support for six months if, for example, you pay for braces, that does not change the court order for you to pay child support, and you could still be sued for contempt.

A sample consent order looks like this:

CONSENT ORDER

IN THE CIRCUIT COURT FOR COUNTY _____ STATE _____

JOHN KEELING   *

  Plaintiff   *

vs.   *   Family Law 5555

PATRICIA KEELING   *

  Defendant   *

CONSENT ORDER

The parties having consented to the passage of this Consent Order on this _____ day of _____, 2013, by the Circuit Court for Montgomery County, Maryland. it is

ORDERED, that the terms and provisions of the parties' Amendment No. 1 to Settlement Agreement, dated August 19, 2013 (attached hereto), be and the same is hereby incorporated, but not merged, into this Consent Order insofar as the Court has jurisdiction; and it is further.

ORDERED, that if the obligor accumulates support payment arrears amounting to more than thirty (30) days of support, he shall be subject to service of an earnings withholding order; and it is further.

ORDERED, that the obligor is required to notify the Court within ten (10) days of any change of address or employment so long as his obligation to pay support remains in effect; and it is further.

ORDERED, that failure to comply with the foregoing requirements of notification of address or employment will subject the obligor to a penalty not to exceed $250.00, and may result in the obligor's not receiving notice of proceedings for earnings withholding.

_____
JUDGE of the Circuit Court

THIS IS A PROPER ORDER
TO BE SIGNED

_____

Family Division Master

AGREED AND CONSENTED TO:

_____

Attorney for Plaintiff

_____

Attorney for Defendant

Breach of Contract

The judge had just rendered her decision in Tom's divorce trial. The judge had ordered Tom to pay child support and alimony. Tom was in the hallway outside the courtroom with his lawyer, Marcia.

"What happens if I don't pay my child support and alimony?" Tom asked her.

"First, your wife can ask the court for an 'earnings withholding order' requiring your employer to take the support payments out of your paycheck and send them directly to her. Or your wife can file a lawsuit for breach of the separation agreement and get a judgment against you," replied Marcia. "The case is fairly straightforward. You promised to pay and did not. She can use the judgment to seize your assets or wages. And don't forget the part of the agreement that says she can also recover her attorney fees if she has to sue you."

"Then, I will just file for bankruptcy," Tom said.

"I'm afraid that won't work. Alimony and child support obligations are not dischargeable in bankruptcy."

"That sounds bad," remarked Tom.

"It gets worse."

"How can it get any worse?" asked Tom.

Violation of Court Order

"She can file a 'show cause' petition," Marcia explained to him.

"What's that?"

"It's full name is 'petition to show cause why defendant should not be held in contempt of court.' The basis of the petition is that the court ordered you to pay and you did not. Therefore you violated a court order."

"What's so bad about that?" inquired Tom.

"If the court finds that you had the ability to pay, it can order what's called a purge provision."

"What's a purge provision?" Tom asked.

"A typical purge provision," Marcia explained, "might require that the defendant be incarcerated for sixty days unless he pays support within the next thirty."

Tip A willful failure to pay child support or alimony or other violation of a court order can have dire consequences including jail time.

Appeals

You will have a certain number of days to file a notice that you intend to appeal the judge's decision. After that, the judge's decision becomes final and unappealable.

In order to do so, you will have to order a copy of the trial transcript or as much of it as you wish to contest. And you will have to prepare an appeal brief, which is your argument about what errors were committed by the trial judge.

The court of appeals is a panel of judges. They do not retry the case. They will review whatever decisions of the trial judge you ask be reviewed and determine whether the trial judge was clearly erroneous or not.

If they find no error, they will affirm the decision. If they do find an error, they may correct the error, or more likely, they will send the case back to the judge for more proceedings.

Remarriage

Many divorced people get married again. Even those who say, "Never again." If you find yourself contemplating remarriage, your experience with your divorce should be enough to convince you to at least have a prenuptial agreement the next time.

Cohabitation

After divorce, you may decide that you prefer to live together instead of remarrying. You may feel burned by your divorce or burned out on marriage. You may be receiving alimony you don't want to lose that would terminate upon remarriage.

Whatever the reason, cohabitation in a marriage-like relationship carries its own share of problems. In the case of a breakup, who owns the furniture that was purchased together? Can the partner who doesn't own the house recover anything for the money contributed to the mortgage?

The best way to deal with these problems is with a cohabitation agreement, similar to a prenuptial agreement for married people, that sets forth what happens in the event of death or separation.

Tax Disputes

If you file a tax return that is inconsistent with your former spouse's tax return, the IRS computers will probably pick it up. One of you will be assessed additional tax and a penalty.

For example, if your ex takes a deduction on her tax return for alimony payments, the IRS will expect to find that alimony reported as income on your tax return.

If both of you report the same child as a tax exemption, your returns are likely to be matched and an investigation triggered. The IRS will give the exemption to the parent who has the child with him most of the year and adjust the taxes of the other parent accordingly.

Watch the Records: Property Sales and Other Indicators of Improved Finances

If you have an award of child support or modifiable alimony in your case, you will want to know when and if there are any significant changes in your ex's income.

The Internet is a good starting point for keeping a watch on your ex's finances. Many states have put their real-estate and corporate records on line. You can now find the salaries of any federal government employee online at www.fedsmith.com. You can also find some corporate and association employees' salaries and bonuses online as well as some pension-plan balances and other perqs.

You can also build financial-updating mechanisms into your separation agreement. For example, you can agree to a provision that the parties will exchange tax and supporting financial documents and recalculate child support each year by a certain date. Some people prefer to recalculate every other year or according to some other period. Another example of a mechanism you could suggest is that alimony and child support will increase by the same percentage as the payor's income or the cost-of-living index, whichever is higher.

Keep After Your Ex to Live Up to the Agreement

It will be up to you to manage your separation agreement. If you spouse fails to pay support or follow the access schedule, you can ask the court to enforce those provisions. The law helps those who help themselves.

If your ex has been difficult all of her life, a divorce can end your marriage, but it will not make her less difficult. You will still have to deal with her after the divorce, whether because of the children, alimony property, debt, or taxes. Your spouse will probably still be difficult to deal with when solving postdivorce problems.

Summary

Even after your divorce, you will still have issues you have to deal with. Use this chapter as your checklist for following up on all the matters addressed in your agreement or decree of divorce.

PART VI

Appendix

APPENDIX A

Sample Forms

The following forms are illustrative examples only, provided so that you will be familiar with similar ones you encounter in your case. The laws, procedures, rules, and forms are different in every state, and the facts are different in every case. So don't try to use these forms in your actual case.

Form #1: Complaint for Absolute Divorce

IN THE CIRCUIT COURT FOR [COUNTY], [STATE]

[plaintiff's name and address]   :
    Plaintiff,   :
    v.   :   Case No. _____
[defendant's name and address]   :
    Defendant,   :
_____   :

COMPLAINT FOR ABSOLUTE DIVORCE

Plaintiff, [name], by and through his undersigned counsel, respectfully states to the Court as follows:

1. Plaintiff and Defendant have been bona fide residents of [state] for more than twelve months preceding the filing of this Complaint.
2. The parties were lawfully married in [city, state] on [date].
3. No children were born of the marriage or adopted.
4. The parties have lived separately without cohabitation since [date], and said separation has continued without interruption or cohabitation for a period of more than twelve months immediately before filing this Complaint.
5. The parties have executed a Marital Settlement Agreement, dated [date] settling all differences existing between them.

WHEREFORE, Plaintiff, [name], prays:

    A. That the Court award him an absolute divorce from Defendant on the ground that the parties have lived separate and apart without cohabitation for more than twelve months prior to the filing of this Complaint;

B. That the parties' Marital Settlement Agreement, dated [date], be incorporated into the Judgment of Absolute Divorce insofar as this Court has jurisdiction, but that the terms of the Separation and Property Settlement Agreement not merge into the Judgment but remain independently enforceable; and

C. That he be awarded such other relief as the Court may deem just and proper.

Respectfully submitted,

_____

[name and address of counsel]

Counsel for Plaintiff

Form #2: Plaintiff's Affidavit

PLAINTIFF'S AFFIDAVIT

State of: _____

County of: _____ ss

I DO SOLEMNLY declare and affirm under the penalties of perjury that the foregoing statements contained in the Complaint for Absolute Divorce are true and correct to the best of my knowledge, information, and belief.

_____
Plaintiff

Subscribed and sworn to before me this ____ day of _____, 2013.

_____
Notary Public
My commission expires:

Form #3: Answer to Complaint for Absolute Divorce

IN THE CIRCUIT COURT FOR [COUNTY], [STATE]

[plaintiff's name]   :
    Plaintiff,   :
    v.   :   Case No. _____
[defendant's name]   :
    Defendant.   :
_____   :

ANSWER TO COMPLAINT FOR ABSOLUTE DIVORCE

Defendant admits all the allegations of the Plaintiff's Complaint for Absolute Divorce.

WHEREFORE, the Defendant prays that the Court:

1. Grant her an Absolute Divorce from the Plaintiff,
2. Permit her to resume the use of her former name, [former name], and
3. Award such other relief as the Court may deem just and proper.

                        Respectfully submitted,

                        _____

                        Defendant

Form #4: Certificate of Mailing

CERTIFICATE OF MAILING

I HEREBY CERTIFY that on this _____ day of _____, 2013, a copy of the foregoing, together with all attachments, was mailed to [name and address], attorney for Plaintiff.

_____
Defendant

Form #5: Interrogatories

IN THE CIRCUIT COURT FOR [COUNTY], [STATE]

[plaintiff's name]   :
      Plaintiff,   :
    v.   :   Case No. _____
[defendant's name]   :
      Defendant.   :
_____   :

INTERROGATORIES

The following Interrogatories are propounded pursuant to Rule [rule number]:

1. Identify yourself and all individuals with whom you reside. For each individual other than yourself, state that individual's age, relationship to you, and marital status. State your own birth date and social security number.

2. Describe your educational background. Include in your answer the highest grade you completed; the name and date of any degree, diploma, or certificate you received; the name of the institution conferring the degree, diploma, or certificate; and any specialized training you have received.

3. If you are currently employed in any capacity, identify each current employer and, for each employment, state: (a) your job title, (b) your duties, (c) the number of hours in your average workweek, (d) your regular pay period, (e) your gross wages per pay period, and (f) the deductions per pay period made by your employer from your wages. If overtime work was available to you during the past twelve months, state: (a) the number of overtime hours you worked during the twelve months and your rate of pay for those hours and (b) the number of overtime hours that were available to you during the twelve months but that you did not work and the rate of pay you would have received if you had worked those hours.

4. Describe the nature and amount of any fringe benefits that you receive as a result of your employment.

5. If you are unemployed, describe your efforts to obtain employment since you became unemployed, identify each prospective employer and employment agency you have contacted while seeking employment, and state the date of each contact.

6. If you claim you are physically or mentally unable to work or your capacity to work is limited, state the facts upon which your claim is based and identify all persons with personal knowledge of those facts.

7. For each employment that you have had during the past five years other than any current employment, identify each employer, and for each employment state: (a) the dates of employment, (b) your duties, (c) your wages, and (d) your reason for leaving the job. If you were unemployed for any period of time, specify the amount and source of any income that you received while unemployed.

8. Identify the sources and amounts of all taxable and non-taxable income you received during the past five years.

9. Identify the sources and amounts of any other moneys and credit(s) you received during the past five years with an aggregate value in excess of $250.00 in any one year, including gifts, loans from others, loans repaid to you by others, sales of assets, and untaxed distributions.

10. List each item of property in which you have any interest. For each item listed, state how it is titled, its value, the amount of any present lien or mortgage on the property, the date of acquisition of the property, and the identity of any other person with an interest in the property. If you claim that any property listed is not marital property, state the facts upon which you base your claim, including all sources of funds used for the acquisition of the property and identify all persons with personal knowledge of those facts.

11. If you, either alone or with anyone other than your spouse, transferred property during the last five years of your marriage with a value in excess of $250.00 to any person other than your spouse without receiving full consideration in money or money's worth for the property transferred, identify each person to whom a transfer

was made and the property transferred, giving the date and method of transfer and the value of the property at the time of transfer.

12. If the information contained on your financial statement submitted pursuant to the court has changed, describe each change.

13. State by type and amount all support provided by you for your spouse and children since the date of your separation.

14. State the date on which you separated from your spouse and describe the circumstances of the separation.

15. If you contend that you are entitled to a divorce because your spouse's conduct toward you or your minor child was cruel or vicious or that your spouse constructively deserted you, describe your spouse's conduct and state the date and nature of any injuries sustained by you or your minor child and the date, nature, and provider of health care services rendered regarding the injuries. Identify all persons with personal knowledge of your spouse's conduct and all persons with knowledge of any injuries you or your minor child sustained as a result of that conduct.

16. State the date on which you and your spouse last had sexual relations with one another.

17. If you have had sexual relations with a person other than your spouse during your marriage, identify the person(s) with whom you have had sexual relations, state the date of each act of sexual relations, and state the location where each act took place. If you refuse to answer this interrogatory as framed because the answer would tend to incriminate you, state so, and answer this interrogatory for the period ending one year prior to the date of your answers.

18. If you have had sexual relations with a person other than your spouse during the marriage and you contend that your spouse has forgiven or condoned your actions, state the facts upon which your contention is based.

19. If you contend that your spouse is unfit to have custody of the children, state the facts upon which your contention is based and identify all persons having personal knowledge of these facts. If your contention is based on

the use of controlled dangerous substances or the abuse of alcohol on specific occasions, identify the substance used, the other persons present at the time of the use, and the date, time, and place of the use. If your contention is based on the repeated use of controlled dangerous substances or the repeated abuse of alcohol, identify the substance and all persons with personal knowledge of the repeated use or abuse.

20. If you have sought or received treatment or therapy at any time during the past 10 years for any physical, mental, or emotional condition, including drug addiction or alcoholism, describe the condition and the treatment or therapy provided, state the date or dates of treatment or therapy, and identify all persons providing treatment or therapy.

21. If you contend that placing the children in your sole, shared, or joint custody will be in their best interest, specify the facts and circumstances upon which you rely.

22. Describe the child care plan you intend to follow when the children are with you. Include in your answer a description of the place where the children will reside, specifying the number of bedrooms, bathrooms, and other rooms, the distance to the school which the children will attend, and the identity of all other persons who will be residing in that household. Identify all persons who will care for the children in your absence, state the hours during which they will care for the children, and the location where the care will be provided.

Respectfully submitted,

_____

[name and address of counsel]

Counsel for Plaintiff

Form #6: Request for Documents

IN THE CIRCUIT COURT FOR [COUNTY], [STATE]

[plaintiff's name]   :
    Plaintiff,   :
      v.   :   Case No. _____
[defendant's name]   :
    Defendant.   :
_____   :

REQUEST FOR PRODUCTION OF DOCUMENTS

Plaintiff, [name], pursuant to Rule [rule number], requests that Defendant, [name], produce and permit Plaintiff to inspect, copy, and photograph all documents and things in Defendant's possession, custody, or control which embody, refer to, or relate to in any way the following subject, other than written materials prepared in anticipation of litigation or for trial.

As used herein, documents and things shall include all types of recorded information, including but not limited to writings, drawings, graphs, charts, photographs, phonorecords, computer disks, and other data compilations from which information can be obtained and translated, if necessary, through dictation devices into reasonably usable form.

Plaintiff requests that the documents and things herein requested be produced within thirty days at the offices of the Plaintiff's attorney, [attorney's name and address]. The Defendant is requested to produce the following documents:

1. All Federal and State income tax returns for the last three years, W-2 forms, 1099s, and all other documents showing savings, income, or other funds received by you for the past three years. The word "funds" is all inclusive, including but not limited to, earnings, income, gifts, non-taxable earnings, and every form of deferred compensation.

2. All documents evidencing source and amounts of all monies or credits of any nature whatsoever not reflected in your Federal and State income tax returns received by you for the last three years to the date of this Request, including but not limited to gifts received by you, loans made to you, repayment of loans to you, sale of assets, disability benefits, nontaxable distributions, and so forth.

3. All documents related to savings, investments, pension funds, retirement funds, profit sharing arrangements, retirement agreements, and deferred compensation of any kind, in which you have or have had an indirect or direct interest for the past three years.

4. All records and documents related to savings, checking, credit union, and any other accounts, including all business accounts, whether presently open or closed, in which you have or have had a direct or indirect interest and/or on which you have been a signatory for the past three years, including signatory cards, deposit slips, passbooks, ledgers, check stubs, canceled checks, and monthly and periodic statements.

5. All signatory cards, deposit slips, passbooks, ledgers, check stubs, canceled checks, monthly and periodic statements and any other documents related to any checking, savings, investment, credit union, and other accounts opened by you jointly or separately, for the benefit of another, whether said accounts are now open or closed, for the past three years.

6. All records, minutes, resolutions, seals, stock certificates, contracts, or other indicia of ownership or interest in any trust, corporation, partnership, joint venture, or any other business venture in which you have or have had a direct or indirect interest for the past three years.

7. All deeds, deeds of trust, mortgages, deed of trust notes, purchase contracts, settlement sheets, leases, tax assessments and bills, checks related to purchase, rental and mortgage payments, checks and receipts related to all repairs, furnishings, decorating, communications with tenants, and any other documents related to purchase, ownership and leasing, for any and all real property in which you have, or have had, any legal or equitable interest, whether direct or indirect, for the past three years.

8. All certificates and documents related to stocks, bonds, mutual funds, or any like asset in which you have, or have had, any interest, direct or indirect, for the past three years.

9. All instruments, documents, or records illustrating indicia of ownership or any other interest of yours in any other item of property, real or personal, not heretofore mentioned.

10. All instruments, documents, or records evidencing purchase, sale, or other disposition of any item of property, real, personal, or mixed, valued in excess of $500.00 in which you have or have had an interest for the past three years.

11. All receipts and billings for credit cards which you have used, illustrating each particular charge, and monthly statements, for the past three years.

12. All documents related to any current debts which are yours personally or joint debts.

13. All statements, not privileged, prepared by you involving any matter which might relate to the facts of this case.

14. All written reports made by an expert hired by you, or any agent for you, whom you propose to call as a witness.

15. Any and all documents reflecting an appraised fair market value obtained by you or any agent for you with regard to any item of real or personal property in which you have or have had any interest, whether direct or indirect, said appraisal having been obtained within the past three years.

16. All financial statements, written applications, balance sheets, income statements, and other documents in which you, or any related business entity, have or have had at least a one percent (1%) interest during the past three years, have presented to any bank, lending institution, partnership, corporation, insurance company, or other business entity for the purpose of obtaining a loan or refinancing a loan.

17. All documents sent to or received from any stockbroker in the past three years.

18. Title documents and settlement sheets for any asset and item of property in which you have or have had any interest, legal or equitable, direct or indirect, within the past three years.

19. All documents currently held, and which were at any time held, in any safety deposit box under your control or to which you have, or have had, access within the past three years.

20. Copies of all documents relating to your ownership or tenancy interest in your current residence.

21. Copies of all documents showing monies expended by you for hobbies in the past three years.

22. All written or recorded statements made by the party making this Request which you intend to use at trial.

23. All agreements with your attorney or attorneys relating to the rendering of legal services in the instant proceeding along with all bills and billing records pertaining to any monies due from you to him, her, or them.

Respectfully submitted,

_____

[name of attorney for plaintiff]

Form #7: Judgment of Absolute Divorce

IN THE CIRCUIT COURT FOR [COUNTY], [STATE]

[plaintiff's name]   :
    Plaintiff,   :
    v.   :   Case No. _____
[defendant's name]   :
    Defendant.   :
_____   :

JUDGMENT OF ABSOLUTE DIVORCE

This cause, being presented for determination; testimony having been taken before the Court on March 11, 2014; it is this ___ day of _____, 20__, by the Circuit Court for [county] County, [state],

ADJUDGED, ORDERED, AND DECREED that the above Plaintiff, be, and she is hereby, awarded an Absolute Divorce from the Defendant, and it is further

ADJUDGED, ORDERED, AND DECREED, that the Plaintiff is hereby awarded rehabilitative alimony in the sum of $600.00 per month for twenty-four consecutive months following the date of this Judgment, and it is further

ADJUDGED, ORDERED, AND DECREED, that the Plaintiff be, and is hereby awarded a monetary award in the sum of $25,000.00 as an adjustment of the rights and equities of the parties, and it is further

ADJUDGED, ORDERED, AND DECREED, that said monetary award be, and the same is hereby, reduced to judgment in favor of the Plaintiff, together with interest at the legal rate, and it is further

ADJUDGED, ORDERED, AND DECREED that the Defendant pay the cost of these proceedings as part of the judgment in favor of the Plaintiff, in the sum of $130.00, and it is further

ADJUDGED, ORDERED, AND DECREED, that the Defendant be ordered to pay, as and for Plaintiff's attorney's fees, the sum of $5,000.00, together with interest at the legal rate; and it is further

ADJUDGED, ORDERED, AND DECREED, that the Plaintiff, whose current married name is [current name], be restored to the use of her former name, [former name].

_____
JUDGE

Glossary

Abandonment. *Desertion.*

Abuse. Cruelty.

Admissible. Description of a testimony, document, or other item that the court allows into evidence to be officially considered in a case.

Adultery. Sexual intercourse between a married person and a third party. Grounds for divorce in some jurisdictions.

Affidavit. A written statement of facts by a witness or party with personal knowledge of the situation, signed under oath.

Agreement/Separation Agreement/Property Settlement Agreement/Marital Settlement Agreement. A written and signed contract between spouses settling all matters in their divorce.

Alimony. Maintenance payments by one spouse or former spouse to the other.

Alimony Pendente Lite. Temporary spousal support during the divorce litigation.

Annulment. An order of the court declaring a marriage invalid.

Answer to Complaint. A pleading that responds to the allegations made in the complaint for divorce.

Antenuptial Agreement. A prenuptial agreement

Appeal. The process by which a higher court reviews the trial judge's decision.

Appearance/Entry of Appearance. An attendance by your attorney-of-record in court or a pleading informing the court of your representation.

Glossary

Arbitration. A proceeding held before a neutral third party who acts as private decision maker.

Arrearages. Any amount owed in the past under a court order, such as past-due child support.

Attachment. A court-ordered lien on personal or real property.

Best-interest attorney. A court-appointed attorney who represents the children.

Best interest of the child. The legal standard the judge uses to determine decisions related to the children.

Bifurcation. The splitting of a case into two separate parts. An example is when custody is tried first and then everything else is tried later.

Child Support. Court-ordered payments from the noncustodial parent to the custodial parent for the expense of raising children. These are neither tax deductible by the payor nor taxable income to the payee.

Child Support Guidelines. State guidelines for determining the amount of child support to be paid.

COBRA (Consolidated Omnibus Budget Reconciliation Act). Federal legislation that allows you to continue to participate in your ex-spouse's health insurance benefits after the divorce for up to eighteen months.

Cohabitation. An arrangement where persons are single but living together as if they were married.

Common-Law Marriage. A recognition of marriage granted by a handful of states even when the parties have not been officially married.

Community Property. A property-distribution system that is applied in divorces. Community property is divided equally no matter in whose name it is held.

Complaint for Divorce. A document that is filed with the court to begin your divorce. The complaint identifies the parties; states the grounds for divorce; alleges all claims against the defendant; and requests the court to grant a divorce, grant custody, divide property, and order support.

Conflict of Interest. The legal contradiction that is said to exist when a lawyer attempts to represent both parties in a divorce.

Consolidation. An order of the court joining two related cases.

Contempt of Court. Failure to obey a court order, usually involving child-support or alimony payments.

Contested and Uncontested Divorce. A contested divorce is one in which the parties cannot reach an agreement and require the judge to decide on matters through a trial. An uncontested divorce is one in which the parties agree to all matters and sign a separation agreement.

Contingency Fee. A charge for legal services based on a percentage of recovery, traditional in auto accident cases, but not permitted in divorce cases.

Counsel Fees Pendente Lite. An court-ordered award of counsel fees made in order to allow a spouse with insufficient funds to be able to pay for legal fees during a divorce.

Counterclaim. A pleading stating the defendant's allegations against the plaintiff, as would be produced if the defendant were the one to initially ask for a divorce.

Court. The place in the courthouse where the trial is held or a reference to the judge.

Court Docket. A formal record of court proceedings prepared by the clerk noting all pleadings and orders.

Cross-examination. The follow-up questioning of a witness by the opposing lawyer following the direct examination.

Cruelty. Physical or emotional harm. Constitutes grounds for divorce in most states.

Curtesy. A husband's legal right to inherit a certain amount of his wife's property in the event of her death.

Custodial Parent. The parent with whom the child(ren) reside most of the time on the basis of her having been awarded physical custody or primary physical custody.

Custody, Legal. The right of a person to make long-term parenting decisions affecting a child.

Custody, Physical. The award to a person to be the one with whom the child lives most of the time.

Decision. The judge's determination in a divorce case.

De Facto. Latin term for "in fact." Refers to facts that may not be court ordered, such as *custody de facto*, which means that one parent has custody as a practical matter although no order has been entered yet.

De Jure. Latin for "in law." Refers to matters that have been ordered by the court, such as *custody de jure*, which means custody ordered by the court.

Desertion. Unjustified leaving of the marital home by one spouse. Grounds for divorce in some states.

Discovery. The procedure and rules for obtaining information before trial. It consists of producing the following:
1. *Interrogatories.* Written questions for you or your spouse that must be answered in writing under penalties of perjury.
2. *A request for production of documents.*
3. *A request for admissions.* Written statements for your spouse that must be admitted or denied. If you do not respond, they will be considered to be admitted by the court.
4. *Depositions.* A series of verbal questions asked of a party or witness that he then answers under oath before a court reporter who produces a transcript of the testimony.
5. *Third-party Subpoenas/Subpoena Duces Tecum.* Requests to a third party, like an employer or bank, to attend a deposition and bring requested documents.

Divorce Decree. The court's final order granting a divorce.

Domicile. A person's residence, which is used in divorce to establish jurisdiction and venue.

Dower. A wife's legal right to inherit a certain amount of her husband's property in the event of his death. In most states, a surviving spouse cannot be written out of the will and has the right to claim against the will one-third to one-half of the husband's property.

Emancipation. The age when a child becomes an adult.

Equitable Distribution. A system of property division in which marital property is divided on an equitable but not necessarily equal basis.

Equity. A set of principles that can be applied by a divorce court, which include fairness in addition to the principles of law.

Evidence. Any testimony, document, or other item introduced in court to prove a person's case. Only admissible evidence will be considered by the court.

Exhibit(s). Any evidence attached to a pleading or introduced at trial; an example would be a husband's pay stub attached to a motion for temporary support.

Ex Parte. The Latin term for "one-sided." It refers to a hearing where the opposing party isn't present.

Expert Witness. Witnesses that are brought in to court to state their opinions on such matters as custody or the value of the marital home, pensions, and businesses.

Fault and No-Fault Grounds for Divorces. Grounds for divorce that must be stated in a complaint for divorce. Fault grounds are adultery, desertion, cruelty, and other misconduct. No-fault grounds may be separation for a certain amount of time or irreconcilable differences.

Fee Agreement/Retainer. A fee agreement is the written contract between you and your lawyer. It usually provides for an advance payment called a retainer.

File/Filing. Submitting a document to the court.

Filing Fee. A charge paid to the court to file a pleading.

Financial Statement. A court form that each party must complete, file, and serve that states their assets and liabilities, and income and expenses.

Find/Findings. A determination made by the judge, after listening to the evidence, about what she believes are the actual facts that will form the basis of her decision.

Fraud. Deception. Misrepresentation.

Garnishment/Wage Assignment/Wage Attachment. A court order requiring an employer to deduct a certain amount from an employee's paycheck and send it to his spouse.

Hold Harmless. An agreement by your spouse to defend and indemnify you against any claims brought upon you by a third party.

Impeach. An attempt to prove that a witness hasn't told the truth in all situations.

Injunction. A court order prohibiting or requiring some act.

Innocent Spouse Rule. Section 434(c)(1) of the Internal Revenue Code, giving a spouse relief from being responsible for an error in a joint tax return that she had no knowledge of.

Interlocutory Order. An order of the court that is not final.

Intestate. A person who dies without a will. Intestacy laws of the state will determine how the person's property will be distributed.

Joint Property. Property held in the name of both spouses.

Jurisdiction. The court's legal authority to decide a couple's case.

Legal Separation. Something filed for in states where it is allowed to decide issues of custody and support before you have grounds for a final or absolute divorce.

Marriage Certificate. An official certification of your marriage with a raised seal.

Glossary

Mediation. A situation in which the parties meet with a neutral mediator to try to work out a separation agreement.

Memorandum. A legal document filed with pleadings by your lawyer setting forth facts and law to support a request to the court.

Modification. A postdivorce procedure undertaken to change custody, child support, or modifiable alimony.

Motion. A pleading asking the court to take a specified action.

Negotiated Settlement. A separation agreement worked out by the parties, usually with counsel.

Nuptial. A description of something that pertains to the marriage.

Order. A decision produced by the court. Violation of a court order is considered contempt of court.

Parens patriae. The right of the state to determine what is in the best interests of your children.

Parental Kidnapping. A parent illegally taking a child in violation of a court order. The Parental Kidnapping Prevention Act is a federal law that requires states to cooperate with each other in returning children kidnapped by a parent. The United States, along with approximately thirty-five other countries, are signatories to the Hague Convention on the Civil Aspects of International Child Abduction, which provides procedures for returning abducted children to their rightful custodian.

Pendente Lite. The Latin term for "during the litigation."

Perjury. Lying under oath.

Pleadings. Documents submitted to the court, such as the complaints for divorce, answers, counterclaims, and motions.

Postnuptial Agreement. An agreement similar to a prenuptial agreement but entered into after the wedding. It should be noted that a separation agreement is technically a postnuptial agreement.

Prayer for Relief. Request made to the court at the end of a pleading.

Premarital Assets. Assets acquired before marriage.

Prenuptial Agreement. A written contract, signed before marriage, that sets forth what happens in the event of death or divorce.

Pretrial Conference. A meeting of all parties and counsel with the trial judge to prepare for the trial.

Privilege. The right to have evidence excluded based on confidential relationships, such as attorney-client communications. You also have the right to assert the privilege against self-incrimination.

Pro Se Divorce. A party who represents herself without a lawyer.

Proposed Order. An order that sets forth how you would like the judge to rule that is usually submitted with motions.

QDRO. A "qualified domestic relations order." It is directed to a plan administrator to divide retirement benefits between spouses.

Recrimination. A counterclaim accusing the plaintiff of marital fault served in response to an accusation to the defendant of marital fault.

Recusal. The disqualification of a judge because of judicial prejudice or bias.

Rehabilitative Alimony. Short-term spousal support designed to help the recipient transition to self-support.

Relocation. Moving the children out of the current area.

Restraining Order/Protective Order. A temporary court order prohibiting a party from conducting certain activities. Issued in response to a motion, it is often issued to protect marital assets and to protect against domestic violence.

Rules. The rules that govern court procedure.

Rules of Evidence. The rules that govern testimony, documents, and demonstrative materials.

Sanctions. The punishment of a party for improper behavior by the court within certain guidelines. This includes failing to respond to discovery requests.

Separate Property. Property that is not part of the marital estate, such as premarital property, inheritances, and gifts from third parties.

Service of Process. The legal process of giving notice to the other party that a complaint or motion is pending.

Stay. The act of suspending a court order or proceeding.

Stipulation. A written document indicating the agreement of the parties.

Strike/Motion to Strike. A move for the court to delete any pleadings or evidence that is improper.

Subpoena. A court order requiring a person to attend a legal proceeding, such as a trial or deposition. If documents are also requested, the subpoena is called a *subpoena duces tecum*, which is Latin for "bring with you." See also "Discovery"

Summary Judgment. The entry of a judgment without a trial when only questions of law, and not fact, are at issue (rare in divorce cases).

Summons. A court's official notice to the defendant requiring him to respond to an attached complaint.

Temporary Restraining Order. A TRO. A court order compelling a party to do something or prohibiting him from doing something.

Temporary Support. A court order to pay child support or spousal support while the case is pending.

Tenancy by the Entirety. The terms on which real estate is usually held by married couples. According to it, the surviving spouse becomes the sole owner of the real estate automatically upon the death of the other if they are still married at the time that the death occurs.

Testimony. Any statement made under oath.

Tort/Marital Tort. Any wrongful act that creates legal liability for the defendant. Some states allow spouses to bring tort actions in addition to divorce actions. Tort claims include assault and battery, fraud, and intentional infliction of mental distress.

Trial/Hearing. A legal proceeding before a judge, who hears testimony under the rules of evidence and makes a final decision relating to the matters presented.

Trustee. A third party who is appointed to carry out the court's orders; for example, to sell the marital residence.

Venue. The location of the court that will hear your case.

Visitation, Grandparent. The visitation rights given to grandparents. The parents' visitation schedule is given preference over the grandparents' schedule unless it excludes them altogether.

Visitation. The time ordered by the court or agreed to by the parties that the noncustodial parent spends with the children.

Index

A

Abbreviated custody, 84
Acts
    The Husband's Lawyer
        (see The Husband's Lawyer)
    The Mediator (see The Mediator)
    The Wife's Lawyer (see The Wife's
        Lawyer)
Agreement. See Separation agreement
Alimony, 255
    changes, 106
    cohabitation, 107
    factors, 105
    health insurance, 111
    job status issues, 106
    life insurance, 111
    marital misconduct, 103
    nonmarried parents, 107
    permanent alimony, 104
    rehabilitative alimony, 104
    state law and varies, 104
    taxes
        child support and payments, 107
        disguise child support, 110
        payments deductible, 108–109
        recapture, 109
    temporary alimony (pendente lite), 103
Alimony vs. Child Support, 166
Arbitration, 203
Assets. See also Bank accounts; Stocks
    airline frequent flyer miles, 161
    automobiles and vehicles, 159
    credit card award points, 161
    furniture and furnishings, 160
    other assets, 161
Attorneys, negotiation, 202

B

Bank accounts, 153. See also
        Assets; Stocks
    attorney, 155
    court, 156
    date of division, 154
    divide marital bank accounts, 154
    divorces, 157
    finding hidden bank accounts, 157
Bargaining
    interest-based bargaining, 199
    position-based bargaining, 199
Best alternative to a negotiated
        settlement (BATNA), 206
Best-interest attorney, 78
Breach of Contract, 259
Business investments, 143
    discounts, 146
        lack of marketability, 146
        personal goodwill, 146
        taxes, 146
    double-dipping, 147
    husband's expert, 145
    income, 150
    intellectual properties, 150
    professional degrees and licenses, 149
    spouse, silent partner, 143

Index

Business investments (cont.)
    divorce, values, 144
    documents, 144
    proceedings, 149
    valuable assessts, 147
    wife's expert, 145

C

Cash vs. stock, 168
Child support, 91
    accounts, 93
    adjustments, 95–96
    calculations, 95
    college, 97
    cover, 92
    deviations, 96
    enforcement, 99
    guidelines cases, 95
    health insurance, 100
    life insurance, 100
    modification, 98
    pays, 93
        direct payments, 91
        income shares, 93
        indirect payments, 92
        Melson method, 94
        percentage-of-income method, 94
    private schools, 96
    starts, 97
    stop, 98
    tax considerations, 99
    URESA or RURESA, 99
Civil Service Retirement System (CSRS), 137
Collaborative law, 201
Communication skills, 199
Countercomplaint, 222
Custody agreements, 232
Custody evaluation
    case study, 77
    recommendations, 76

D

Debts, 118. See also Property and debt
Defense Finance and Accounting Service (DFAS), 139
Defense of Marriage Act (DOMA), 246

Deferred Pay
    direct pay, 139
    disposable retired pay vs. disability pay, 139
Different negotiating techniques, 211
    nibbler, 212
    quid pro quo, 212
    segmentation, 211
Divorce information and evidence.
        See also Finances
    about information, 19
    domestic violence, 22
    inventory and safeguard, 19
        collections and valuables, 20
        documents, 20
        safe deposit boxes
            and storage units, 20
    lawyer, 23
        divorce calendar, 24
        divorce notebook/file, 24
        divorce to do list, 24
        financial statement, 25
        marriage history, 24
        war chest, 23
    power of attorney, 21
    social security
        benefits, 20–21
        ex-spouse dies, 21
Divorce lawyers. See Meeting (with lawyer)
Divorce of same-sex couples, 248

E

Employee Retirement Income Security Act (ERISA), 133
Equitable distribution factors
    case study, 119
    marital award, 118
Evidence, 225
    answering questions, 225
    direct examination
        background facts, 227
        children, 228
        child support, 230
        custody arrangements, 230
        divorce, 229
        incorporation, 230
        judge rules, 231
        marriage certificate, 228
        name change, 231

retirement funds, 230
separation agreement, 229
divorce case
   direct examination, 227
   preliminary matter, 226
   witness stand, 226
important tips, 234
rules, 234
separation agreement
   custody, 231
   property, 234
   support, 233

F

Federal Marriage Amendment, 245
Finances
   bank accounts, 15
   bills, 18
   credit cards, 16
   health insurance, 18
   life insurance, 18
   loans and lines, 17
   retirement accounts, 19
   stocks, money market funds, deposit and brokerage accounts, 16

G

Gather tax, 59

H

Health insurance, 111
The Husband's Lawyer
   Scott, Marvin
      bank statements, 126
      Brandenburg formula, 126
      calculation of property, 126
      premarital property, 125
      tenancy, 125
      transfer of title, 127

I

Individual Retirement Accounts (IRAs), 137, 170
Interest-based bargaining vs. position-based bargaining, 199
Internal Revenue Code, 165

J, K

Joint legal custody, 72

L

Lawyer, 35
   benefits, 35
   contested divorce, 39
      alimony, 40
      business interests and investments, 40
      children, 39
      domestic abuse, 40
      government employees, 40
      high conflicts, 39
      high-income earner, 40
      house, 40
      military, 41
      missing spouse, 41
      retirement funds, 40
      same-sex, 41
      simple, 39
      spouse, 41
      stakes, 39
   costs of, 36
      conflict, 36
      expensive, 36
      hidden costs, 38
      knowledge, 38
      litigation costs, 37
   divorce consideration
      contested, 39
      simple or complex, 38
      uncontested, 38
   mediation, 41
      advantages of, 41
      disadvantages of, 43
   No Fault, 43
Lawyer identification, 45
   attorney (male or female), 50
   divorce, 45
   experience, 46
   internet, 46
   litigator, 50
   phone calls and emails, 51
   retainers and fees, 51
   save money, 52
      alimony and child support, 53
      budget, 54
      business value, 52

Index

Lawyer identification (*cont.*)
    collaborative law, 53
    custody plan, 55
    divorce, 53
    emotions, lawyer, 52
    financial statements, 52
    hanging, 54
    house value, 52
    lawyer, 53–55
    printer or copies, 53
    research knowledge, 52
    resolution, 53
    settlement with spouse, 54
    spouse for divorce, 54
    staff, lawyer, 53
    stuff division, 55
  skill of, 47
  style, 48
    negotiator, 50
    pushover, 49
    shark, 48
    technician, 49
    traffic cop, 48
    zen lawyer, 49
  trust, 47
  word of mouth, 46
Legal custody
  best interests doctrine, 69
  chances, 70
  constitutional rights, 67
  factors, 69
  future, 71
  general terms, 71
  joint legal custody, 72
  notebook, 71
  parens patriae, 67
  sole legal custody, 72
  tender years doctrine, 68
Life insurance, 111

M

Marital property, 115
Marriage
  same-sex marriage (see Same-sex marriage)
  penalty, 250
The Mediator
  Davis, Brooke, 127
  Silverstein, Stephanie, 127
    aggrement, 130
    custody in court, 128
    payments and taxes, 128
    taxes, 129
    transfer of amount, 129
    work of a mediator, 127
Mediation, 200
Meeting (with lawyer), 57
  bad lawyer, 66
  before meeting, 57–58
  consultation, 65
  divorce lawyers pratice, 66
  first meeting
    bank and stock accounts, 59
    debts, 61
    income evidences, 59
    legal documents, 58
    miscellaneous items, 60–61
    nonfinancial items, 61
    real estate, 60
    retirement funds, 60
  goals, objectives
    and priorities, 64–65
  lawyer questions, 64
  legal advice and counsel, 65
  marshaling the facts
    attorney's goal, 62
    children, 63
    finances, 63
    marriage, 63
    proceedings, 63
Melson model, 94

N, O

Negotiation
  by attorneys, 202
  good communication skills, 199
  information gathering, 198
  interest-based bargaining *vs.* position-based bargaining, 199
Nonmarital property, 116

P

Part marital and part nonmarital property, 117
Pendente lite hearing, 238

Pensions
  plans, 131
    defined benefit, 132
    defined contribution, 132
    nonqualified, 136
    qualified (see Qualified Plans)
Percentage-of-income method, 94
Permanent alimony, 104
Physical custody, 75
  best-interest attorney, 78
  custody evaluation
    case study, 77
    recommendations, 76
  custody modification, 78
  practical considerations, 80
  relocation cases, 79
  shared physical custody, 75
  sole physical custody, 76
  split physical custody, 76
  thrid-party custody, 80
Pleadings, 215
  answer, 221
  complaint
    attachments, 218
    caption, 216
    children, 216
    debt, 217
    grounds for divorce, 217
    marriage, 216
    parties, 216
    prayer for relief, 217–218
    property, 217
    signature and verification, 218
    support, 217
  complaint for divorce, 216
  countercomplaint, 222
  preliminary motions
    default judgment, 221
    motions, 220
  respond-to-countercomplaint, 222
  rules, 215
  summons
    alternative service, 219
    certified mail, 219
    personal service, 219
    service copy, 219
    service of process, 219
Position-based bargaining vs.
    interest-based bargaining, 199

Postdivorce, 253
  alimony, 255
  amendments, 255
  appeals, 260
  Breach of Contract, 259
  checklist, 253
  child support, 254
  cohabitation, 261
  consent orders, 258
  court order violation, 259
  custody and access, 254
  financial-updating mechanisms, 262
  life insurance and pension plans, 253
  real-estate and corporate records, 261
  remarriage, 260
  separation agreement, 262
  tax disputes, 261
  the House, 254
Postnuptial agreement.
    See Separation agreements
Preliminary motions
  default judgment, 221
  motions, 220
Premarital agreements.
    See Prenuptial agreements
Prenuptial agreements, 175
  background, 175
  bulletproof prenup, 179
  elements
    conditions, 177
    full disclosure, 177
    no duress, 178
    no overreaching, 178
    proper form, 179
  lifestyle clauses, 182
  people don't think they need, 176
  prenup before
    bring up the subject, 181
    can help you answer
      this questions, 180
    legal system is adversarial, 181
    UPAA, 181
  prenup current, 183
  in writing, 176
Property and debt
  equitable distribution
    case, 115, 119
    changing property classification, 116
    community property, 114–115

Property and debt (cont.)
    date of valuation, 117
    earning and appreciation, 117
    marital award, 118
    marital property, 115–116
    nonmarital property, 116
    part marital and nonmarital property, 117
  gets rover, 119
  hiding assets, 120
  marital dissipation, 119
  uncooperative spouse, 113
Public Policy Polling, 250

Q

Qualified Plans, 133
  alienation, 133
  individual retirement accounts (IRAs), 133
  mechanics of a QRDO, 134
    issue of, 135
    marital settlement aggrement, 135
    plan administrator, 134
    retirement benefits, 134
  QRDO, Congress to Rescue, 133
  survival benefit, 136

R

Rehabilitative alimony, 104
Relocation cases, 79
Remarriage, 260
Research and documents, 27
  additional records, 32
  assets
    automobiles and vehicles, 29
    bank statements, 28
    business interests, 29
    collections and jewelry, 29
    furnishings and furniture, 29
    inheritance/trust interests, 29
    insurance policies, 28
    retirement funds, 28
    safe and safe deposite boxes, 28
    stocks and bonds, 28
    tax benefits, 29
    time-shares, 29
  expenses, 31
  fault and private investigators, 32–33
  income, 31
  law research
    cases, 33
    code, 33
    constitution, 33
    courtroom, 34
    Internet, 34
    rules, 33
  liabilities, 30
  organization, 32
  records, 27
Residential custody. See Physical custody
Retirement funds
  individual retirement account, 170
  401(k) plans, 169
Retirement plans
  federal government plan, 137
    civil service, 137
    federal employees retirement system, 138
  individual retirement accounts, 137
  international organizations, 138
  military pensions, 138
Revised Uniform Reciprocal Enforcement of Support Act (RURESA), 99

S

Same-sex marriage, 245
  benefits, 249
  capital gains taxes/estate taxes, 249
  Defense of Marriage Act, 246
  divorce, 248
  Edith Windsor and Thea Spyer, 246
  future case, 250
  health insurance, 249
  IRS, 249
  Kristin Perry and Sandra Stier, 247
  marriage penalty, 250
  opponents, 245
  Public Policy Polling, 250
  in United States, 251
    California, 251
    Columbia, 252
    Connecticut, 251
    Delaware, 252
    Iowa, 251

Maine, 252
Maryland, 252
Massachusetts, 251
Minnesota, 252
New Hampshire, 252
New York, 252
Rhode Island, 252
Vermont, 251
Washington, 252
Separation agreement, 197, 205, 256, 262
　answering questions, 208
　arbitration, 203
　avoid vague statements, 212
　BATNA, 206
　checklist
　　access to children, 192
　　alimony, 193
　　child support, 192
　　consideration, 191
　　facts, 190
　　legal custody of children, 191
　　personal property, 194
　　real property, 193
　　retirement funds, 194
　　separation, 191
　　taxes, 194
　conversation, 213
　different negotiating techniques, 211
　　nibbler, 212
　　quid pro quo, 212
　　segmentation, 211
　divorce
　　actual agreement, 189
　　advantages, 189
　　disadvantages, 190
　　lawyer, 187
　　when to get a divorce, 189
　formal agreement, 213
　information gathering, 207
　items, 208
　mediation, 200
　negotiation, 198
　　by attorneys, 202
　　collaborative law, 201
　　good communication skills, 199
　　information gathering, 198
　　interest-based bargaining *vs.*
　　　position-based bargaining, 199
　prenuptial agreements, 187

　push buttons, 209
　substance, 209
　time and place, 207
　trial, 203
　value of questions, 208
　verbal clues, 210
Shared physical custody, 75
Social Security, 140
Sole legal custody, 72
Sole physical custody, 76
Split physical custody, 76
Stocks. *See also* Assests;
　　　Bank account
　certificates, 158
　options, 159
Summons
　alternative service, 219
　certified mail, 219
　personal service, 219
　service copy, 219
　service of process, 219

T

Taxes, 163
　alimony
　　child support payments, 166
　　Internal Revenue Code, 165
　　vs. property transfer, 167
　children
　　child care expenses, 173
　　child tax credit, 172
　　dependency exemption, 171
　　tax planning, 172
　family home
　　deductions, 167
　　sale, 167
　property transfers
　　cash *vs.* stock, 168
　　retirement funds, 169
　tax filing status
　　file separate tax returns, 163
　　head of household, 165
　　joint tax return, 163
　　third-lowest tax rates, 164
Temporary alimony (pendente lite), 103
Thrid-party custody, 80

Index

Timesharing
    abbreviated custody, 84
    changes, 89
    children-others, 89
    child spends, 87
    holidays, 86
        schedule, 86
        special days, 87
    judge, 83
    parent, 88
    parenting issues and scheduling, 84–85
    provisions, 89
    supervised, 88
    third-party timesharing, 88
Timing considerations, 3
    agreement, 13
    burning, 13
    companionship, 4
    dating, 4
    divorce is a process, not an event, 14
    employment, 5–6
    familiarity, 4
    family finances, 11
    finances, 4, 6–7
    investment and children, 4
    issues, 7–10
    lawyer sense, 13
    start dating, 12
    state courts, 5
Trial procedure, 203, 237
    closing arguments, 244
    court-ordered mediation, 242
    cross-examination, 243
    decision, 244
    defendant rests, 243
    direct examination, 243
    discovery
        depositions, 241
        document requests, 240
        interrogatories, 239
        meaning, 239
        request for admissions, 240
        scope, 239
        thrid-party subpoena, 241
    opening statements, 242
    pendente lite, 238
    pretrial statement, 242
    rebuttal, 244
    redirect examination, 243
    scheduling hearing
        dates, 238
        services, 237
    stipulations, 242
    trial, 242
    witnesses, 243

U, V

Uniformed Services Former Spouse Protection Act (USFSPA), 138
Uniform Interstate Family Support Act (UIFSA), 99
Uniform Premarital Agreement Act (UPAA), 175
Uniform Reciprocal Enforcement of Support Act (URESA), 99
United States
    same-sex marriage, 251
        California, 251
        Columbia, 252
        Connecticut, 251
        Delaware, 252
        Iowa, 251
        Maine, 252
        Maryland, 252
        Massachusetts, 251
        Minnesota, 252
        New Hampshire, 252
        New York, 252
        Rhode Island, 252
        Vermont, 251
        Washington, 252

W, X, Y, Z

The Wife's Lawyer, 123
    Davis, Brooke, 123
        aggrement, 125
        home, 124
        property rights, 124
    Nicholas, Simon, 124
        financial situation, 124
        house, 124
        mutual aggrement, 125
        ownership details, 125
        possibility of selling, 124

Get the eBook for only $10!

Now you can take the weightless companion with you anywhere, anytime. Your purchase of this book entitles you to 3 electronic versions for only $10.

This Apress title will prove so indispensible that you'll want to carry it with you everywhere, which is why we are offering the eBook in 3 formats for only $10 if you have already purchased the print book.

Convenient and fully searchable, the PDF version enables you to easily find and copy code—or perform examples by quickly toggling between instructions and applications. The MOBI format is ideal for your Kindle, while the ePUB can be utilized on a variety of mobile devices.

Go to www.apress.com/promo/tendollars to purchase your companion eBook.

All Apress eBooks are subject to copyright. All rights are reserved by the Publisher, whether the whole or part of the material is concerned, specifically the rights of translation, reprinting, reuse of illustrations, recitation, broadcasting, reproduction on microfilms or in any other physical way, and transmission or information storage and retrieval, electronic adaptation, computer software, or by similar or dissimilar methodology now known or hereafter developed. Exempted from this legal reservation are brief excerpts in connection with reviews or scholarly analysis or material supplied specifically for the purpose of being entered and executed on a computer system, for exclusive use by the purchaser of the work. Duplication of this publication or parts thereof is permitted only under the provisions of the Copyright Law of the Publisher's location, in its current version, and permission for use must always be obtained from Springer. Permissions for use may be obtained through RightsLink at the Copyright Clearance Center. Violations are liable to prosecution under the respective Copyright Law.

Other Apress Business Titles You Will Find Useful

Control Your Retirement Destiny
Anspach
978-1-4302-5022-7

Plan Your Own Estate
Wheatley-Liss
978-1-4302-4494-3

Tax Insight
Murdock
978-1-4302-6310-4

Healthcare, Insurance, and You
Zamosky
978-1-4302-4953-5

Common Sense
Tanner
978-1-4302-4152-2

Underwater
Lauer
978-1-4302-4470-7

Tech Job Hunt Handbook
Grossman
978-1-4302-4548-3

The Employer Bill of Rights
Hyman
978-1-4302-4551-3

Unite the Tribes, 2nd Edition
Duncan
978-1-4302-5872-8

Available at www.apress.com

GPSR Compliance

The European Union's (EU) General Product Safety Regulation (GPSR) is a set of rules that requires consumer products to be safe and our obligations to ensure this.

If you have any concerns about our products, you can contact us on

ProductSafety@springernature.com

In case Publisher is established outside the EU, the EU authorized representative is:

Springer Nature Customer Service Center GmbH
Europaplatz 3
69115 Heidelberg, Germany

www.ingramcontent.com/pod-product-compliance
Lightning Source LLC
LaVergne TN
LVHW040732250326
834688LV00031B/265